Marcel Proust
and the
Creative Encounter

Marcel Proust
and the
Creative Encounter

George Stambolian

The University of Chicago Press

CHICAGO AND LONDON

THE UNIVERSITY OF CHICAGO PRESS, CHICAGO 60637
THE UNIVERSITY OF CHICAGO PRESS, LTD., LONDON

© 1972 by The University of Chicago
All rights reserved. Published 1972
Printed in the United States of America

INTERNATIONAL STANDARD BOOK NUMBER: 0–226–77068–0
LIBRARY OF CONGRESS CATALOG CARD NUMBER: 72–77645

To My Parents

Contents

Preface

I wish to express my deepest gratitude to Germaine Brée, whose lectures and critical studies first awakened my interest in Proust, and whose guidance was invaluable during the preparation of my doctoral dissertation on which this book is largely based. I am also indebted to Allan Pasco, who made useful suggestions for improving my manuscript, and to Dennis Spininger for helping me to refine many of my ideas. He, Barbara Gerber, and Gerald Storzer generously offered their assistance whenever they sensed my need of it. My special thanks go to Michael Hampton, without whose patience and kind attention this book would not have been completed.

I am grateful to my colleagues in the French Department at Wellesley College for their encouragement and advice, and to the Fulbright Commission, the Ford Foundation, and the Presidents and Trustees of both the University of Wisconsin and Wellesley College for the financial support granted me at different times during the last nine years.

Although this study is based on my readings of Proust in French, I have decided, for the convenience of English-speaking readers, to use the Moncrieff-Blossom translation for the passages I quote from the novel. In each case, however, the reference to the English edition is immediately followed by the reference to the French edition. The French titles of the seven volumes of *A la Recherche* and their English equivalents are: *Du Côté de chez Swann—Swann's Way, A l'Ombre des jeunes filles en fleurs—Within a Budding Grove, Le Côté de Guermantes—The Guermantes Way, Sodome et Gomorrhe—Cities of the Plain, La Prisonnière—The Captive, La Fugitive—The Sweet Cheat Gone, Le Temps retrouvé—The Past Recaptured.* Only the French titles have been retained in the body of this study and in the notes, where they are given in an abbreviated form.

The 1954 edition of *A la Recherche,* which was based on Proust's manuscripts and corrections, contains passages not found in the translation of Moncrieff and Blossom, who worked with the *Nouvelle Revue Française* text published from 1919 to 1927. Some passages in this early text have also been changed by Clarac and Ferré for a variety of reasons that are explained in their notes. I have translated the passages not present in the Random House edition and, whenever necessary, have changed the English translation to make it correspond more closely to the new Gallimard edition. I have also made changes in the translation when I have found Moncrieff's or Blossom's reading of the French to be inaccurate or inconsistent. For example, certain important words such as *esprit, attention, espace,* and *perception* which Proust uses repeatedly were not always translated in the same way. While such variations may have been justified at times, if only for reasons of sentence harmony, they do tend to hide the consistency of Proust's aesthetic vocabulary. I have bracketed all the passages from the novel that I myself have translated, and each change has been identified in the corresponding note. Occasionally I have included words and phrases from the French text whenever the meaning of the original cannot be adequately rendered in English.

I have followed the same procedures in quoting from Proust's other works, for which I have used as often as possible the existing English translations. All translations of works by Proust or by other French writers which exist only in the original are my own and have not been bracketed.

Unless otherwise indicated, all italics in the quoted passages are also my own.

Wellesley, Massachusetts   G.S.
October 1971

Nous ne connaissons vraiment que ce qui est nouveau, ce qui introduit brusquement dans notre sensibilité un changement de ton qui nous frappe, ce à quoi l'habitude n'a pas encore substitué ses pâles fac-similés.

La Fugitive

Introduction

In *Du Côté de chez Swann* there is a group of passages in which Proust's narrator recalls the happy hours he spent during his youth reading the novels of Bergotte. At first, he says, he was unable to distinguish those aspects of Bergotte's style that he would later love so much:

> Then I observed the rare, almost archaic phrases which he liked to employ at certain points, where a hidden flow of harmony, a prelude contained and concealed in the work itself would animate and elevate his style. . . . One of these passages of Bergotte, the third or fourth which I had detached from the rest, filled me with a joy to which the meager joy I had tasted in the first passage bore no comparison, a joy which I felt myself to have experienced in some innermost chamber of my soul, deep, undivided, vast, from which all obstructions and partitions seemed to have been swept away. For what had happened was that, while I recognised in this passage the same taste for uncommon phrases, the same bursts of music, the same idealist philosophy which had been present in the earlier passages without my having taken them into account as the source of my pleasure, I now no longer had the impression of being confronted by a particular passage in one of Bergotte's works, which traced a purely bi-dimensional figure in outline upon the surface of my mind, but rather of the "ideal passage" of Bergotte, common to every one of his books, and to which all the earlier, similar passages, now becoming merged in it, had added a kind of density and volume, by which my own [*mind*] seemed to be enlarged.[1]

1. Marcel Proust, *Remembrance of Things Past*, tr. C. K. Scott Moncrieff and, for *Le Temps retrouvé*, Frederick A. Blossom, 2 vols. (New York: Random House, 1934), I, 71–72; Proust, *Du Côté de chez Swann*, in *A la Recherche du temps perdu*, ed. Pierre Clarac and André Ferré, 3 vols. (Paris: Gallimard, 1954), I, 94.

1

The experience the narrator describes here is familiar to most readers. It is only gradually, and because of their recurrence in different works, that one is able to recognize the various themes, images, and patterns of expression that characterize an author's particular vision of reality. For Proust, these *phrases-types,* or "typical phrases," show that great writers "have never created more than a single work, or rather have never done more than refract through various mediums an identical beauty which they bring into the world."[2] If the discovery of these *phrases-types* defines the experience of reading, their elucidation for others defines the activity of criticism. The first task of every critic, writes Proust, is "to help the reader to feel the impact of an artist's unique characteristics, to put before him those traits whose similarity with what he is reading at the moment may enable him to realize the essential part they play in the genius of a particular writer."[3]

Proust himself uses this method of criticism both in *A la Recherche du temps perdu* and in his essays on various writers and artists, for whether he describes how Stendhal associates the life of the spirit with a certain sense of altitude, the way Flaubert uses the imperfect tense, or Dostoevsky's special love for mysterious women and houses, his effort is always to define a writer's uniqueness and originality.[4] It is of course true that Proust usually limits himself to discussing only the two or three traits of a writer that are of interest to him and generally neglects what he describes as the second task of the critic—that of reconstructing "the peculiar life of the spirit which belongs to every writer who is obsessed by his own special view of reality."[5] Yet it is also true that all of Proust's criticism moves in this direction, for he values the *phrases-types* primarily for what they reveal about the inner structure of a writer's creative personality and about the particular acts or processes of creation

---

In this passage I have replaced the word "understanding" by "mind," which is the word Moncrieff himself most often used to translate the French *esprit* (see chapter 1, note 7).

2. II, 643; *Prisonnière,* III, 375.

3. *Marcel Proust: A Selection from his Miscellaneous Writings,* tr. Gerard Hopkins (London: Allan Wingate, 1948), p. 24 n; Proust, *Pastiches et mélanges* (Paris: Gallimard, 1919), p. 108 n. See also John Ruskin, *La Bible d'Amiens,* tr. Marcel Proust (Paris: Mercure de France, 1947), p. 10.

4. For a concise and lucid discussion of Proust's literary criticism, see Walter A. Strauss, *Proust and Literature: The Novelist as Critic* (Cambridge: Harvard University Press, 1957). A more extensive study of the same subject can be found in René de Chantal, *Marcel Proust: Critique littéraire,* 2 vols. (Montreal: Presses de l'Université de Montréal, 1967).

5. *Proust: A Selection,* p. 25 n; *Pastiches,* p. 109 n.

by which the writer transformed his experience in life into a work of art.

The critic who would apply Proust's own method to his novel and attempt to distinguish those *phrases-types* that best reveal not only Proust's vision of reality and the way he expressed it, but also the structure of his spiritual or creative life, confronts a curious situation. *A la Recherche du temps perdu,* like all works of art, is the product of a complex creative process and, like many great novels, it is also a kind of fictionalized autobiography. This last aspect of Proust's novel is complicated by the fact that although its hero is not Proust, he is nonetheless, if inadvertently, called Marcel, says "I," becomes a novelist, and possesses a character that closely resembles his creator's. What is especially fascinating about Proust's novel is not so much the existence of this resemblance but the form that it takes. *A la Recherche* is not simply the biography of a novelist who resembles Proust, it is the description of the very experiences by means of which the hero becomes a novelist who shares Proust's own conception of art and of the creative process. It is because of this emphasis on the creative "becoming" of its hero that Proust's novel can be seen as the fictionalized description of its own genesis. It is as if Proust, having read his life like a critic, were presenting to his readers the very structure of his creative personality. In the novel, of course, it is Proust's hero, Marcel, who reads his life critically by discovering those *phrases-types* of his existence in time that reveal to him his vision of reality and the form of his spiritual life. A study of these *phrases-types* would show, therefore, not only some of the ways Proust himself discovered the life of his spirit, but also, because the novel is a work of fiction, the techniques Proust employed in expressing his vision.

When after discovering his "vocation" in *Le Temps retrouvé* Marcel looks back on his life, he perceives that certain joyful moments in his past contained the secret of his artistic vision and concealed a "fundamental trait" of his nature. He divides these *moments bienheureux* into two groups: *impressions* and *réminiscences.* In the first group Marcel places those moments, which occurred mostly during his youth at Combray, when he experienced an intense joy before an object or scene in the exterior world that seemed to hide beneath its beauty some secret he felt called upon to discover and, at times, to express. The *réminiscences,* on the other hand, are for Marcel the miraculous resurrections of the past caused by involuntary memory. It is through involuntary memory, he realizes, that he has not only regained the time he had lost but has also discovered within himself the material for the novel he will write in order to redeem the time he had wasted. Indeed, the important truths

3

revealed during these joyful moments can be elucidated only in a work of art:

> In short, in this case as in the other, whether objective impressions such as I had received from the sight of the spires of Martinville, or subjective memories like the unevenness of the two steps or the taste of the *madeleine,* I must try to interpret the sensations as the indications of corresponding laws and ideas; I must try to think, that is to say, bring out of the obscurity what I had felt, and convert it into a spiritual equivalent. Now this method, which seemed to me the only one, what was it other than to create a work of art?[6]

Given the undeniably important role played by these *moments bienheureux* in Proust's novel, it is not surprising that almost all the critics who have written on *A la Recherche* have devoted considerable attention to them. Despite differences in approach and emphasis, critics have generally agreed that in his description of these moments Proust treats the most essential aesthetic problems and themes of his novel. It is here, for example, that he discusses in depth the relationship between sensitivity and intelligence, impression and expression, and reveals his particular conception of time and memory. In these moments Proust reconstructs the fundamental aspects of his own creative vision and describes the "laws" that governed the way he transformed his experiences into a work of art.

Since Marcel's *moments bienheureux* and similar experiences will be referred to as "creative encounters," this expression requires a brief explanation.[7] In an article entitled "The Nature of Creativity," published in 1959, the noted existential psychologist Rollo May writes that "the first thing we notice in a creative act is that it is an *encounter.* The artist encounters the landscape he proposes to paint—looks at it, observes it from this angle and that, is, as we say, absorbed by it." During such encounters the artist experiences joy, "joy defined as the affect which goes with heightened consciousness, the affect that accompanies the experience of actualizing one's own potentialities." The artist feels himself capable of making something, of bringing something new into birth, of

6. II, 1000–1001; *Temps retrouvé,* III, 878–79.

7. Proust's use of various types of encounters in the composition and plot development of his novel is discussed in Henry M. Kopman, "The Phenomenon of *Rencontre* in *A La Recherche Du Temps Perdu*" (Ph.D. dissertation, New York University, 1960).

expressing at once a new reality and his own being. His joy is in this sense a feeling of "ecstasy" for it results from his ability to "stand out from" himself, "to be freed from the usual split between subject and object which is an almost insurmountable barrier in most human activity." These encounters cannot, however, be willed. "We cannot *will* to have insights," writes May, "we cannot *will* creativity; but we can will to give ourselves to the encounter with intensity of dedication and commitment. The deeper aspects of awareness are activated to the extent that the person is committed to the encounter." Finally, an artist's encounters are always with his "world," which does not mean his environment but "the pattern of meaningful relations in which the person exists and in the design of which he participates." "Creativity," May concludes, "is the encounter of the intensively conscious human being with his world."[8]

Marcel's *moments bienheureux* clearly resemble the type of creative encounter May describes. They are joyful moments of heightened consciousness caused by impressions that lift Marcel out of himself and enable him to enter into a profound communion either with an object of the exterior world or with his own inner world. The impressions are not willed but strike him suddenly and by chance. He realizes, however, that he must give himself to his impressions, must seek to elucidate with his intelligence the new reality his sensitivity reveals. Finally, to express his impressions, to bring into being this new reality, is for him tantamount to expressing his own inner self. Indeed, if *A la Recherche du temps perdu* is, as Howard Moss writes, "the story of how a little boy becomes a writer,"[9] it is also the story of how a man comes to discover the spiritual life of his true self, which, for Proust, is the same as the creative self.

Now although these *moments bienheureux* play an important role in Proust's novel, they alone cannot explain his particular vision of reality or of the creative process. They reveal what Proust calls "essential truths," truths related to the intemporal "essence" of the self and its world; but they do not reveal all the complex laws governing man's existence in time, which was Proust's avowed purpose in writing his novel. Also when in *Le Temps retrouvé* Marcel contemplates his future work, he remarks that *all* his past life is the material for his novel, and

8. Rollo May, "The Nature of Creativity," *Etc.*, XVI, no. 3 (Spring 1959), 261–76. May's italics.

9. Howard Moss, *The Magic Lantern of Marcel Proust* (New York: Grosset and Dunlap, 1966), p. 2.

5

that he must decipher this "inner book" in order to express the truths it contains concerning love, suffering, society, and human behavior.[10] Marcel's mind and the material of his novel were formed, therefore, not only by the *moments bienheureux* but also by other experiences. The question now arises whether these other experiences can be considered as different examples of the fundamental *phrase-type* established by Marcel's joyful moments of creativity.

In a relatively early study one critic, Ramon Fernandez, did discover analogies between different types of experiences described in *A la Recherche*. Fernandez points to the importance in Proust of "the moment when an impression, or an apparition, attracts him as if by a call from its depths."[11] By "impression" Fernandez means, as Proust does, those moments when Marcel experiences a total communion with the objects of the exterior world and attempts to interpret their meaning. "Proustian analysis," remarks Fernandez, "rests on the will and power to hold before the mind's gaze a sudden encounter between consciousness and things, and to maintain this gaze in its state . . . of a first, fresh glance."[12] Expanding on this idea, Fernandez discovers that the same type of "sudden encounter" takes place when Marcel meets many of the characters in the novel. Whereas in Flaubert the description of a character's face coincides with the description of the action of the novel, and whereas in Balzac such a description reveals almost the entire psychological makeup of a character, in Proust characters simply *appear* in their pure physical reality; they are *seen* before their life and thoughts are *known*. Since Marcel often dreams of different persons or places before encountering them, each apparition or impression, by revealing a reality that does not conform to his expectations, strikes his eye all the more powerfully because it provokes "a kind of explosion which pulverizes all the imaginary content" he originally attributed to the individual or object.[13]

Admitting his debt to Fernandez, Gaëtan Picon has more recently developed these ideas in his *Lecture de Proust*. Proust's characters, writes Picon,

> have this privilege of being seen either because, expected, hoped for, they reveal themselves to be different from their mental model—by lack or by excess,—or because, unexpected, unfore-

10. II, 1015–16; *Temps retrouvé*, III, 899.
11. Ramon Fernandez, *Proust* (Paris: Nouvelle Revue Critique, 1944), p. 83.
12. Ibid., p. 91.   13. Ibid., p. 93.

seen, they impose themselves without the mind being prepared in any way to deaden the shock. Whether this vision be tied to an experience of disappointment, wonderment, or surprise, it explodes with such force precisely because it is the vision of a strange body that the mind had not been capable of producing. It always has this character of "striking the eye for the first time," of being "a sudden breach opening onto the real world."[14]

What Picon says here about "apparitions" is equally true of Marcel's impressions of the exterior world. Just as these sudden apparitions govern, for Picon, the relationship between "the self and the other" in Proust's novel, so certain startling impressions determine the relationship between "the self and the world." Beneath these relationships Picon finds evidence of Proust's ambiguous attitude toward the real. Proust is torn, he writes, "between the desire and fear of the real, between curiosity and the inclination toward habit."[15] This conflict is resolved only by involuntary memory which provides Proust with a world that is at once real yet contained within himself.

Both Fernandez and Picon show in their work an interest in what Proust himself calls the Dostoevsky and Mme de Sévigné "side" of his style: "Mme. de Sévigné . . . like Dostoievski, instead of presenting things in their logical sequence, that is to say beginning with the cause, shows us first of all the effect, the illusion that strikes us."[16] Although many critics have discussed this aspect of Proust's style and have investigated the complex problem of the relationship between consciousness and reality raised in the novel when such "illusions" or impressions strike Marcel, the importance of Fernandez, and particularly of Picon, to the present study, derives from the fact that they explore this problem in the context of certain fundamental types of encounter which they consider an essential part of Proust's unique vision of reality.

In an interesting and neglected study published in 1929 Clive Bell wrote: "*A la Recherche du temps perdu* is a series of carefully planned explosions by means of which the submerged past is brought into the present, the deep-sea monsters of memory to the surface. The pursuit, capture and exhibition of these is the motive of the book."[17] As the work of Fernandez and Picon would suggest, Bell's definition of Proust's

14. Gaëtan Picon, *Lecture de Proust* (Paris: Mercure de France, 1963), pp. 49–50.
15. Ibid., p. 131.   16. II, 645; *Prisonnière,* III, 378.
17. Clive Bell, *Proust* (New York: Harcourt, Brace, 1929), p. 51.

novel would be excellent if it were not limited to the instances of involuntary memory. The reader of *A la Recherche* does indeed have the impression that the novel is a series of "explosions" carefully planned and timed by Proust. Expressions like *tout d'un coup, tout à coup, brusquement* are encountered so often that they strike the reader as being more characteristically, more inevitably "Proustian" than even the ubiquitous *çà et là* is for Flaubert. The most important of these explosions can be placed in the following categories: (1) moments of involuntary memory; (2) profound or "poetic" impressions of the exterior world; (3) the impression produced by the reality of a place previously imagined, for example, Marcel's encounter with the "real" Balbec; (4) the "apparition" of persons previously imagined; (5) a sudden change in Marcel's habitual world that reveals some new aspect of a known person, place, or thing; (6) the revelation of some startling new fact or truth, as when Albertine inadvertently reveals her possible homosexuality; (7) encounters with various works of art. These categories are not always mutually exclusive. For example, Marcel's first encounter with the actress La Berma is at once an encounter with a person previously imagined and with a "work of art" since he sees her in a theatrical performance.

It is certainly true that all these experiences do not exactly conform to May's conception of the creative encounter. While some produce in Marcel a feeling of joy, others cause surprise, disappointment, and often intense suffering. Instead of experiencing the union of subject and object, Marcel is often confronted by a situation in which his self seems completely divorced from its world. Yet all these encounters represent moments of heightened consciousness produced by the explosive revelation of something unforeseen, unexpected, strange, new, or unknown. They are all in the strictest sense of the word *paradoxical* in that they reveal some aspect of reality that is "counter or against human expectation." These expectations need not be the positive projections of the imagination, but simply what Marcel habitually expects of the world. The reality revealed, on the other hand, need not be that of the actual world, but can be a spiritual or transcendent reality. What is needed is that Marcel's habitual or imaginary conceptions of the world be disrupted or destroyed, that he be forced, consequently, to see his self, his world, and their relationship in a new light. "We really know," writes Proust, "only what is novel, what suddenly introduces into our sensibility a change of tone which strikes us, the things for which habit has

8

not yet substituted its colourless facsimiles."[18] The known world, the world of habit, must be destroyed by the shock of an encounter produced by the new or unknown which alone is a source of knowledge. Even though this destruction often causes suffering, the truth it reveals may ultimately become a means of transcending suffering.

In one of the most perceptive sentences ever written on Proust's novel, Samuel Beckett remarks: "In Proust each spear may be a spear of Telephus."[19] Beckett reveals here the essence of Proust's vision of life in time. All of *A la Recherche* is based on the dual paradox that time must be lost in order to be regained, wasted to be redeemed. But Marcel is also subjected to the paradoxical action of time itself that destroys in order to create, and it is precisely during his painful encounters that he becomes most acutely aware of the way time forces him out of his self. This destruction of Marcel's habitual world and self not only exposes aspects of reality that he will describe in his novel, it also teaches him eventually that the secrets of creation and personal salvation also rest on paradoxes, for the artist must destroy the "real" world in order to create the virtual world of art, must lose his superficial self in order to find his true self. Thus, *all* of Marcel's chance encounters determine the course of his becoming, and form at once the material of his novel and his vision of art and reality. "Proust's first gift," writes Clive Bell, "the gift that conditioned his method, was his capacity for giving himself shocks."[20] A study of Marcel's encounters, his "shocks," should reveal not only how Proust's own "method" was conditioned, but also the methods he used to express his vision.

My object is to examine these different types of creative encounter as variations on a fundamental *phrase-type* in Proust's novel. This study proposes, therefore, to reveal both the similarities that exist between these encounters and the way each differs from the other. It will be shown why some encounters cause suffering and others joy, and why even within the same group of encounters Marcel sometimes succeeds in elucidating his impressions and at other times fails. Indeed, Marcel's failures are so frequent that *A la Recherche du temps perdu* might more accurately be called the story of how a little boy almost does *not* become a writer. Yet Marcel's failures, as well as those of other characters like Swann, prepare and help explain his ultimate success. Proust would

18. II, 754; *Fugitive*, III, 529.
19. Samuel Beckett, *Proust* (New York: Grove Press, 1957), p. 1.
20. Bell, p. 53.

have agreed with the art historian E. H. Gombrich that "in the study of art no less than in the study of man, the mysteries of success are frequently best revealed through an investigation of failures."[21] Marcel's encounters will, therefore, be studied in depth, for if Proust's primary interest is to show *how* Marcel becomes a writer, and if the nature of this becoming is most clearly revealed in his encounters, then the way Marcel acts during such moments must be thoroughly elucidated if the meaning of the novel and the form of Proust's vision are to be understood.

Such an elucidation would necessarily involve an examination of Proust's psychology. As has been noted, Picon devotes considerable attention to Proust's ambiguous attitude toward reality, which is at once feared and desired. Another critic, Leo Bersani, also discusses the way Marcel is often torn between his desire for a real world existing outside of himself and his need for a secure world that reflects his own presence.[22] Since an analysis of Marcel's conflicting attitudes toward reality is one of the objects of this study, the work of both these critics will be referred to again. Like all Proust's critics, Picon and Bersani demonstrate in their work that an understanding of Proust's psychology is fundamental to an accurate appreciation of his aesthetics. Like many others, however, they do not show that Proust's particular vision of art and of the creative process is based not only on his conception of the human psyche but also on his conception of the creative spirit, or *esprit*.

Thanks to the work of a small group of critics and scholars, it is now known that Proust began to devote serious attention to the nature and function of the mind, or *esprit*, during his last year at the Lycée Condorcet. André Ferré in his book *Les Années de collège de Marcel Proust*,[23] and Henri Bonnet in a study of Alphonse Darlu,[24] Proust's professor of philosophy, have reconstructed this important period in Proust's intellectual development. What emerges from their work is an affirmation of the influence of Darlu's idealist philosophy on Proust's

21. E. H. Gombrich, *Art and Illusion: A Study in the Psychology of Pictorial Representation* (New York: Pantheon Books, 1965), p. 77.

22. Leo Bersani, *Marcel Proust: The Fictions of Life and of Art* (New York: Oxford University Press, 1966).

23. André Ferré, *Les Années de collège de Marcel Proust* (Paris: Gallimard, 1959).

24. Henri Bonnet, *Alphonse Darlu (1849–1921): Le Maître de philosophie de Marcel Proust. Suivi d'une étude critique du "Contre Sainte-Beuve"* (Paris: Nizet, 1961).

thought. For Darlu, the *esprit* was neither material nor purely abstract but a living, liberating force defined by its activity of perceiving unity in multiplicity and identity in the successive. To turn inward, to know the world by knowing one's impression of it, was for Darlu man's moral duty. In a seminal article Germaine Brée has shown how Proust developed around this conception of the *esprit* a rich and complex group of images.[25] In Proust the *esprit* becomes an inner god whose laws must be obeyed by the artist, an active, creative force that plunges into the darkness of its own inner world and brings its truth to light. The *esprit* is transformed by Proust into a kind of creative imagination, the source of an artist's vision and the means by which he expresses it.

"In any period," writes M. H. Abrams, "the theory of mind and the theory of art tend to be integrally related and to turn upon similar analogues, explicit or submerged."[26] I shall show how Proust's conception of the *esprit* is in fact integrally related both to his theory of art and to his vision of the creative process exemplified by Marcel's encounters. The images Proust employs to describe the *esprit* also reveal how closely his personal morality is related to his conception of artistic creation. For Proust, as for Darlu, the activity of the *esprit* is a moral activity. Indeed, when discussing his novel Proust insisted that "the metaphysical and [moral] point of view predominates throughout the work."[27] Since in Proust the metaphysical is the transcendent reality of art, the *esprit* is the essential link that connects his psychology and ethics to his aesthetics. It is this moral dimension that expands the significance of Marcel's encounters, for it reveals beneath his search for an artistic vocation the need for personal salvation.

Finally, I shall demonstrate that all of Marcel's encounters are related to each other through the presence of certain essential images associated with an archetypal structural pattern Proust discovered as early as *Les Plaisirs et les jours.* Among the most important of these images are the room and the door. All readers of *A la Recherche* are familiar with the rooms Proust describes—the child's bedroom at Combray, the hotel room at Balbec, and many others. As enclosed spaces these rooms

25. Germaine Brée, "La Conception proustienne de 'l'esprit'," *CAIEF,* XII (1960), 199–210.

26. M. H. Abrams, *The Mirror and the Lamp: Romantic Theory and the Critical Tradition* (New York: Norton and Co., 1958), p. 69.

27. *Letters of Marcel Proust,* tr. Mina Curtiss (New York: Random House, 1966), p. 231; Proust, *Lettres à la NRF* (Paris: Gallimard, 1932), p. 104. Curtiss translates "moral" as "intellectual."

are related to other autonomous places in the novel—the gardens, the salons, the world of Combray, and, in fact, all the different "sites" and "milieux" Marcel encounters in the course of his quest.[28] But it is not only within the confines of a room that many of Marcel's most intense encounters take place, it is also the room that most clearly symbolizes certain fundamental relationships between the self and its world. The room may represent the habitual, secure space in which the self feels at ease or seeks refuge from suffering.[29] It can become a hostile, alien space when the habits of the self are destroyed. It may be related to the imprisoning space of the self Marcel often desires to leave. Finally, the room may represent the inner creative space of the *esprit,* similar to that "inner-most chamber" of his soul Marcel enters when he joyfully discovers the "ideal passage" of Bergotte.

Yet it is not these spaces alone that interest Proust, but how one is transformed into another. These moments of sudden transformation when the self enters one space as it exits from another are the moments of encounter. It is during such moments of change that an intense drama takes place between the self and the reality of time. Proust's novel describes a threshold world whose tensions are not completely resolved until the end, when involuntary memory opens for Marcel the inner door leading to the world of artistic creation.[30] It is the existence of this door that gives meaning to all the others. With such recurring images as these Marcel's encounters have an even greater claim to being considered Proust's *phrases-types.*

Despite the fact that all of Marcel's encounters and the sudden revelations of reality he experiences help form the world he eventually transforms into a novel, I shall analyze only those encounters which most powerfully determine his creative vision and which most clearly reveal the particular structure or pattern of events, ideas, and images that will be discussed in greater detail in chapter 1. This concept of the creative encounter, by adding a new dimension to the work of earlier critics, will, I hope, provide a more accurate key to the understanding not only of the other "shocks" and "explosions" of truth in the novel, but also of *A la Recherche* as a whole.

It should be noted also that my purpose is not to examine all of

28. These more extensive spaces in Proust's novel are studied by Georges Poulet in *L'Espace proustien* (Paris: Gallimard, 1963).

29. Picon discusses several such places of refuge in his *Lecture de Proust.*

30. II, 991; *Temps retrouvé,* III, 866.

12

Proust's works or to trace in stages the evolution of his thought. *Jean Santeuil,* for example, will not be discussed in any detail, because the encounters Proust describes there are found in a more fully developed form in *A la Recherche du temps perdu.* On the other hand, material from Proust's critical writings, letters, and early works like *Les Plaisirs et les jours* will be utilized only to the extent that it sheds new light on the fundamental pattern of the creative encounter. It is to his early writings that one must turn, however, to understand his conception of the *esprit* and of the images associated with it.

1
Lessons

In 1888 at the age of seventeen Proust wrote a remarkable letter to his professor of philosophy, Alphonse Darlu, after only two days at the Lycée Condorcet. Proust begins his letter by recalling that Darlu had spoken in class of certain young men who too soon in life seem to split in two and find themselves unable "to do anything or think of anything without their consciousness studying and analyzing these acts and thoughts." Wondering if Darlu can provide him with a cure for this "malady," if indeed it is one, Proust gives his professor a brief history of his own difficulties:

> When I began, at about 14 or 15, to retire within myself and to study my inner life, it was not painful, on the contrary.
> Later, toward 16, it became intolerable, above all physically, causing me extreme fatigue, and becoming a kind of obsession. Now, it no longer has this character at all. My health, once very poor, having become almost good, I have been able to react against the exhaustion and despair that this constant splitting [dédoublement] causes.

Despite this change in its character, Proust insists that his suffering is no less acute. Rather, it has become intellectualized to the point that he can no longer find complete pleasure in what was once his source of greatest joy—works of literature:

> When I read for example a poem by Lecomte [sic] de Lisle, while I still enjoy the same infinite sensual pleasures as in the past, my other self [l'autre moi] considers, amuses itself in considering the causes of my pleasure, sees them in a certain affinity between myself and the work, in this way destroys my certainty

14

of the *intrinsic* beauty of the work, above all immediately imagines the opposite conditions of beauty, finally kills all my pleasure.

Unable to judge anything, Proust states that he is consumed particularly by the need to have "fixed rules" by which to evaluate works of art. Yet the very hope that his professor might know the cure for his condition creates an even more disturbing doubt in his mind: "But then, in order to cure myself, I cannot avoid destroying my inner life, or rather that gaze ceaselessly open on my inner life, and this seems frightening to me."[1]

Already present in this letter are some of the essential themes and ideas Proust will present and discuss throughout his works: the love of literature and the joys associated with reading, the uncompromising need for certainty in the face of doubt, the problem of consciousness that prevents a direct contact with the exterior world, the nature of the relationship that exists between sensitivity and intelligence or between the self that feels and the self that observes and judges. Above all, Proust affirms here the value of the inner, spiritual life of the mind revealed by that particular form of creative activity he will later define as "autocontemplation."

When in his semiautobiographical novel *Jean Santeuil* Proust describes this inner life again, he suggests that the "cure" he sought was indeed found in philosophy. The excitement and dreams produced by Jean's reading of modern poetry had developed in him, writes Proust, "a habit of self-examination for which the study of philosophy had not provided the necessary food." Seeking a way "to keep hold of the elusive nature of his thoughts," Jean reads books which, "no matter how superficially, gave him the sense of a philosophic background."[2] He delights in them just as the hero of *A la Recherche* finds pleasure in discovering passages that reveal Bergotte's "idealist philosophy." In the earlier novel it is Jean's professor of philosophy, Monsieur Beulier, an only slightly fictionalized Darlu, who teaches him how to discipline his thought. Jean is at first surprised to hear the man speak of goodness, truth, and certainty, but Beulier's intelligence, his idealism, his "doctrines spiritua-

1. Bonnet, *Darlu*, pp. 61–62. Proust's italics.
2. Marcel Proust, *Jean Santeuil*, tr. Gerard Hopkins (New York: Simon and Schuster, 1955), pp. 72–73; Proust, *Jean Santeuil*, 3 vols. (Paris: Gallimard, 1952), I, 124.

listes" quickly destroy in Jean's mind "the sophistical doctrines of scepti-
cal materialism."[3] Beulier reaffirms the value of the inner life by revealing
to Jean the nature and function of the *esprit*.

André Ferré remarks that it would be inaccurate to speak of the "philosophy" of Darlu, since Proust's professor never constructed a complete
philosophical system. Ferré does offer a succinct definition of what he
calls Darlu's "philosophical position," which was born from a double
reaction. On the one hand, Darlu rejected

> the materialistic positivism which was then officially in vogue,
> and which claimed, following Taine and his essay *On Intelli-
> gence,* to explain thought by the mechanisms of the brain, the
> movements of the soul by physiological modifications, and to
> see the mind only as a kind of emanation or property of matter.

On the other hand, Darlu balanced his position by reacting no less
strongly against

> the mystical tendency which was opposed to this apparently sci-
> entific conception, and which refused to apply to the mind the
> law of determinism, placed the soul in an empyrean cut off from
> reality, postulated the ordering of the universe by divine will,
> and founded ethics and morality on religious beliefs.

Accepting "neither the reduction of thought, the ideal, and duty to a
pre-determined play of mechanical forces, nor the resignation of reason
and the abandonment of the scientific spirit," Darlu was, in his effort to
know and to explain the world and man, a realist. But, concludes Ferré,
the first reality Darlu encountered in his search for facts and their causes
was "that of the mind, of the activity and demands of his own mind."[4]

Put simply, for Darlu the mind or *esprit* was *real without being material, ideal without being abstract.* His "philosophy" was an idealistic
positivism that refused to acknowledge the validity of any approach
that judged the superior by the inferior, spirit by matter. Believing that
reality is intelligible, he rejected as futile and deceptive any attempt to
explain the world by forces exterior to man himself. Darlu, like Descartes
before him, realized that the most direct and immediate experience and
knowledge that thought has of the world is in fact the experience and
knowledge it has of its own existence. The world is first of all in the
mind and can be apprehended only by and because of the mind.

Proust's professor also considered himself an heir of Kant's idealism.

3. *Jean Santeuil,* p. 240; II, 13.   4. Ferré, *Années de collège,* p. 221.

According to Darlu, Kant had made a clear distinction between the natural world of contingency and unintelligible necessities, and man's spiritual nature, which was a *point fixe* and analogous, in a Platonic fashion, to the divine. A "fixed point" of certainty, an autonomous source and center of truth transcending all systems, the *esprit* was indeed for Darlu "un Dieu intérieur." Man had a "religious duty" to turn toward this inner god in order to understand the truth. And, he insisted, "No one can understand the truth except in himself. No one can *know it,* unless he discovers it in a new light [avec un visage nouveau]."[5] Above all, man's pursuit of truth was an active and, therefore, moral process: "in all things philosophy considers their unity, and the unity of things, or to speak more simply, the unity of human life is accomplished in action. Thus philosophy necessarily tends toward morality"[6]—toward a morality itself independent of any established religion.

Although Darlu's philosophical position is not without ambiguity, it shows why the French word *esprit* is perhaps the only one that can accurately describe his conception of the human mind. While *esprit* is generally, and more or less accurately, translated as "mind" when it refers to the processes of thought and perception, it is also related to the English word "spirit" with its religious, and even mystical, connotations. The same poles of meaning can be ascribed to the adjective *spirituel,* which can be translated both as "mental" or "intellectual" and as "spiritual" depending on the context in which it is used. For Darlu, man's intelligence is supreme precisely because it can completely transcend the limits of discursive reasoning. On the other hand, when he speaks of the divine nature of the mind and its activity he carefully avoids falling into any spiritualism or mysticism that would imply the existence of a supraintellectual or supernatural way of comprehending and explaining the world. He does insist on affirming, however, the *metaphysical* dimension of human thought. Using its richness to his advantage, Darlu defines *esprit* by placing its meaning in a region lying between the somewhat neutral value of "mind" or "intellect" and the more charged significance of "spirit" or "soul."[7]

Two nonliterary texts show how closely Proust himself shared the

5. Bonnet, *Darlu,* p. 52. Darlu's italics.   6. Ibid., p. 18.

7. In this study the French word *esprit* will often be left in the original, particularly when it refers to the creative mind or spirit. The adjective *spirituel* will be translated as "spiritual," but occasionally as "mental" or "intellectual" when the sense of the text requires it. In the Moncrieff-Blossom translation of *A la Recherche, esprit* is usually rendered as "mind." This word has *not* been changed

17

basic tenets of his professor's idealism. The first is a letter Proust wrote in 1904 to his friend and former classmate Fernand Gregh. The letter reflects Darlu's fundamental belief that the *esprit* is at once real and ideal without being material or abstract:

> Do you recall what they told us about the *Metaphysics* of Aristotle? How before him the error of the materialists was to believe they could by analysis find reality in matter, how the error of the Platonists was to search for it, outside of matter, in abstractions; how Aristotle understood that reality could not be an abstraction, that it could not, however, be matter itself, but was rather that which, in each individual thing, is in some way behind matter, being the sense of its form and the law of its development.

Although Proust speaks here of reality and not of the mind, he quickly shows that for him there is no fundamental difference between the two. Turning to Gregh's poetry he transforms his philosophical position into an aesthetic principle:

> So one could say of your poetry that it is neither materialistically descriptive, nor abstractly rational, but that it extricates from the very form of things the individual and transcendent spirit [esprit] that there is in each thing, in each thing belonging to nature or to man. . . .[8]

The true reality of man is his *esprit* which, particularly in the artist, is alone able to seize and to express what is analogous to it—the "spirit" of each thing or, as Proust often notes elsewhere, its "essence."

Of greater importance is a much earlier and longer text drawn from Proust's juvenilia and written either during his year of study with Darlu or later, in 1895, when Proust was preparing for his *licence* in philosophy.[9] It is a philosophical dissertation bearing the interesting title, "The Spirituality of the Soul."

---

back into the original in order to avoid disrupting once again the harmony of Proust's sentences. For the sake of consistency, however, *esprit* has been translated as "mind" also in those instances when Moncrieff or Blossom uses another word (see Introduction, note 1). Finally, as an aid to the reader, the word "mind" has been placed in italics in the translation whenever it represents the *esprit*.

8. Fernand Gregh, *Mon Amitié avec Marcel Proust: Souvenirs et lettres inédites* (Paris: Grasset, 1958), pp. 92–93.

9. While Ferré seems certain that the text is an echo of the course taught by Darlu, *Années de collège,* p. 229, Bonnet suggests that it may date from the later year, *Darlu,* p. 67, n 1.

Proust begins by asking whether our belief in the existence of the soul will not be destroyed by philosophy or made obsolete by science. All our life, he answers, the soul is subjected to the influences of the body. While psychologically different from cerebral matter, thought is no less dependent on the health of the brain. The body and soul must be seen as existing in a state of mutual dependence. But once we attempt to explore this notion of our body, we are forced to recognize that we can understand it only in terms of mental images [représentations spirituelles]. Sensations are organized by the *esprit* according to its own laws and are localized by it in the forms of time and space. The *esprit* is not the product of matter; it is that which constructs matter. The soul cannot be reduced to material elements, but matter can be reduced to psychological elements.

Matter cannot be the substance of the soul, because it is itself not a substance. We do not have the intuition of material objects, but of a multitude of phenomena which our thought unites when it sees in them a certain relation toward the same end. But, Proust adds, when we turn to the soul, it too seems to dissolve into phenomena, for "we have no more the intuition of a single and identical self [un moi un et identique] than we have the intuition of a material substance." All that we apprehend is only what we grasp with our knowledge, only what is, consequently, in time, passing, and particular:

> An emotion, a sensation, an idea, that is what we apprehend of ourselves, those are the limits of the series among which we establish relations in order to forge a fiction of substance as we have already forged one for the things of the exterior world. The mental THING exists no more than material THINGS. The soul, like matter, breaks down into phenomena united by thought.

But in order to unite phenomena and to have an idea of them, the *esprit* must be more than a phenomenon. Unity is not given in the phenomenon, nor is it formed simply by the consciousness that survives the phenomenon or the memory that preserves it. For consciousness or memory to attribute this phenomenon to the self, thought must know the unity and identity of the self:

> Thought is not a reality hidden beneath phenomena, it is rather the single and identical conception of phenomena. That is the substance that in truth does not support phenomena and is not distinct from them but is the consciousness of their unity and

their identity. It is an action which consists in reducing multiplicity to unity, what is successive to what is identical. The substance thus comprised is completely spiritual.

This "substance" is simply thought, the *esprit,* the self. Proust calls it our essence [le fond de nous-même], an essence common to all who think. Yet if we participate by means of it in what is universal, it is only individually that we can realize and express it. We do not perceive our thought as an "immobile abstraction," but rather as "an activity which is proper to us, namely to convert [résoudre] the multiplicity of phenomena into the unity of the mind, to order our most particular acts with a view to their universal ends." Although this higher unity of the mind may be considered to be more real than the individual, it still "leaves a place for individual effort, in the progress of which our soul manifests itself to us as a relatively free spiritual activity." And Proust concludes:

> Our final word is that the soul in each man's consciousness is a kind of dominion, or universe within the universal dominion. This is not completely intelligible: but it is the truth of moral freedom. Therefore, if the spirituality of the soul must be defined, we shall say: *it is freedom.*[10]

Proust's dissertation can clearly be placed in the grand tradition of philosophical idealism going back to Kant, if not beyond.[11] It is also true that Proust belonged to a generation of writers, artists, and aestheticians which meditated on the nature of perception, on the activity of the mind, and on the role of consciousness and of the unconscious.[12] Well before the publication in 1889 of Bergson's *Essai sur les données immédiates*

10. Ferré, pp. 224–29. Proust's italics.
11. Proust's idealism is the subject of one major study. See: Noël Martin-Deslias, *Idéalisme de Marcel Proust* (Paris: Nagel, 1952). This book was published before documents from Proust's student years were made available to scholars. An excellent presentation of the basic principles of French idealism at the turn of the century can be found in two early works by one of Darlu's disciples, the philosopher Léon Brunschvicg: *L'Idéalisme contemporain* (Paris: Alcan, 1905); *Introduction à la vie de l'esprit* (Paris: Alcan, 1932). Proust knew Brunschvicg at the Lycée Condorcet and mentions having read the second of the above works, which was first published in 1903 (*Bible d'Amiens,* p. 254, n 1).
12. Germaine Brée discusses the intellectual climate in France at the end of the nineteenth century in her article, "La Conception proustienne de 'l'esprit'," pp. 202–3.

de la conscience,[13] they read the works of Schopenhauer, Hartmann, Fouillée, and Charcot. I do not intend to examine the real or probable influence of these or other philosophers on the development of Proust's thought. While Darlu was the only one to whom Proust himself acknowledged a truly substantial debt, even this influence should be placed in the proper perspective. Proust's letter to Darlu shows that he was already conscious of some aspects of his inner life before beginning his study of philosophy. Although his dissertation on the soul demonstrates his profound understanding of Darlu's conception of the *esprit,* it also reveals the presence of certain ideas, which, because they are found elsewhere in Proust's work, must be considered as part of a highly individual and personal vision of the self's relationship with its world.

When in *Le Temps retrouvé* Proust's narrator looks back on his life, he remarks: "I realised that only superficial and defective [perception] attaches all importance to the object, when the *mind* is everything."[14] It is certainly this erroneous perception that Proust describes in his dissertation when he speaks of our tendency to create "fictions of substance" for the things of the exterior world as well as for our own selves. Throughout *A la Recherche* Marcel repeatedly witnesses the destruction of these fictions. Not only do things and persons fail to correspond to his images of them, but they also "break down" through their existence in time into a succession of individual and often incompatible impressions. He discovers the same void whenever he attempts to seize his own identity, since he also seems to dissolve into a multiplicity and succession of selves in space and time. This inability to grasp the identity of others or to discover within himself "a single and identical self" is for Marcel a source of intense anguish, particularly during and after his love for Albertine. He does not, however, remain in this state. Just as philosophy "cured" Proust by teaching him that he must think not in terms of

13. For a discussion of the influence of Schopenhauer and Hartmann on French literature at the turn of the century, see Guy Michaud, *Message poétique du symbolisme* (Paris: Nizet, 1961). Robert Champigny compares Proust's thought to that of Bergson, Spinoza, Schopenhauer, and Kierkegaard in his article, "Temps et reconnaissance chez Proust et quelques philosophes," *PMLA*, LXXIII (March 1958), 129–135. Henri Bonnet compares Darlu's philosophy with Bergson's in *Darlu*, pp. 79–82. Bonnet also gives an excellent analysis of the similarities and differences between Proust's thought and Bergson's in his book, *Le Progrès spirituel dans l'oeuvre de Marcel Proust*, vol. II: *L'Eudémonisme esthétique de Proust* (Paris: Vrin, 1949), pp. 212–36.

14. II, 1025; *Temps retrouvé*, III, 912. Blossom translates "perception" as "observation."

"things," but in terms of the spiritual *activity* that comprehends things, so Marcel passes from a rather naive materialism through a period of skepticism and disenchantment until he finally discovers within his own *esprit* the ultimate source of truth and certainty. In the novel, of course, it is neither a philosopher nor philosophy but experience that forces Marcel to acknowledge "the purely mental character of reality."[15] For Proust also philosophy could not and did not replace experience, and life was, as his professor himself would have wished, a greater teacher than Darlu.

Proust's definition of spiritual activity as "an action which consists in reducing multiplicity to unity, what is successive to what is identical" is for this very reason of the greatest importance to an understanding of his work. Although Proust describes an activity that *reduces* multiplicity to unity, his entire discussion suggests that he is not referring simply to the activity of ordinary perception but to a higher form of perception. In *A la Recherche* Proust ascribes this reductive action either to habit, which creates a false unity by eliminating the rich complexity of experience, or to the rational intellect, which reduces experience to the general "laws" of behavior. He speaks there of the power of the *esprit* to *discover* unity in multiplicity and identity in the successive. He shows also that the creative *esprit* reveals new forms of unity through a metamorphosis of reality. In this sense Proust's *esprit* resembles Kant's "transcendental faculty of imagination" that remodels experience[16] or Coleridge's "Secondary Imagination" that "dissolves, diffuses, dissipates, in order to recreate."[17]

It should be noted that Proust does not use the word "imagination" in quite the same way to describe the creative faculty. In *A la Recherche* Marcel's imagination can function only when directed toward an absent person, place, or thing. The primary source of his dreams and desires that reality invariably destroys, his imagination is not fully satisfied until involuntary memory brings forth a world at once absent or past yet capable of being experienced in the present. The narrator does call imagination "the only organ with which I could enjoy beauty."[18] But when he

15. II, 1026; *Temps retrouvé*, III, 914.
16. Immanuel Kant, *The Critique of Pure Reason*, tr. F. Max Muller (New York and London: Oxford University Press, 1907), pp. 82–85; *The Critique of Judgment*, tr. J. C. Meredith (Oxford: Oxford University Press, 1952), pp. 172–79.
17. Samuel Taylor Coleridge, *Biographia Literaria*, ed. J. Shawcross (Oxford, Clarendon Press, 1907), I, p. 202.
18. II, 996; *Temps retrouvé*, III, 872. Proust describes the role of the imagination in *Jean Santeuil*, pp. 406–10; II, 228–34.

relates those privileged moments of his youth when he was struck by the beauties of nature, he uses words like *pensée, attention,* and *esprit* to describe the creative activity of his mind. Certainly, the imagination also operates during such moments, but it should be seen as a vital part of the *esprit* itself. In Proust's aesthetic vocabulary it is the *esprit* that occupies the central position, for it is not only the source of a rich variety of images or the key to all the functions of the artist's mind, but also the most *active* element in the creative process.

Proust does not describe this creative power of the *esprit* in his short dissertation. Indeed, he makes no mention of artistic creation as such. Yet his remarks on the *esprit* reveal the sources of his aesthetics and of his vision of reality. In *A la Recherche* Marcel discovers his own identity when he recognizes within himself the existence of a permanent and individual way of seeing the world that exposes "the sense of its form and the law of its development." He discovers, in other words, that while each of his impressions was determined by a different set of phenomena, all were perceived and formed by an identical spiritual activity.[19] In Proust's novel it is the discovery of unity in multiplicity and identity in the successive that gives form to space and time. The *esprit* is seen as the creator of *metaphors* that "spiritualize" the matter of reality. Through its creation of "spiritual substances" the *esprit liberates* the self from the limits of contingency and unites the self with its world. The *esprit* creates, therefore, a world analogous to itself—a world that is at once real and ideal, individual and universal.

"At bottom," writes Proust in the conclusion to *Contre Sainte-Beuve,* "all my philosophy, like all true philosophy, comes back to vindicating and re-establishing [what exists]."[20] Through Darlu and above all through his own experience Proust did indeed learn that what *exists* is the *esprit* and not the "fictions of substance" which, like idols, prevent us from recognizing our "inner god." Unlike Darlu, Proust will vindicate and reestablish the existence of the *esprit* through art, for only by means of the individual activity of artistic creation will he be able to express the universal and liberate his "soul."

19. A similar idea is expressed by Benedetto Croce: "It is the matter, the content, which differentiates one of our intuitions from another: the form is constant: it is spiritual activity, while matter is changeable." *Aesthetic,* tr. Douglas Ainslie (New York: The Noonday Press, 1960), p. 6.

20. *Marcel Proust on Art and Literature: 1896–1919,* tr. Sylvia Townsend Warner (New York: Dell, 1958), p. 272; Proust, *Contre Sainte-Beuve suivi de Nouveaux mélanges* (Paris: Gallimard, 1954), p. 308. Warner translates "ce qui est," literally "that which is," as "the actual."

The Will

When Proust left Darlu's philosophy class in 1889, he did begin to write a series of short pieces which in 1896 were published as *Les Plaisirs et les jours*. All these stories and descriptive fragments, despite their apparently disparate nature, are united, as Henri Bonnet remarks, by a common theme: "the theme of the superiority of the inner life, of the life of the *esprit*, of the contemplative life."[21] Although Proust recognizes from the beginning his debt to Darlu, whom he praises as "the great philosopher whose inspired words, more certain to last than a written text, have in me, as in so many others, engendered thought,"[22] the way he expresses this theme reveals its profoundly personal origin. In fact, in *Les Plaisirs et les jours* Darlu's ideas undergo a certain transformation and even lose temporarily part of their original meaning.

In the dedication to his dead friend Willie Heath, Proust describes the nature of the inner life. "Our harsh life presses us too closely," he writes, "and perpetually inflicts pain on our soul." But there are times when we experience "the sweetness of a suspension of living, of a true 'Divine Truce'" that interrupts "our tasks and evil desires."[23] These periods of "grace" when we feel closer to our soul occur for lovers at the beginning of their love, for poets when they create, and for those who suffer illness. Placing himself in this last group, Proust recalls his own experiences:

> When I was just a child, the fate of no character in the holy scriptures seemed to me as miserable as that of Noah, because of the flood which kept him imprisoned in the ark for forty days. Later, I was often ill, and for long days I too had to remain in the "ark." I understood then that Noah had never seen the world so well as from the ark, despite the fact that it was closed and that darkness covered the earth.[24]

Here, as in his letter to Darlu, Proust attributes his knowledge of the inner life to his frequent illnesses. What is most striking about this passage, however, is the image of the ark. By describing his bedroom as an ark, Proust transforms it into a symbol for the enclosed, autonomous inner space of the soul. He is careful to note that his childhood fear of

21. Bonnet, *Le Progrès spirituel*, II, p. 162.
22. Marcel Proust, *Les Plaisirs et les jours* (Paris: Gallimard, 1924), p. 16. The dedication to Willie Heath, in which this passage and the one below are found, is not in the Dupee edition.
23. Ibid., pp. 13–14.   24. Ibid., p. 13.

entering this space and of abandoning his habitual life was itself transformed into joy, once he realized that the voyage through darkness could provide him with a new vision of the world, of a world that could be truly seen only from within the soul.

The first story of *Les Plaisirs*, "La Mort de Baldassare Silvande," develops these themes and images. Forced by illness to suspend his active social life, Baldassare spends in his bedroom "long and charming hours tête-à-tête with himself, the only guest he had neglected to invite to supper during his lifetime."[25] So completely does his illness change him, that when he begins to regain his health the thought of resuming his former life frightens him:

> He . . . vaguely felt that it would be wrong to lose himself in pleasure and in action again, now that he had made the acquaintance of his other self, of that fraternal stranger with whom, so remote and yet so close, he had conversed for hours.[26]

This self-examination remains incomplete, and when his rapidly approaching death brings Baldassare once more in contact with his soul, he realizes that it is too late to redeem his wasted life and to satisfy his mother's dream that he would someday become a great musician.

Another story, "Violante ou la mondanité," also describes how a life can be wasted in society. After a childhood passed in dreaming and meditation, Violante marries a duke and begins to desire a brilliant social career. Her old servant, Augustin, warns her of the dangers inherent in her desire, for, he says, "happiness is to be found only in doing what one loves, following the soul's profoundest bent."[27] Convinced that she will be able to return when she wishes to her life of thoughtful solitude, Violante enters the social world, but there her old self is replaced by a new one. Each day her egoism, desires, and social ambitions take her farther and farther away from "the noble destiny that might have been hers."[28] A whole side of her now seems lost forever, and even her moments of solitude no longer enable her to enter into contact with her inner self:

> Mornings in bed she would still read or dream, but with a distorted mind that stopped short at the outside of things and

25. *Pleasures and Days and Other Writings by Marcel Proust*, ed. F. W. Dupee, tr. Louise Varese, Gerard Hopkins, and Barbara Dupee (Garden City: Doubleday, 1957), p. 14; *Plaisirs*, p. 32.

26. *Pleasures*, p. 16; *Plaisirs*, p. 36.   27. *Pleasures*, p. 32; *Plaisirs*, p. 61.

28. *Pleasures*, p. 33; *Plaisirs*, p. 63.

would contemplate itself not with a desire to penetrate more profoundly, but to admire itself voluptuously and coquettishly, as in a mirror.[29]

This false self-consciousness is the mark of Violante's failure. Her social world has become so much a part of her self-identity that she cannot abandon one without losing the other. She is, in fact, no longer capable of abandoning society, for her will has been completely destroyed by habit, which hides her disgust and even her boredom.

The weakness of the will and the force of habit are treated again in "La Confession d'une jeune fille." The heroine, who is dying of a self-inflicted gunshot wound, relates the events that led to her present state. Her youth was filled with promise, and her mother early conceived for her a bright, productive future. Her character suffered, however, from a dangerous flaw. "What grieved my mother was my lack of will. I did everything on the impulse of the moment." All her mother's efforts were directed toward helping her to create by herself and within herself the necessary strength of will. But she always postponed her own efforts:

> I would give myself time, miserable sometimes to see it passing, but, after all, for me there was still so much ahead! I was a little frightened, nevertheless, and felt vaguely that this habit of getting along without using my will weighed on me more and more with the years, sadly suspecting that things would not change suddenly, that I could scarcely count on a miracle which would cost me nothing to change my life and create a will for me. To wish to possess a will was not enough. What I had to do was precisely what I could not do without a will: to will to have one.[30]

This weakness of the will led her to abandon herself to her sexual desires whose demands habit rendered increasingly more imperative. By giving herself to pleasures that destroyed her will, she says, "I was committing the worst crime against my mother."[31] Through the help of a young man whom she was to marry, she was able for a time to triumph over her habits. One night shortly before her marriage, however, she could not resist the desire to embrace one of her former lovers. Her mother witnessed the scene from the balcony and died from the shock. All that remained for her after that was to take her own life.

29. *Pleasures*, p. 33; *Plaisirs*, p. 64.
30. *Pleasures*, pp. 83–84; *Plaisirs*, pp. 148–49.
31. *Pleasures*, p. 86; *Plaisirs*, p. 152.

These stories clearly reflect Proust's own experience, his interests, desires, fears, and obsessions. If in all of them he demonstrates the value of the inner life, he does so by describing the emptiness of the social or sensual life. Throughout *Les Plaisirs et les jours* Proust condemns *divertissement* with a moral fervor at times equal to Pascal's. His heroes and heroines, like Baldassare, are perpetually "losing themselves" in pleasure and action, particularly the pleasures and activities of elegant society from which their egos derive an uneasy satisfaction. They are centrifugal beings trapped by the need to "get out of" themselves. These early stories reveal how acutely Proust sensed the paradoxical nature of his own social success—it was nothing less than the reverse side of a personal failure. In a letter to his friend Reynaldo Hahn written in 1896 Proust speaks of "those persons who could have been great men if . . . (*Tu Marcellus eris*)."[32] Virgil's sad vision of a promise that was never fulfilled must have seemed particularly prophetic to Proust. He was wasting his time and his talent in society, and might become, like Baldassare, an *artiste manqué*.

"Complete natures being rare," writes Proust in *A la Recherche,* "a man who is highly sensitive and highly intelligent will generally have little will-power, will be the plaything of habit and of that fear of suffering in the immediate present which condemns us to perpetual suffering."[33] Baldassare, Violante, and the young girl all reflect in varying degrees this "incomplete nature" Proust early discovered in himself. Endowed with an extraordinarily acute sensitivity and a remarkable intelligence, he recognized that the tragic flaw in his character was the weakness of his will. This weakness made him at once the victim of his habits which alone could protect him against suffering, and of his sensitivity which was the primary source of his suffering. Also, without a strong will his intelligence could not be directed toward the necessary task of elucidating the impressions provided by his sensitivity and thereby drawing from them the knowledge that could fortify him against suffering and free him from his habits.

Hoping to discover the sources of his weakness, Proust read Ribot's *Les Maladies de la volonté,* which taught him that the exercise of will power was an illusion because man's choices were determined by preceding moral and physical causes. He also read Schopenhauer, who

32. Marcel Proust, *Lettres à Reynaldo Hahn,* ed. Philip Kolb (Paris: Gallimard, 1956), p. 63.
33. II, 814; *Fugitive,* III, 616.

claimed that man was the victim of the blind will of his unconscious self. But Schopenhauer also wrote that whereas ordinary perception could not reveal true reality or "idea," a man of genius could discover this reality through another form of perception—contemplation. By means of contemplation, which is also the source of art, man could free himself from the barriers that exist between subject and object.[34] It is important to note that when Proust speaks of the will, he means the *conscious* will by means of which man is able to enter into contact with his inner life. The danger of possessing a weak will is that it is unable to resist the demands of the "unconscious" will, of habit, or of the desire for social and sensual pleasures.

In this respect "La Confession d'une jeune fille" is particularly revealing. Certainly, the girl is Proust, and the guilt she feels because of her inability to resist her sexual desires is a reflection of Proust's own feelings of guilt related to his homosexuality. But what makes the girl's failure a "crime" is that it represents the defeat of the conscious will and, therefore, the cruel destruction of the mother's dreams. Proust early considered his mother as representing the best part of himself. It is she who remains within the bedroom during his illnesses, and when she leaves through "the door of the ark" her departure signals the end of the period of "grace."[35] She is the voice of the inner life and the living reminder of the commitment Proust felt each man must make to himself, "which is to live in order to be worthy and to merit respect."[36] The mother is also the embodiment of the past, of the lost world of childhood innocence and promise. This world can be recaptured, success assured, and the inner life truly lived when the moral obligations and responsibilities represented by the mother are fulfilled. It is for this reason that no word in Proust's early vocabulary has greater weight than "duty." As the young girl's story shows, Proust made no distinction between his duty to himself and his duty to fulfill his mother's dreams. But the accomplishment of one's duty requires a strong will. In "La Confession d'une jeune fille" the girl's impulsive will for pleasure triumphs over the moral will represented by the mother. At the end her suicide merely destroys

34. For an analysis of the importance of Ribot and Schopenhauer to Proust's conception of the will, see Harold March, *The Two Worlds of Marcel Proust* (New York: A. S. Barnes and Co., 1961), pp. 1–18. For Proust's own remarks on these two thinkers, see, for Ribot, *Pastiches,* p. 251, n 1; and, for Schopenhauer, *Pastiches,* pp. 259–61.

35. *Plaisirs,* pp. 13–14.   36. *Plaisirs,* p. 15.

her body, for the final act of weakness that kills her mother also kills the girl's soul.

The themes in "La Confession d'une jeune fille" will be developed in *A la Recherche* when Proust describes the relationship between Marcel and his mother and grandmother, and between Mlle Vinteuil and her father.[37] This story, like many of the others in *Les Plaisirs et les jours,* already reveals Proust's method of expressing in the dramatic conflicts of his characters his own inner conflicts. "The real elements . . . of any work of fiction," writes Edmund Wilson in a now famous passage,

> are the elements of the author's personality: his imagination embodies in the images of characters, situations and scenes the fundamental conflicts of his nature or the cycle of phases through which it habitually passes. His personages are personifications of the author's various impulses and emotions: and the relations between them in his stories are really the relations between these.[38]

In "La Confession d'une jeune fille" the characters are indeed personifications of the fundamental elements of Proust's nature, for just as the mother represents the inner life, the conscious will, and the soul, so the girl represents the superficial self, the impulses of the unconscious, and the body. The same basic conflict is expressed in the dialogue between Augustin and Violante, and in Baldassare's "conversation" with his soul.

It is in fact possible to consider these early stories as so many variations on the often described conflict of body and soul. Proust himself knew that his writings contained images and ideas that had already been expressed by other writers. Throughout *Les Plaisirs et les jours* passages from their works are used to introduce the different sections of each story. Among the most interesting of these works is the *Imitation of Jesus Christ.* Although the passages from it that Proust quotes generally describe the self-destructive power of the senses, he was certainly aware that its argument was based on the fundamental Christian vision of man's paradoxical nature. In the *Imitation* man is shown as being at once a sinful earthbound creature and an *imago dei* capable of self-

---

37. Proust's interest in the macabre relationship between child and parent can be seen in another early work, "Sentiments filiaux d'un parricide," *Pastiches,* pp. 211–24.

38. Edmund Wilson, *Axel's Castle: A Study in the Imaginative Literature of 1870–1930* (New York: Scribner's, 1931), p. 176.

transcendence. Proust found a similar vision in Emerson. A phrase from the works of the American transcendentalist introduces "La Mort de Baldassare Silvande": "The poets say that Apollo tended the flocks of Admetus; so too, each man is a God in disguise who plays the fool."[39]

In quoting Emerson, Proust was careful to translate "God" simply as "dieu" in order to avoid any direct allusion to the biblical divinity. Although Darlu also admired Emerson, Proust had learned from his professor and from his mother a fundamentally secular morality. Yet it is significant that the different sources of Proust's early vision of life and reality coalesced in this conception of an inner god and of man's paradoxical nature. To stop "playing the fool" and to "imitate" the god within became for Proust the essence of moral duty.

The Stranger

As dramatizations of Proust's own paradoxical nature the three stories that have been discussed contain many of the important conflicts that Proust will develop in *A la Recherche*. There is one story, however, in which the same themes and images are expressed in a particularly significant form. Although the story, entitled "L'Etranger," is hardly more than a sketch, it comes close to being a prototype of those creative encounters described in the Introduction to this study. Because of its importance, the story is given here in a somewhat reduced form:

> Dominique was sitting in front of the dying fire waiting for his guests to arrive. Every evening he invited some great nobleman to sup with him in the company of men of wit, and as he was wellborn, rich, and charming, he was never alone. The candles had not been lighted and in the room the day was sadly dying. All at once he heard a voice saying, a faraway and intimate voice saying: "Dominique," and only to hear the way it uttered, uttered from so far away and yet so close, "Dominique," froze him with fear.

The voice seems that of a "noble victim sacrificed by him" reproaching Dominique for a past crime which he cannot recall, but for which he is responsible. Looking up he sees "a stranger with a vague and striking air," who asks: "Dominique, am I to be the only one not invited to your supper? [There are wrongs you have done me to be repaired, old wrongs. After that, I shall teach you to do without the others who, when you are

39. *Pleasures*, p. 4; *Plaisirs*, p. 17.

old, will come to you no longer.]" "But I do invite you to my supper," answers Dominique with "a grave warmth" in his voice that even he finds unusual; for already the "fraternal gaze" of the stranger has changed Dominique's fear into "a novel happiness." "But if you wish me to stay, you must send the other guests away," says the stranger. With his guests knocking at the door and the room now completely dark, Dominique replies: "I cannot send them away, *I cannot bear to be alone.*" "Choose quickly," cries the stranger after warning him again of his future solitude, but Dominique has already gone to open the door for his guests. "But who are you?" he asks. And the stranger who is vanishing answers:

> "Habit, to which you sacrifice me this evening, tomorrow, nourished by the blood of the wounds you have inflicted on me, will be stronger than ever. Each day more exigent for having been obeyed again, it will lead you a little farther from me, force you to make me suffer even more. Soon you will have killed me. You will never see me again. Yet you owe more to me than to the others, who will soon desert you. I am within you, yet I am now very far away; I hardly exist any longer. I am your soul, I am yourself."

Later at the table with his guests Dominique attempts to relate his encounter with the stranger, but already those past moments seem a dream he can no longer recall. "Then they all began drinking again. Dominique chatted gaily but without joy, flattered by the brilliance of the company."[40]

This story is hardly a masterpiece. Its style is pretentious and inflated. The rather awkward repetitions of words and phrases never quite succeed in fulfilling their obvious intent, that of creating the peculiar atmosphere of oracular mystery Proust must have judged proper to the expression of "eternal moral truths." Although here again Proust is condemning *divertissement* and habit while praising the value of solitude and the inner life, his description of the conflict between body and soul seems at first glance shallow when compared with the more realistic description he achieves in the longer stories. The mother in "La Confession d'une jeune fille" is certainly more convincing in the role of the "noble victim" who embodies the demands of the soul. Violante's addic-

40. *Pleasures,* pp. 120–22; *Plaisirs,* pp. 207–10. The bracketed passage is not found in the English translation.

tion to social pleasures and Baldassare's encounter with his own "fraternal dinner guest" are also presented with greater subtlety. Indeed, "L'Etranger" seems to be a relatively early work, for it more blatantly reveals the influence of certain literary models.[41] Proust's mysterious stranger resembles Musset's dark visitor in the "Nuit" poems, while his description of a supernatural dinner guest seeking retribution for past crimes recalls the "feast of stone" scene in Molière's *Don Juan.* Also, Proust appears to be dramatizing in this story Pascal's discovery that "all the unhappiness of men arises from one single fact, that they cannot stay quietly in their own chamber."[42]

Despite its weaknesses, "L'Etranger" is a remarkable story. Proust is not describing here the calm moments of "grace" during which the self communes with its inner life. He is presenting with dramatic economy a man's confrontation and struggle with himself. This encounter does not take place because of illness but is precipitated by a *sudden apparition* which, because it is totally unexpected, is truly "strange." As in "La Mort de Baldassare Silvande" the soul is described as possessing a mysterious life of its own. It is far and near, absent and present, at once distant and intimate, unknown and known. In "L'Etranger," however, this paradoxical nature of the soul is an integral part of the action. Having forgotten during most of his life the existence of his inner god, Dominique must now redeem his past "crimes" by making his soul fully present and known to himself. He must, in other words, bring it into being through an act of will, for if the soul is always present in man, it remains forever absent until it is recognized and accepted as the true self. But in order to become what he truly is, Dominique knows that he must detach himself from his habitual world and must accept the loss of the self that is tied to that world. The fear he feels at the sight of the stranger is really his fear of losing this self and the feeling of certainty attached to it. In Proust as in the Bible, however, "he who would save his life must lose it." Dominique almost achieves this paradoxical transformation of his life when he asks the stranger to be his guest.

Dominique's struggle with his soul also reveals important aspects of Proust's vision of life in time. Dominique has wasted and lost his time

41. "L'Etranger" is one of the few stories in *Les Plaisirs et les jours* for which no date of composition has been discovered.
42. Blaise Pascal, *Pensées/The Provincial Letters,* tr. W. F. Trotter (New York: Random House, 1941), p. 48; Pascal, *Pensées,* ed. Louis Allard (Montreal: Editions Variétés, 1945), p. 116.

in the pursuit of social pleasures, and his soul represents both the wasted time that must be redeemed and the lost time that must be regained. Instead of turning inward to this permanent world within himself, Dominique seeks for permanence in society. "Every evening" he must have his guests, who must "always" come. He refuses to accept his own or his friends' existence in time, and that is indeed the lesson of the stranger. Dominique will grow old and his friends will abandon him. Age and death are already in Proust, if somewhat prematurely, the inescapable faces of time. Instead of marching backward toward death with his eyes turned toward life, Dominique must reverse his vision and become himself a stranger to his world. His soul invites him to step outside of time and to contemplate not his reflection in the exterior world of illusion, but his true self contained in the world within him. To step outside of time is to abandon one's ego, the self-satisfied and self-indulgent social being who is the victim of time.

In "L'Etranger" Proust incorporates time into the very fabric of the encounter. A situation that necessitates a choice is thrust upon Dominique "all at once," and he must not only choose, but choose "quickly." The guests are knocking on the door, and time is being wasted and lost at the very moment of decision. Dominique's encounter is truly a privileged *moment*. It is a race against time with all the odds in favor of habit, automatic responses, and inertia. It already points to another fundamental theme in Proust's work closely related to the conflict of body and soul—the struggle between *l'Esprit et le Temps*.

Dominique's choice also reveals the importance of the role played by the will in an encounter. The apparition of the stranger is not willed. If it were, it would not disrupt Dominique's habitual world and produce a heightening of his consciousness. But he must will to give himself to his encounter in order to bring forth his soul. Although his failure represents the triumph of his habits and of his fear of solitude, it is nevertheless the result of a conscious choice. Like Darlu, Proust never accepted a purely deterministic vision of life that would deny to the mind its freedom of action and destroy the meaning of moral responsibility. The stranger's parting remarks to Dominique, like the young girl's description of her weak will, reveal Proust's underlying conception of life as *a series of choices made in time*. For the girl and for Dominique time is running out. As each day and year passes, their failure to resist the force of habit makes them more and more its victims. Through their choices in favor of habit they are destroying instead of creating themselves.

33

Although it is true that for Proust the choices made in the past largely determine the choices that will be made in the future, it is also true that the possibility always exists to choose in favor of the inner life. Dominique, like the young girl, loses his chance for salvation through an *abdication* of his will to habit.

What is most significant in this story is the way Proust relates Dominique's entire encounter, and particularly his final abdication, to the images of the room and the door. The stranger's presence transforms the room into the autonomous inner space of the soul. This presence, acknowledged by the happiness Dominique feels, encloses him within an "ark" and, for a moment at least, *excludes* the world of habit represented by the guests, who are in this respect merely extensions of the superficial self. Unable to remain within the ark by accepting his solitude and this loss of his familiar identity, Dominique abandons the activity of self-examination for the actions of society. His failure is complete once he opens the door to his guests, for by doing so he *corrupts* the space of his heightened consciousness. The new world and the new self promised by the encounter are in turn excluded and replaced by the "colorless facsimiles" of habit. The threshold of the inner life is not crossed. The door opens in the wrong direction.

"L'Etranger" doubtless contains certain modes of expression that Proust soon abandoned. In *Jean Santeuil* and, of course, in *A la Recherche* encounters are not caused by the supernatural apparition of a personified soul, but by elements in the real world of experience. Indeed, there are times in *Les Plaisirs et les jours* when Proust's praise of the inner life seems too absolute. "I have thought, and that is to live," remarks Augustin to Violante.[43] Proust had certainly not forgotten the lessons of Darlu and his own early definition of thought as an activity which is developed through its contacts with reality. It seems, however, that his youthful disillusionment and perhaps his desire to create certain "poetic" effects in the manner of the decadent writers of the time led him to neglect the importance and necessity of a continuing experience of life.

But if "L'Etranger" does not show that the discovery of the true self can be achieved only through the discovery of the truth or essence hidden within the sensations and impressions produced by reality, it nonetheless provides a structure that is admirably suited to the description of

43. *Pleasures,* p. 32; *Plaisirs,* p. 62.

such experiences. In *A la Recherche* also the revelations of reality take the form of a sudden encounter that has not been willed. There again Proust repeatedly demonstrates how the most intense activity of the *esprit* and efforts of the will take place within the context of a specific *event*.

This need of a particular context or, as the existentialists would say, "situation," in relation to which decisions are made and acts performed modifies somewhat the nature of the moral imperatives associated with self-redemption. The girl in "La Confession" knows that she cannot "count on a miracle" to change her life suddenly by giving her the will she lacks. Although Proust emphasizes in this way that there can be no substitute for an individual decision and act in favor of the inner life, he does not have his heroine experience a moment of heightened consciousness in which such a decision *must* be made. The apparition of Dominique's soul does not suddenly change his life. It confronts him with a sudden opportunity for a change to be brought about by his own efforts with regard to a "situation" that is far more immediate and specific than any in which the girl, Violante, or Baldassare find themselves. While Proust does not abandon the idea that one can choose the inner life at any time, he suggests in "L'Etranger" that life occasionally *gives* us moments that demand a choice. Moral duty involves, therefore, not so much the search for opportunities, but the attempt to find a way of realizing fully those that confront us. In *A la Recherche* sudden sensations and impressions will be the given elements of experience by means of which Marcel will discover the meaning of his life in time.

Once duty is associated with the actual *process* of creation it takes on an even greater moral significance, for it must be directed also toward *resisting* anything that could weaken or arrest this process. In "L'Etranger" Dominique does not bring his self into being and enter the ark completely because he fails to resist the pressures of habit that threaten and finally destroy the self's purity and autonomy. This danger of the *corruption of consciousness* will be a fundamental part of all the encounters Proust describes in which the will must struggle against the temptation to abdicate. In the following chapters I shall demonstrate that Proust's concern with such corruption is not only an important key to an understanding of his psychology, but that it is also an essential element in his aesthetics. For example, in an essay on the painter Gustave Moreau written a few years after the publication of *Les Plaisirs*, he notes that an artist's or poet's creations are the "fragmentary apparitions" of his deepest soul. Then in order to describe the creative process, Proust turns again to the image of the inner space: "Inspiration is the moment when the poet is able to break through into that innermost soul. Being at work is the struggle to remain entirely there, so that while he is writing or painting there may be no contamination from the outer world [pour ne pas . . . y rien mêler du dehors]."[44] Just as the absence of "contamination" from whatever source is the hallmark of greatness in the works of all artists, real or fictional, that Proust discusses, so its presence is immediately seen as a sign of failure. Duty in Proust will become in its most meaningful form a question of artistic integrity.

Judging by his later work it is certain that Proust realized after *Les Plaisirs* that he must attempt to unite more thoroughly his literary mind and poetic imagination with the solid philosophical concepts he had inherited from Darlu. He knew that he must define more clearly the *esprit,* the self, and the soul; that he must discover how and why something that is near and far away, present and absent is related to what is real and ideal, individual and universal, particular and general; how and why all forms of true reality are in one way or another paradoxical. All of Proust's works before *A la Recherche,* his numerous essays on writers and artists, *Jean Santeuil,* his writings on Ruskin, the *Contre Sainte-Beuve,* represent a long meditation on these questions and an intensive study of those moments of encounter that set the mind and the creative process in motion. Yet whatever their nature, Proust's discoveries have their roots in the past and always reflect the particular moral vision he acquired early in life. Morally superior, mysterious, and the very opposite of that other "esprit" or wit that in Dominique, as later in the Guermantes, is the superficial and wasteful expression of the social self, the "creative spirit" is always seen as something divine within man. "Art cannot be defined," wrote Georges de Lauris many years after Proust's death. "Marcel considered it to be a god who had the power to resuscitate that which, without it, would remain forever dead."[45]

44. *Proust on Art,* pp. 348–49; *Sainte-Beuve,* pp. 389–90. Proust's essay on Moreau was probably written between 1898 and 1904.

45. Marcel Proust, *A un ami,* préface de Georges de Lauris (Paris: Amiot-Dumont, 1948), p. 17.

2
Suffering

The Ways of Habit

The man described in the opening pages of *A la Recherche du temps perdu* is, like Dominique, alone and in a room. The strangeness he encounters is not, however, that of his soul but of his own past life. Existing on the borderline between sleep and wakefulness, he is plunged into "the shifting kaleidoscope of the darkness" composed of the disparate images of past selves and places and set in motion by the temporary suspension of his present habits. His mind, carried off on a rapid voyage through time and space, is pushed to the threshold of existence. For brief, fleeting moments he becomes each of his past selves—the child whose curls are pulled by a great uncle, the man dressing for dinner at the home of Mme de Saint-Loup. He even becomes at times the subject of the book he is reading—"a church, a quartet, the rivalry between François I and Charles V."[1]

The artistic merits of this introduction or "overture" are evident. Proust is carefully presenting the fragments of the world his novel will explore and develop. Yet what is for the author a conscious plan is for his hero only confusion, for he cannot even control these endless metamorphoses of his own being. The becoming in which he is involved is in no sense qualitative. Each metamorphosis is of equal value, and he can become any of his past selves or anything. He can also awake to find himself stripped of all identity. At such times the memory, first of the other places where he had lived, draws him up out of "the abyss of not-being."[2] But this memory that saves him is essentially the memory of the body or, more particularly, of the body's habits. The void created by the suspension of present habits is filled by former ones which contain the identity of each succeeding place and self from the past. Finally, it

---

1. I, 3; *Swann*, I, 3.   2. I, 5; *Swann*, I, 5.

is habit itself that stops the turning kaleidoscope, reconstructs the present, and gives back to the mind a room in which it can dwell in peace.

This praise of habit seems far removed from Proust's condemnation of it in "L'Etranger." But the experience described in the overture is not entirely comparable to Dominique's encounter with his soul. For the man lost in time and space, conscious choice and moral responsibility have little meaning. Habit may be the great enemy of creativity, but it is shown here as a necessary and indispensable element of existence. Without habit there could be no recognition or identification of objects and persons. In fact, *the narrator's experience teaches him that his own self-identity depends on his ability to find himself in the things of the exterior world*. Habit alone, he realizes, maintains the stability of that world: "Perhaps the immobility of the things that surround us is forced upon them by our conviction that they are themselves, and not anything else, and by the immobility of our conceptions of them."[3] To preserve the immobility of his world is for the narrator the surest way to avoid the suffering that would result from the loss of the self.

The stable space that habit creates for the self is, nevertheless, a negation of time. The strange kaleidoscopic world is not understood; it is excluded, reduced to a simple identity devoid of mystery. "As a rule it is with our being reduced to a minimum that we live," remarks the narrator later; "most of our faculties lie dormant because they can rely upon habit, which knows what there is to be done and has no need of their services."[4] This reduction of his being is the price he pays for the certainty and security he desires.

The themes of the overture and the bedroom motif are again present in the narrator's first, and voluntary, memory of Combray. Recalling the nights of his childhood, he describes the magic lantern his family had given him in the hope that it would alleviate the sadness of being alone in his room. Paradoxically, the effect produced by its luminous projections is just the opposite of the one desired. The magic lantern, like the "kaleidoscope of the darkness," transforms the familiar world into a strange one. Although Marcel acknowledges the charm of these brilliant images and is fascinated by the way they metamorphose the objects of his room, he is deeply disturbed, for the "intrusion of mystery and beauty" fills the room with an alien presence that *excludes* him.[5] The projections of the magic lantern replace the reassuring projections of the

3. I, 5; *Swann*, I, 6.   4. I, 498; *Jeunes filles*, I, 656.
5. I, 8; *Swann*, I, 10.

38

self onto the objects of the room, and these objects, whose function had been to reflect his presence, now serve a new function. Marcel suddenly realizes that objects have an existence outside of himself. A distance has been created between himself and his world, and that world is no longer simply seen; it is looked at. This separation between self and world is immediately felt *within* Marcel as a splitting, or *dédoublement,* of his being. Forced to pay attention to his room because of its strangeness, he must also confront the stranger he has become, must make of himself the object of his attention. To think, to feel, to question the self in this way are for Marcel sources of suffering.

In his dissertation on the soul Proust had noted that the mind is dependent on the health of the body, and had implied, as in his letter to Darlu, that any change in the one directly affects the other. In these opening pages of *A la Recherche* the conflict of body and soul has become the conflict of the self and its world. And here it is the room, particularly the bedroom, which is the most immediate manifestation of the world's presence. The room, like the body, is the dwelling place of the mind, and each particular room is for each succeeding self in time the frame of reference that determines and reveals the self's identity. Like the body again, the room is seen as the unconscious extension of the self, ignored and forgotten until something disturbs its "immobility." Just as illness provokes self-examination, so the world's dislocation causes the self to question its own being.

Proust's purpose in describing such dislocations obviously goes beyond the revelation of certain psychological laws governing the self and its world. Not only do modifications in our habits expose "the purely mental character of reality," they also uncover what habit hides so effectively—the poetry of existence. It is not by chance that Proust speaks of kaleidoscopes and magic lanterns, for these instruments, which transform reality by changing one thing into another, reveal the rich possibilities for metaphor that exist beneath the surface of life. These transformations will be discussed again when Proust describes the activity of the artist. Yet what strikes the reader at the beginning of the novel is the way Proust repeatedly demonstrates his hero's extreme sensitivity to change. So delicate is the balance between Marcel's inner and outer worlds that a change in either is capable of producing a disruptive effect on the psyche. In this respect the kaleidoscope of time and space and the magic lantern have as their immediate function to set the stage for the first real "event" in the novel—the drama of suffering and abdication that takes place when Marcel, unable to do without his mother's good-night kiss, succeeds in forcing her to spend the night in his room.

The Bedroom Drama

The anguish of solitude Marcel encounters each night can be eased only by his mother:

> My sole consolation when I went upstairs for the night was that Mamma would come in and kiss me after I was in bed. But this good night lasted for so short a time: she went down again so soon that the moment in which I heard her climb the stairs . . . was for me a moment of the keenest sorrow. [It announced the one that was going to follow, when she would have left me, when she would have gone down again.] So much did I love that good night that I reached the stage of hoping that it would come as late as possible, so as to prolong the time of respite during which Mamma would not yet have appeared.[6]

What Marcel desires, what his habit demands, is his mother's presence. He longs to kiss her face which he regards as "a Host, for an act of Communion in which my lips might drink deeply the sense of her real presence, and with it the power to sleep." Yet his need for his mother's presence is not free from the knowledge of her eventual absence. Indeed, as Proust carefully reveals, Marcel possesses an exceptionally acute sense of time, a sense which perceives privation in satisfaction, future emptiness in present fulfillment, absence in presence. Marcel's tactic is to arrest the flow of time by denying it a future and, consequently, the past which the future will reveal as a loss. Expectation, unlike fulfillment, does not bear the mark of an event in time. To wait for something in the certainty that it will occur is preferable to the occurrence whose brevity vitiates its value. Yet expectation only increases the need for the event, which becomes all the more necessary as the certainty that it will take place diminishes. It is this loss of certainty that precipitates the particular crisis the narrator relates.

One night, because of Swann's visit, Marcel is forced to remain alone in his room. Although he knows that such visits always preclude the communion he desires, the question of the good-night kiss becomes the object of his "maniacal attention." At first he desperately attempts to create a bridge across the immediate future that confronts him—the time

6. I, 10; *Swann,* I, 13.

when he will be deprived of his mother's presence—by imagining a future created by a change in his thoughts, a time of detachment from the anguish of the present. But Marcel's obsession will not allow him this escape from time, and the certainty of eventual forgetfulness is only an empty idea that finds no place in the limited and exclusive focus of his mind.

In his confrontation with the projections of the magic lantern it was the strangeness of the exterior world that created within Marcel a sense of separation from that world. Now it is his separation from his mother that makes him imagine her world, enclosed in "that forbidden and unfriendly dining-room," as being not only strange but also evil. It is an alien space from which he is excluded—an unknown, mysterious world indifferent to him and to his anguish. In his solitude he senses the otherness of his mother's life, her separate existence and, consequently, his own otherness.

Marcel's desire, therefore, is twofold: to penetrate his mother's world and to force her to return to his. He decides to write a letter to his mother asking her to come up to his room, and when Françoise, who takes the letter down, returns to announce that a way will be found for giving it to her, Marcel's anxiety immediately subsides. The dining-room, he feels, "had opened its doors to me and, like a ripe fruit which bursts through its skin, was going to pour out into my intoxicated heart the gushing sweetness of Mamma's attention."[7] The first result of Marcel's success in attracting his mother's attention is that it frees him momentarily from the necessity of paying attention to himself, of thinking about his own suffering. By destroying the "barriers" of his mother's world, he escapes from the prison of his obsessive desire. A new thought enters his mind—the certainty of his mother's arrival.

Marcel thinks that Swann would mock him if he knew of the letter, but he will later learn, the narrator remarks, that Swann's own experience with love had made of him a person who could well understand "that anguish which lies in knowing that the creature one adores is in some place of enjoyment where oneself is not and cannot follow."[8] Proust is here adumbrating part of his theory of love and jealous anxiety. Separated from the beloved, the lover imagines that she is participating in an "inconceivable, infernal scene of gaiety" and giving herself to "unknown pleasures." His desire is to penetrate the unknown world of her

7. I, 23; *Swann*, I, 30.   8. I, 23; *Swann*, I, 30.

pleasures and there to possess, indeed to create, at least a moment of time when she will belong to him because forced to think of him. Proust will later show that love itself is often born from this very sense of separation, the lover being attracted by the otherness of the beloved and by the unknown mystery of her life. "Certainly, personal charm is a less frequent cause of love," he writes, "than a speech such as: 'No, this evening I shall not be free.' "[9]

At Combray, however, Marcel's tactic fails. His mother's message is simply, "Il n'y a pas de réponse." He knows now that sleep is impossible, for the expectations aroused by his letter have become too insistent to forgo satisfaction. But once again he is saved from his suffering by a new plan for fulfilling his desires. He resolves not to sleep without seeing his mother. This final choice represents Marcel's *abdication* in the face of his solitude. By yielding to a "nervous impulse" he commits the very fault his family education constantly taught him to resist. He waits for his mother, confronts her at the top of the stairs, and, despite her own resistance, triumphs with the help of his father. His mother enters the bedroom; and while her presence brings the calm and security Marcel desires, it also destroys the atmosphere of intense self-confrontation he could not endure. The pattern of the encounter is complete.

But Marcel's victory does not give him the happiness he longed for:

> I ought then to have been happy; I was not. It struck me that my mother had just made a first concession which must have been painful to her, that it was a first [abdication of] the ideal she had formed for me, and that for the first time she, with all her courage, had to confess herself beaten.[10]

What was only partially expressed throughout the narrator's account of the bedroom drama is here placed in sharp relief—namely, its profound moral significance. As early as his thirteenth year Proust had written that his idea of misery was to be "séparé de maman."[11] The description of the way Marcel experiences the same misery at Combray clearly reveals the intensity of that attachment, for to be separated from his mother is for Marcel tantamount to being separated from his self. When she enters his room, it is as if he recovers his lost self. But if this recovery

9. II, 142; *Sodome,* II, 797–98.
10. I, 29; *Swann,* I, 38. Moncrieff translates "abdication" as "a step down."
11. André Maurois, *A la recherche de Marcel Proust* (Paris: Hachette, 1947), p. 17.

does not bring happiness, it is bceause his mother represents much more than a necessary physical presence.

As the preceding chapter revealed, Proust early associated his mother with the best part of his being, with his *ideal* self. It is she, in fact, who often remains *within* the ark during the periods of "grace." Although the bedroom at Combray because of Marcel's own weakness does not quite become an ark during this particular crisis, it still represents the privileged place for self-examination. The fact that it is now the mother's entrance into the room rather than her departure that marks the end of this period doubtless shows that Proust grew to see his mother as the most important, if not dangerous, object of his habitual desires and pleasures. This modification in Proust's attitude is, as was just noted, clearly discernible in the novel. It does not change in any way, however, the moral imperatives his hero confronts. On the contrary, since the mother now represents both the "soul" and the "guests" of "L'Etranger," both the ideal self and the self of habit, Marcel's drama is more intense, for what has become more complex is the paradox that requires him to sacrifice one self for the other.

Marcel's moral duty was to live up to the ideal his mother had conceived for him by enduring his suffering and by resisting the demands of his habits, particularly in this case of the habits associated with her. Such resistance would not only have strengthened his will, it would also have enabled him to bring that ideal self into being. It is his inability to perform this act of *self-creation* that determines his moral failure. The narrator can speak of his mother's abdication while describing his own because both acts represent the surrender of the ideal self to a contingent one. Indeed, Marcel feels that his mother has died in her ideal form in order to become the servant of his habits: "I felt that I had with an impious and secret finger traced a first wrinkle upon her soul and made the first white hair shew upon her head."[12] Marcel, like Dominique and the girl in "La Confession," is guilty of killing his soul.

It can certainly be said that Marcel's moral failure will work to the advantage of the novelist he will become, for it guarantees the preservation of his acute sensitivity and, therefore, of his capacity for suffering. As for the value of possessing a nervous nature, Proust writes: "All the greatest things we know have come to us from neurotics. It is they and they only who have founded religions and created great works of art."[13]

12. I, 30; *Swann*, I, 39.   13. I, 933; *Guermantes*, II, 305.

All this may be true, but it does not lessen the importance of Marcel's failure. As will be shown, Swann also suffers intensely, but he lacks the will to endure his suffering and the will to devote himself to an elucidation of its causes. Therefore, if Marcel's abdication favors the development of his artistic sensitivity, it also exposes him to the possibility that this sensitivity will never be utilized. The narrator himself does not forget the importance of his early failure to strengthen his will. "It was that evening, when my mother abdicated her authority," he says in *Le Temps retrouvé*, "which marked the commencement of the waning of my will power and my health, as well as the beginning of my grandmother's lingering death."[14]

Absence and Presence

Many years later, in an interesting variant of the abdication drama at Combray, Marcel again tests his will against his mother's. Moments before their planned departure from Venice, Marcel asks his mother if they might remain a few days longer. He has just learned of the imminent arrival of Baronne Putbus, and hopes to satisfy his desire to possess her chambermaid. His mother's refusal to take his request seriously awakens in Marcel "that old desire to rebel against an imaginary plot woven against me by my parents." With his mother's departure Marcel is left alone on the terrace of the hotel to listen to the song *Sole mio*, yet the Venice he now sees takes on a frightening aspect: "Things had become alien to me. I was no longer calm enough to draw from my throbbing heart and introduce into them a measure of stability. The town that I saw before me had ceased to be Venice."[15]

The mother's departure has set off a violent chain reaction. She has taken away not only her own being but that of her son as well, and the Venice that remains without her, that no longer "contains" her, resists through the anxiety it causes him all of Marcel's attempts to project back onto its forms the images of a self that has ceased to exist. Just as he is stripped of his former self, so Venice is stripped of its personality, of the whole context of personal and historical associations. Proust once thought of dividing his novel into three consecutive "Ages"—Names, Words, and Things; and perhaps nowhere in *A la Recherche* is this reduction of names to things presented more dramatically. Marcel, reduced to a beating heart, is confronted by a Venice of purely material

14. II, 1122; *Temps retrouvé*, III, 1044.   15. II, 837; *Fugitive*, III, 652.

forms existing outside of human time, a "real" Venice that makes the former city seem a "fiction." The void of the mother's absence is filled by a strange presence that once again excludes Marcel, is indifferent to him, neither "knows" him nor can be "known" by him. The Venice of the Doges and of Turner enters a new context of images at once disgusting and frightening to Marcel, who sees the city as the murky entrance to the underworld.

He must now make an agonizing decision: either to remain in Venice and endure his solitude, or to run to the railroad station and rejoin his mother. The immanent departure of the train intensifies Marcel's anguish, for he knows that he must (like Dominique) choose quickly. Soon his mother will be gone, and his solitude, becoming "minute by minute" more complete, will be irrevocable. He feels that he should make up his mind to leave without wasting another instant, yet he remains listening to *Sole mio* as if doing so were a "duty." Unable to say directly to himself that he is not leaving, he finds in the decision to hear yet another phrase of the song an excuse for his continued presence. He realizes that such a decision can only mean that he will remain alone: "Thus I remained motionless with a disintegrated will power, with no apparent decision; doubtless at such moments our decision has already been made: our friends can often predict it themselves. But we, we are unable to do so, otherwise how much suffering would we be spared!" The drama of Marcel's inner conflict derives precisely from this two-sided resistance to the inevitable, that is, to the inevitability of his solitude if he remains, and to the inevitability of the decision not to remain. Incapable of accepting a future of solitude and able for the moment to resist the determinism of the past, he is suspended in the flow of time. But soon time dissolves what will power remains, and he moves in the line of least resistance. "Thanks to the unimaginable defensive force of inveterate habit," he runs away to the train and leaves Venice with his mother.[16]

There is no question here of a return to the "virtues of Combray." It is not Marcel's sense of moral duty that triumphs over his desire for pleasure, but rather his habits that destroy his will to resist by revealing the impossibility of the pleasure he seeks outside their context. Marcel's experience in Venice points up once again the extreme interdependence of all the elements of his habitual world, in which the slightest change destroys his personal stability and feeling of security. "But the absence

16. II, 839; *Fugitive*, III, 655.

45

of one part from a whole is not only that, it is not simply a partial omission," writes Proust, "it is a disturbance of all the other parts, a new state which it was impossible to foresee from the old.[17]

If the absence of one element can destroy the whole structure of habit, there are also moments when a single element divorced from its habitual context can evoke a totally new vision of reality or, rather, expose the reality hidden by habit.

While at Doncières on a visit with his friend Saint-Loup, Marcel makes a telephone call to his grandmother in Paris. The telephone itself, at that time still a mysterious and inhabitual means of communication, gives him a strange new sense of space. His grandmother's voice, like that of Dominique's soul, is at once near and far away. It has been isolated from its usual context, "the open score of her face." In the newly felt "sweetness" of his grandmother's voice Marcel senses all the suffering she has endured, which her face, like a mask, had hidden. The isolated voice becomes as well a symbol of her separation from him and the mark, therefore, of her eventual death: "A real presence indeed that voice so near—in actual separation. But a premonition also of an eternal separation!"[18] And when like Orpheus he loses contact with her voice, the anguish of his separation drives him back to Paris. He surprises his grandmother reading, yet he is not really there, because she does not know that he is there. For a brief moment he has the sensation of being present at his own absence. He is like a photographer taking a shot of an unknown woman. His gaze, stripped of habit, confronts the reality of the present, for the face he sees is no longer a mirror of the past. All that his own habits and her efforts had concealed now strike his eye like a painful revelation. Seeing her as though he were a stranger, he sees her own strangeness:

> I, for whom my grandmother was still myself, I who had never seen her save in my own soul, always at the same place in the past, through the transparent sheets of contiguous, overlapping memories, suddenly in our drawing-room which formed part of a new world, that of time, that in which dwell the strangers of whom we say "He's begun to age a good deal," for the first time and for a moment only, since she vanished at once, I saw, sitting on the sofa, beneath the lamp, red-faced, heavy and common, sick, lost in thought, following the lines of a book with eyes that

17. I, 234; *Swann*, I, 305.   18. I, 810; *Guermantes*, II, 134.

seemed hardly sane, a dejected old woman whom I did not know.[19]

To be aware of one's own exclusion, to be present at one's own absence is perhaps the most succinct definition that can be given to Proust's conception of suffering. Although Marcel compares himself to a photographer who does not know his subject, it is obvious that it is because he does know, or did know, his grandmother that a shock is produced at all. The new image of the grandmother does indeed exclude the old image, but it does not, for the moment, obliterate it. The old image, existing in Marcel's mind, is there to confront the new one. It is not enough to say that Marcel does not recognize his grandmother, for he does recognize her as being strange, that is, different from what she was. In this episode, Marcel's conscious vision of the old woman he sees supposes a simultaneous, if perhaps unconscious, *recognition of difference itself*. An encounter, in its simplest form, is just this sort of experience. Marcel, the images in his mind, his grandmother, and her voice, are all near and far, absent and present, the same yet different. It is because he is caught in this "in between" state that Marcel feels directly the effects of spatial distances and of temporal change. These same remarks can be applied to the encounters already discussed. If in Venice Marcel suffers because of the loss of his self, it is because there also he is present at his own absence. And if his suffering is caused by the inner perception of change and loss in time and space, the even greater suffering derives from the fear that time and space will continue to do their work, that the absence of his mother or grandmother will become permanent and their separation from him total. Habit in these instances seems the only source of salvation because it replaces change and distance by a limited, immobile, and "timeless" image. Marcel learns at Balbec, however, that the reality of time and space is most acutely felt when an encounter with the unknown initiates a period of painful transition during which an old habit must be replaced by a new one.

The Prison of Time and Space

A few moments after his arrival at the Grand Hotel at Balbec in the company of his grandmother, Marcel, exhausted from his voyage, enters his room in order to sleep. Instead of sleep, however, what he encounters is the strangeness of a room filled with unknown objects. His senses are

19. I, 815; *Guermantes,* II, 141.

suddenly placed on the defensive, and he feels as tortured as the cardinal La Balue in his cage where he could neither stand erect nor sit down. "It is our [attention] that puts things in a room," remarks the narrator, "[and habit] that takes them away again and clears a space for us."[20] With his habit suspended, Marcel is forced once again to look at things that do not know him, that take no account of his existence. He feels his own exclusion as if, in a Sartrean sense, he were *de trop*. The furniture strikes him as having a mobile, monstrous life of its own. "The things in my room in Paris disturbed no more than did my eyelids themselves," says the narrator, "for they were merely extensions of my organs, an enlargement of myself."[21] But at Balbec the memory of the low ceiling of his Paris room makes Marcel all the more conscious of the hotel room's high ceiling, and the furniture, now the object of his acute attention, seems to penetrate to the very center of his being.

Here as earlier, in the bedroom at Combray, Marcel's suffering is calmed by the entrance of a soothing presence:

> Having no world, no room, no body now that was not menaced by the enemies thronging round me, invaded to the very bones by fever, I was utterly alone; I longed to die. Then my grandmother came in, and to the expansion of my ebbing heart there opened at once an *infinity of space*.[22]

Just as his grandmother, like his old room, is an extension of his being, so Marcel is a part of her. Escaping from the frightening mobility of the unknown room he buries himself like a child in the immobility and calm of his grandmother's breast. Throughout the rest of his stay at Balbec Marcel is comforted by his grandmother's presence in the next room, and by the fact that, whenever the need arises, he has only to knock on the partition wall for her to appear.

His suffering is not, however, easily forgotten, for it has revealed important truths:

> Perhaps this fear that I had—and shared with so many of my fellow-men—of sleeping in a strange room, perhaps this fear is only the most humble, obscure, organic, almost unconscious form of that great and desperate resistance set up by the things that constitute the better part of our present life towards our

---

20. I, 506; *Jeunes filles,* I, 666. Moncrieff translates "notre attention" as "our noticing them" and "et l'habitude" as "our growing used to them."
21. I, 506; *Jeunes filles,* I, 667.   22. I, 506–7; *Jeunes filles,* I, 667.

mentally assuming, by accepting it as true, the formula of a future in which those things are to have no part.[23]

Marcel knows that habit will assume the task of rendering familiar the new room as well as the new friends and places of the future, and that the old ones will be forgotten. But here as at Combray the knowledge supplied by his intelligence cannot console the anguish of his heart:

> And our dread of a future in which we must forego the sight of faces, the sound of voices that we love, friends from whom we derive to-day our keenest joys, this dread, far from being dissipated, is intensified, if to the grief of such a privation we reflect that there will be added what seems to us now in anticipation an even more cruel grief; not to feel it as a grief at all—to remain indifferent; for if that should occur, our ego would have changed . . . so that it would be in a real sense the death of ourselves, a death followed, it is true, by resurrection but in a different ego, the life, the love of which are beyond the reach of those elements of the existing ego that are doomed to die. It is they—even the meanest of them, such as our obscure attachments to the dimensions, to the atmosphere of a bedroom—that grow stubborn and refuse, in acts of rebellion which we must recognise to be a secret, partial, tangible and true aspect of our resistance to death, of the long resistance, desperate and daily renewed, to a fragmentary and gradual death such as interpolates itself throughout the whole course of our life, tearing away from us at every moment a shred of ourselves, dead matter on which new cells will multiply, and grow.[24]

These passages reveal once again Marcel's particularly acute sense of time. The future he fears is, of course, a future only in respect to the "present life" it will replace. From the perspective of the present that future can be felt only as a void in which the present will be lost. And it is because his present life has not yet been lost that the opposite perspective, that of an indifferent future become itself the present, can cause only suffering by revealing the present to itself as a dead and lost past. Even this interpretation, however, does not quite succeed in revealing the full temporal dimensions of the encounter.

In these moments of suffering Marcel is not living what he calls his present life *in the present*. Indeed, that life was itself never a product of

23. I, 508–9; *Jeunes filles*, I, 670.   24. I, 509–10; *Jeunes filles*, I, 671–72.

the present but rather a creation of Marcel's habits, that is, of the past. Although lived as a present and determined by the past, that life was in fact lived outside of time insofar as it hid from him the truth of his own and of the world's existence in time. Now the presence of the strange room, by excluding his habitual life, forces Marcel into a true temporal present, one that creates a past and a future and makes him aware of them. Although fragments of his past are preserved with the help of his grandmother, other fragments move on into the future, which, once it becomes a new present life, will again hide the face of time. Marcel finds himself, therefore, suspended in a movement over an inner void between a self not fully dead and another not yet fully born, between a world his habits refuse to relinquish and another to which they have not yet learned to attach themselves.

Samuel Beckett has well described these "periods of transition" in Marcel's life:

> Habit . . . is the generic term for the countless treaties concluded between the countless subjects that constitute the individual and their countless correlative objects. The periods of transition that separate consecutive adaptations . . . represent the perilous zones in the life of the individual, dangerous, precarious, painful, mysterious and fertile, when for a moment the boredom of living is replaced by the suffering of being.[25]

This "suffering of being," or "the free play of every faculty" is the opposite of that "life reduced to a minimum" that is the world of habit. Marcel does not, of course, experience this heightening of consciousness as a liberation from habit. It is rather habit, or his body's organic memory, that makes him "suffer" his freedom as a loss. While Beckett's remarks on habit and suffering are universally applicable, they emphasize again the close interrelationship of self and world that Proust, through his hero and narrator, never ceases to put into relief. The treaties concluded by Marcel's habits are particularly strict, because his habits are exceptionally inflexible. What are for most of us most of the time moments of mild surprise or uneasiness are for him violent shocks. It is this ability to be shocked to the point of extreme joy or suffering that is one of the sources of Marcel's eventual creativity. He is made constantly and painfully aware of the distance that separates the inner model of his world created by habit and the outer reality that suddenly bursts upon him and resists,

25. Beckett, *Proust,* p. 8.

however briefly, his attempts to reduce it to an acceptable ally of the self, devoid of all mystery and strangeness.

Marcel's struggle against the indifference of space makes him above all aware of the fundamental destructive-creative action of time itself that appears to him equally indifferent to his suffering. Habit's fight against Time is the basic conflict present in all the encounters discussed thus far. Because it is an "instinct of self-preservation," habit opposes the action of time and tries to establish and preserve fragile islands of stability in the general flux. Curiously, the action of habit resembles that of time in so far as habit is unconscious and automatic. Marcel knows that given enough time, habit will do its work in hiding the force of time. Being automatic, the action of habit does not bear any moral weight, yet a moral dimension is added whenever a deliberate turning toward habit represents a conscious flight from suffering, as in the bedroom drama at Combray. Even such an escape from strangeness through a return to a familiar presence does not constitute an act in the strict sense of the word. It is less Marcel who acts in these encounters, than it is circumstances that act upon him. Something happens to him, and faced by the activity of time, he seeks to return to the status quo that existed before the event. In the Proustian world there is no such thing as the passive endurance of suffering, for to endure means to resist the desire to escape suffering, and such resistance, requiring as it does the strength of the will, is closer to a truly moral act than the decision to seek out the more passive existence of habit. To resist the temptation of habit means to accept the destruction of the old self, and, therefore, to play a more active part in the birth of the new self.

It must be remembered that Proust's central purpose in *A la Recherche* is to show man in time. It is this sense of his own existence in time which strikes Marcel so powerfully in the hotel room at Balbec. He suffers only so long as he feels directly the movement of time—for the time, that is, during which the memory of his old room and the self linked to it resists the excluding force of the new room with its new self. His suffering ends when the exclusion of the old self is complete, when the new present completely replaces the past. He does not change the room, it changes him. He does not impose his memory, he forgets. At the beginning of the novel the narrator was saved from the void by memory, which helped him to identify alien objects. Here it is forgetfulness that saves Marcel from suffering by allowing a new identity to come into being. It is not the old self that forgets; for the new self the past is already forgotten.

Marcel's experience at Balbec directly supports the Proustian thesis of the multiplicity of the self in time. Life is seen as a succession of selves, successively lost, and being as a set of fragments that chance forces into new patterns. Each self is unique, each carries with it its own world, and each is incomparable and incompatible with any other. It is because of this autonomy and exclusiveness of each successive self that Proust sees life as a discontinuous or intermittent becoming ending eventually in death. Yet the very specificity of each self which forgetting guarantees makes possible its rebirth. The self that dies during Marcel's first night at Balbec is reborn later when he returns to the resort after the death of his grandmother. The passage in question is the famous description of the *intermittences du coeur* in *Sodome et Gomorrhe*.

The Intermittences du Coeur

Alone, tired, and ill in his room at the hotel Marcel stoops to unbutton his boots when suddenly he is filled by "an unknown, a divine presence." The being who saves him from the dryness of his soul, who restores him to himself, is once again his grandmother. She is not the dead woman who until now had existed as little more than a name in his memory, but his real grandmother, restored to him through the miracle of involuntary memory. He is overwhelmed by a desire to embrace her, but because of "that anachronism which so often prevents the calendar of facts from corresponding to that of our feelings," he realizes for the first time that she is dead. Although he had thought of her and talked about her during the year since her burial, the memory of what she had really been had existed in him in a purely virtual state:

> At whatever moment we estimate it, the total value of our spiritual nature is more or less fictitious, notwithstanding the long inventory of its treasures, for now one, now another of these is unrealisable, whether we are considering actual treasures or those of the imagination, and, in my own case, fully as much as the ancient name of Guermantes, this other, how far more important item, my real memory of my grandmother. For with the troubles of memory are closely linked the heart's intermissions. It is, no doubt, the existence of our body, which we may compare to a jar containing our spiritual nature, that leads us to suppose that all our inward wealth, our past joys, all our sorrows, are perpetually in our possession. Perhaps it is equally inexact to suppose that they escape or return. In any case, if they

remain within us, it is, for most of the time, in an unknown region where they are of no service to us, and where even the most ordinary are crowded out by memories of a different kind, which *preclude any simultaneous occurrence of them in our consciousness.* But if the setting of sensations in which they are preserved be recaptured, they acquire in turn *the same power of expelling everything that is incompatible with them,* of installing alone in us the self that originally lived them.[26]

Together with the lost reality of his grandmother Marcel has recovered in its full reality, and without any solution of continuity, the self he was when he sought refuge in his grandmother's arms. It is as difficult for him now to imagine any of the selves he had been during the period of intermittence, as it was for those selves to feel his present emotion. But the desires of the former self he has become can no longer be satisfied, for Marcel is now faced by a painful contradiction. On the one hand, he experiences the certainty and joy of his grandmother's presence; on the other hand, he realizes her eternal absence. She seems to him "a mere stranger whom chance had allowed to spend a few years in my company, as it might have been in anyone's else, but to whom, before and after those years, I was, I could be nothing."[27]

The only pleasure now possible for him is the impossible one of diminishing the suffering his grandmother had endured, above all, the suffering he had caused her. Filled with guilt he turns to strike himself, to submit to the inner anguish which is the proof of his grandmother's presence within him. He must struggle, not to escape from his suffering, but to force himself to endure it. Despite all his efforts, however, Marcel is unable to resist the action of time. His "instinct of self-preservation" begins its useful and nefarious work of protecting him against suffering. One by one he recalls those very images of his grandmother that his will had struggled to exclude from his mind, images of their past life together which hide the truth of her eternal absence, which make him act as if she still existed, as if he continued to exist for her. By replacing his original impression with these comforting and false images supplied by his voluntary memory, Marcel corrupts his consciousness and creates a kind of idol of his grandmother that takes the place of the "real" woman his suffering had briefly kept alive within him. After having been miraculously resurrected by involuntary memory, his grandmother dies again because he is unable to accept the truth of her death.

26. II, 114; *Sodome,* II, 756–57.   27. II, 115; *Sodome,* II, 758.

Nevertheless, Marcel does sense that his experience contains an important truth:

> This painful and, at the moment, incomprehensible impression, I knew—not, forsooth, whether I should one day distil a grain of truth from it—but that if I ever should succeed in extracting that grain of truth, it could only be from it, from so singular, so spontaneous an impression, which had been neither traced by my intellect nor attenuated by my pusillanimity, but which death itself, the sudden revelation of death, had, like a stroke of lightning, carved upon me, along a supernatural, inhuman channel, a two-fold and mysterious furrow.[28]

Although Marcel's total comprehension of this truth, that of the nature and artistic value of involuntary memory, will not take place until he discovers it again at the "matinée des Guermantes" in *Le Temps retrouvé,* it is possible to describe certain aspects of his present experience while postponing a more complete discussion until later.

Whereas during the first night of his earlier visit to Balbec Marcel had witnessed the destructive-creative action of time as producing a succession of selves in time, he is now confronted by the simultaneity of two different times. It is true, and Proust through his narrator insists upon it, that the recovered past completely replaces the present. Marcel not only becomes what he was, for a moment he is what he was. Here the difference between voluntary and involuntary memory is evident. Just as habit provides Marcel with a false present attached to the past, so voluntary memory gives only a false past attached to and determined by the present. Voluntary memory denies the past its fundamental characteristic, that of being past. By making him relive the past in its reality, involuntary memory introduces a presence which is not a loss but a gain, not a void but plenitude. Marcel experiences a present which is no longer a period of transition between past and future, but a moment of real time existing outside of time. He attains for an instant a full unity of being as distinct from the limited and false unity of habit as it is from the fragmentary multiplicity of the self in time. Yet it is only in becoming completely present that the past reveals itself as past. It is precisely because he is the self he was *then,* with the same desires and needs, that Marcel must acknowledge the inability of this new present to satisfy him *now.* Although the past recovered by involuntary memory has the effect

28. II, 116; *Sodome,* II, 759.

of reality, it cannot be lived in because it also is *virtual*. Consequently, his grandmother's loving presence forces Marcel to recognize her actual absence and indifference. She has been reborn but only within him. Marcel's experience does more, therefore, than reveal the contradictory nature of forms in time. He is confronted by the form of time itself— time that has built absence into every presence, that will continually show him the impossibility of possessing anyone except in himself. It is this virtual or "purely mental" character of reality that is confirmed again by Marcel's dream of his grandmother, when sleep reflects and refracts "the agonising synthesis of survival and annihilation."

Filled with suffering, Marcel is for a time freed from his desire for pleasure. He cancels his visit to Mme de Cambremer and sends Albertine away without seeing her. Despite this redemption through suffering and momentary return to virtue, Marcel realizes that his own anguish cannot equal that of his mother, who must live every moment of her life confronted by a being within her who is at once near and far away.

If Marcel's experience of involuntary memory at Balbec causes suffering instead of joy, it is because he is still too attached to his actual needs not to regard the intangible presence of his grandmother as a loss. Years will pass before he is able to find joy in that presence by seeing it as a spiritual reality that can be possessed by the mind and expressed in art. Thanks to the *intermittences du coeur* Marcel recovers a lost self, but he does not discover within himself a qualitatively different being capable of viewing his inner world from the perspective of art and outside of time. In other words, his encounters with suffering, conditioned as they are by his love or need for individuals who are also caught in time, remain for the moment the experiences of his *heart* and not of the creative *esprit*. Just as Darlu taught Proust to think not of things, but of the mental activity that perceives them, so time iself will teach Marcel to see the objects and persons of his world in terms of the truths they reveal about his perception of them.

The Dimensions of Suffering

Throughout *A la Recherche* Proust insists on this paradoxical relationship between the suffering of the man and the joy of the artist. Happiness is alone salutary for the body, he writes, but to experience the joy of discovery such happiness must be sacrificed, for "it is grief that develops the powers of the *mind*." The ideas our mind possesses take the place of our sorrows, and "when the latter are transformed into ideas, they at once lose part of their noxious effect on the heart and from the very first moment the transformation itself radiates joy." Truth, reality, and the extensive pattern of "laws" that govern life are exposed by suffering precisely because the painful agitation and "mobility" it creates in our inner world uproots each time, like a storm, "the tangled growth of habits, skepticism, flippancy, indifference" that blocks our vision.[29] But a life of endless suffering would also be meaningless, for if there were no happiness, Proust remarks, unhappiness would not be possible:

> In our happiness, we should form very sweet bonds, full of con-
> fidence and attachment, in order that the sundering of them
> may cause us that priceless rending of the heart which is called
> unhappiness. If one had not been happy, though only in hope
> and anticipation, the misfortunes would have no cruelty and
> therefore no good result.[30]

What Proust says here about happiness can be equally applied to habit, which so often guarantees our daily pleasures. "If habit is a second nature," remarks the narrator, "it prevents us from knowing our original nature, whose cruelties it lacks and also its enchantments."[31] Although there is always the danger that this second nature will become perma- nent, or that it will continually destroy the roots of any meaningful im- pression, it is also true that habit makes it possible for our original nature to *affect* us as cruel or enchanting. Without habit we could not be im- pressed by strangeness. All these paradoxes show again that in Proust's world the enemies of art may also be its greatest allies.

The "laws" and "ideas" revealed by suffering have already been dis- cussed, for they are related essentially to the nature of man's existence in time. Marcel is himself, of course, still too much a victim of time's action to be able to discover and express fully its meaning. Indeed, *to replace the blind creations of time by the conscious creations of art will be his fundamental problem.* But once one begins to speak of the creations of art, that is, of expressive *forms,* one must also recognize that Proust's laws and ideas cannot be understood apart from these forms. Behind the lessons of suffering is the structure of the encounter.

All of the events discussed above reflect, if at times only partially, this fundamental structure. Each experience presents strangers or strange

29. II, 1020–21; *Temps retrouvé*, III, 906.
30. II, 1021; *Temps retrouvé*, III, 907.   31. II, 112; *Sodome*, II, 754.

places, describes the struggle of the will or the force of habit, presents various patterns of exclusion, corruption, and abdication. What is particularly striking in these encounters is the way Proust utilizes the concept of space to reveal the complexity and reality of Marcel's world. The rooms at Combray and Balbec, the grandmother's face, Venice—all are spaces, as is the refuge Marcel finds in his mother's or grandmother's presence which, by freeing him from the prison of his anxiety, causes his heart to "expand," but also causes the loss of his heightened consciousness. It should be noted that in each encounter the new space Marcel confronts, while it produces the shock of strangeness that initiates the inner conflict, is itself *created* by that shock. Confronted by something that appears indifferent to him, that pays no attention to him, Marcel is forced to pay attention to it. Space is created because, for anything to be seen, for it to *exist* for the mind, attention must place it in focus by excluding, as Proust remarks, all that is incompatible with it. Marcel's encounters not only describe how the world enters and leaves the spaces of his heightened consciousness, they also trace the dimensions and boundaries of vision.

And of time. By focusing on space, attention also puts time into focus, gives it, as it were, a space in which to exist. Marcel's encounters suggest that time can be felt only when space is seen stripped of the blinds of habit. This conjunction of vision and temporality can be partly explained by the fact that in these encounters *attention,* the act of fixing one's mind on something, is closely related to *attendre,* the action of waiting for something in the hope or expectation of its arrival. In his moments of intense suffering Marcel is always waiting for someone to arrive, some decision to be made, or simply for something to happen that will put an end to his anxiety, even if the result is only the reestablishment of his habitual vision. Normally, waiting implies the negation of the present in favor of the future. But during these moments the shock of strangeness and the tension it produces are such that the resulting anticipation of the future draws even greater attention to the objects that confront the mind and that seem to exclude both the future and the past.

These encounters show that in Proust's novel the causes and nature of suffering cannot be reduced to established psychological concepts. Marcel's attachment to his mother and the weakness of his will are revealed within the context of a "world" or "situation" which is not simply Oedipal or existential, but more strictly spatial and temporal. Even the intellectual and artistic aspects of Marcel's life will reflect this basic ground of his existence. It is as if Proust were suggesting that our emotions are determined, or at least can be explained, by the equations in a geometry of time. This emphasis on the *forms* of time in Proust's novel reveals once again the importance of the creative encounter, whose structure in turn determines and explains these forms.

Proust's psychology of time and space as well as his ideas concerning vision will be discussed again. It is already evident that if Marcel "sees" the world during his moments of suffering he does not go beyond the surface of things. Only the truly creative vision of metaphor will reveal to him a way to transcend time by completely spatializing it. Marcel begins to make this discovery in his joyful encounters in which attention is related to the efforts of the creative spirit, and in which the anxiety of waiting is replaced by the artistic activity of searching.

3
Joy

The Madeleine

If the child's bedroom drama at Combray stands as a model for the encounters with suffering Marcel will endure, it represents only one half of the thematic dyptic Proust has carefully placed in the opening pages of his novel. Juxtaposed to the memory of childhood suffering is the narrator's joyous encounter with his past, born from the savor of a madeleine dipped in tea. Unlike the voluntary, if obsessive, memory of Combray evoked by the intellect and restricted to the limits of a kind of "luminous panel" containing a few isolated images of the past and surrounded by indistinct shadows, the involuntary memory provoked by the madeleine gives back a complete living past with its full temporal and spatial dimensions.

The structural function of the madeleine episode is obvious. This involuntary memory brings forth the very past the narrator will describe, without as yet revealing in that past the artistic values he will discover only at the end of the novel, when the full meaning of his joy is finally grasped. Yet beyond its function of evoking the past and preparing for the future, the madeleine episode is presented as the model of a variety of encounters Proust will relate in the course of the narration. Nowhere else in the novel is the actual *process* of involuntary memory given such close attention. If the inner structure of the encounter itself is so meticulously described, it is because Proust wants to reveal from the very beginning of his novel certain fundamental aspects of the mind's activity, which, with modifications, will form the basis of all similar encounters, related either to the process of involuntary memory or to those *instants profonds* when Marcel is struck by deep impressions of nature's beauty.

As in his encounters with suffering, the taste of the madeleine confronts the narrator with a new reality that makes his former life appear a fiction. But now this sudden disruption of his existence gives him "an exquisite pleasure." The reality whose threshold he has reached is not indifferent to him, but makes him indifferent to the world. It does not reveal the horror of time and contingency, but lifts him out of time and transcends mortality. It is not a frightening, alien presence that excludes the self and its cherished images, but the pure essence of the self that replaces a life judged as mediocre. The narrator feels liberated rather than imprisoned, and his attention turns toward the joy of his gain and not to the sorrow, inexistent here, of his loss. Filled by a pure, autonomous presence divorced from the needs and desires of his contingent life, he attempts to discover the cause of his joy.

Although the narrator senses that his joy is tied to the taste of the tea and cake, he realizes that it is of a different nature and goes infinitely beyond the taste. He takes a second and a third swallow, but each time the effect of the drink grows weaker. Proust is presenting a kind of law of diminishing returns whose operation he will show again in the novel. The value of the encounter rests with the original sensation or impression, which, because it is by definition unique and completely individual, cannot be readily reproduced. Any attempt at repetition is already dangerous, for repetition is the hallmark of habit, and habit is the negation of originality. Above all, the narrator realizes that the truth he is seeking does not lie in the object or in the repeated sensations whose value time is now destroying, but in himself, in the original sensation still fresh and intact in his *memory* and still resistant to temporal change. The heightened attention awakened by the encounter is now directed inward:

> I put down my cup and examine my own *mind*. It is for it to discover the truth. But how? What an abyss of uncertainty whenever the *mind* feels that some part of it has strayed beyond its own borders; when it, the seeker, is at once the dark region through which it must go seeking, where all its equipment will avail it nothing. *Seek? More than that: create.* It is face to face with something which does not so far exist, to which it alone can give reality and substance, which it alone can bring into [its light].[1]

The images Proust employs here to describe the *esprit* and its activity can also be found in the narrator's accounts of his experiences with suffer-

1. I, 34–35; *Swann*, I, 45. Moncrieff translates "faire entrer dans sa lumière" as "bring into the light of day."

ing in which "darkness" is often associated with the misery of solitude and uncertainty, and "light" with whatever presence or change that alleviates his anguish. Once they are applied more directly to the *esprit,* however, these same images acquire a new meaning. While darkness still refers to the domain of the soul, it is also an attribute of the inner world of the *artist.* As early as 1896, in an article entitled "Contre l'Obscurité," Proust attacked certain young writers of his time who put a false or arbitrary obscurity into their works. All great works that truly reflect the essence of life are obscure, writes Proust, but their obscurity is of a different kind, since it is *féconde à approfondir;* that is, an obscurity that lends itself to a fruitful and in-depth exploration by the mind of the reader. This richness and depth are in the work because the artist's own mind was able to elucidate (*éclaircir*) the obscurity of life by giving it an intelligible form. If the artist traverses the night, writes Proust, "may he do so like the Angel of Darkness, by bringing light to it."[2]

While the metaphor of light for the mind has been used for centuries, Proust's own use of it is particularly interesting for what it reveals about his aesthetics. In *Jean Santeuil* he speaks of certain "moments of profound illumination [when] the spirit drives deep into all things, and floods them with light, as when the sun sinks into the sea."[3] The madeleine encounter describes such a moment, for the *esprit* is again called upon to plunge into its world, into the obscurity of the inner region or "country," which must be brought into the light of consciousness and comprehension. This inner country represents more than just a single memory or past experience. It is a virtual, autonomous world, a forgotten pattern of relationships between a lost subject and its correlative objects. What is to be resurrected is not only the past experience but also the self that experienced it. Having become through the joy produced by the encounter a *qualitatively different person,* the narrator asks his mind to discover the identity of this self, to bring it into being through the liberating act of creation.

By insisting that the mind's search is ultimately a creation, Proust is revealing from the beginning of the novel the essential significance of his hero's quest. The search for lost time will be completed by the creation of time regained. But if in Proust's novel search must lead to creation, *creation itself is always described as a searching activity*—the same

2. Marcel Proust, *Chroniques* (Paris: Gallimard, 1927), pp. 137–44.
3. *Jean Santeuil,* p. 12; I, 45.

plunging into the depths of the self and bringing into light that the narrator is involved in here.

The spirit that creates and that, as Proust carefully notes, can *alone* complete the task before it, is itself a creation of the encounter and of the emotion of joy. In other words, the encounter, by producing a new object of attention, has produced as well its attending subject. The presence of the impression has created quite literally a new "presence of mind." For the moment, however, the narrator finds himself again in an "in-between" situation—between an object not yet fully "realized" and a subject not yet completely in command of its powers. In order to bring the virtual world of the past into being, the mind must meet it on its own terms, must become, as Darlu had taught, "analogous" to its object.

Proust describes this fundamental law of creativity in a note to his translation of *Sesame and Lilies*. Attempting to explain why his own statements about Ruskin's ideas were so readily confirmed by his subsequent readings of the Englishman's work, Proust writes:

> in order to behold his thought (one can see only with something analogous to what is beheld; if light were not in the eye, said Goethe, the eye would not see the light; for the world to be grasped by the thought of the scholar it must itself be thought) I found myself apprehending an idea so analogous to one of his ideas, a glass so pure that his light easily penetrated it; for between my contemplation and his thought I had introduced so little foreign, opaque, and refractory matter.[4]

In the madeleine encounter the subject becomes analogous to its object by becoming memory, with the essential difference that the spirit that seeks and creates represents the *activity* of recollection, while the spirit that is the inner country is *that* which is to be recollected. This need for analogy explains why all the "equipment" of the *esprit,* its reason and analytical knowledge, are of no use for its task. The mind must strip itself of these forms of intelligence in order to approach more closely the nature of its object—the realm of memory that also lies beyond the reach of discursive reasoning. Just as Dominique becomes for a moment like his soul, so the spirit enters here into its own life.

Faced by the felicity of this "unknown state," the evidence of whose reality goes beyond any "logical proof," the narrator continues his search

4. John Ruskin, *Sésame et les lys,* translation, notes, and preface by Marcel Proust (Paris: Mercure de France, 1906), p. 76, n 1.

by "retrograding" his thought to the moment when he first tasted the tea. He finds the same state, but it is "illumined by no fresh light":

> I compel my *mind* to make one further effort, to follow and recapture once again the fleeting sensation. And that nothing may interrupt it in its course I shut out every obstacle, every extraneous idea, I stop my ears and inhibit all attention to the sounds which come from the next room.[5]

The mind's race against time has been entered upon in earnest, and the law of analogy must be obeyed with even greater rigor. All extraneous ideas, all refractory matter are willfully moved aside in order to assure a greater purity of vision and sharpness of focus. The narrator attempts to create, *now by his own efforts,* an enclosed autonomous space for his mind to work in, a kind of mental shelter against the distractions of the neighboring world. The door to the inner life must be opened for the mind and kept closed to all outside corruption.

But his attempts meet with failure. The mind's élan, its spontaneous intuitive movement, has been weakened and fatigued by the very force of the effort. The narrator now decides to direct his will in the opposite direction, to force his mind to take the very distraction he refused it, to think of something else in order that it may refresh itself for a supreme effort.

This tactic is known to anyone who has tried to remember something; yet in Proust's novel the simplest mental processes are constantly shown as correlatives of the most fully developed creative acts. The narrator is repeating consciously and in miniature certain fundamental patterns of the novel itself. He is moving away from center in order to return to it. He is seeking to find directions by indirections. He is also affirming a truth whose meaning he will not completely understand until *Le Temps retrouvé,* namely, the important role played by forgetting in the process of involuntary memory. By breaking all ties that link the past to the present, forgetting assures the autonomy of the past and therefore makes possible its resurrection in the full shock of newness. The taste of the madeleine had to be forgotten in order to be remembered. In attempting to forget for a moment the object of his search the narrator is in fact reproducing the very process that initiated the encounter. His effort is to give back to the impression its original affective force. What is involved here is a kind of regression to the state that existed before the

5. I, 35; *Swann,* I, 46.

encounter. In his book *The Act of Creation,* Arthur Koestler devotes considerable attention to this very tactic which he calls the process of "reculer pour mieux sauter."[6] This paradox of the *recul* will be present in other encounters, but in the madeleine episode it can already be seen in more than one aspect of the creative search. On the one hand, in thinking about something else the mind not only gives itself a different object, it returns as well to a different kind of thinking. On the other hand, the intuitive élan demanded by the encounter itself represents a *recul* to deeper levels of thought. The plunge into the dark world of the mind precedes the jump back into the light of knowledge. The paradox of the *recul* is in this way related to the paradox that requires the loss of the self in order to find the self.

Having momentarily returned to the world of actuality, the narrator excludes it for a second time, and turning again to the *esprit,* recreates the necessary void of purified space before it:

> I place in position before my mind's eye the still recent taste of that first mouthful, and I feel something start within me, something that leaves its resting-place and attempts to rise, something that has been embedded like an anchor at a great depth; I do not know yet what it is, but I can feel it mounting slowly; *I can measure the resistance, I can hear the echo of great spaces traversed.*[7]

The word "resistance" is an important one in Proust's vocabulary. It was shown how in Marcel's encounters with suffering the alien objects that confront him "resist" his efforts to project back upon them the reassuring images of habit. By intensifying the anguish of waiting, such resistance makes him all the more aware of time. It also gives him a new sense of space, for it forces him to "measure" the distance, which he must somehow traverse, that separates the self from its world. Here, it is the inner world of memory that resists the narrator's efforts, not to escape from it or destroy it, but to discover and create it. Although it is a particular lost time and space that is sought, the mind's search and the resistance it encounters make possible the direct experience of the spatial and temporal dimensions that exist within the mind itself and that the mind alone can measure. *Each of Marcel's encounters is the dramatization of a resistance*

6. Arthur Koestler, *The Act of Creation* (New York: Macmillan, 1964), pp. 454–66.

7. I, 35; *Swann,* I, 46.

overcome. Whether change be feared or desired, it is the struggle itself that most clearly reveals the truth of experience. What interests Proust in the madeleine encounter is, therefore, the *process* of memory, the form of its *becoming*, the *movement* toward recognition and into unity across an inner distance. The mind's progress in space and time in relation to the resistance of something that is at once near and far away make up the essence of what Proust calls elsewhere "all the poetry of memory."[8] The past "moves" the narrator emotionally by the very movement that affirms its life within him. Voluntary memory lacks this poetry precisely because forgetting has not created the distance to be traversed.

The narrator feels that what is moving within him must be the image, "the visual memory" tied to the savor of the madeleine and tea; but the form of the memory seems lost in an "uncapturable whirling medley of radiant hues" recalling the "kaleidoscope" of the overture. He tries again and again to lift the memory out of its night. And now what threatens his consciousness and the success of his endeavor is not the fatigue of the mind but of the will.

Then, suddenly, the memory appears, bringing forth the living past of Combray, now "consistent and recognizable," having "form and solidity," freed from the confusion and darkness into which it had almost been lost again. The smell and taste of the madeleine and tea, so long forgotten, have, "like *souls*," carried "in the tiny and almost impalpable drop of their essence, the vast structure of recollection."[9]

It should be noted that Proust, through his narrator, insists from the beginning of his description that the encounter with the madeleine and tea, or with the sensation that provokes the involuntary memory, was the result of pure chance: "And as for that object, it depends on chance whether we come upon it or not before we ourselves must die."[10] Yet it is certainly true that it is not by chance that Proust begins with an involuntary memory of Combray—the beginning of his hero's quest. Nor is it by chance that the narrator, given his particular character and sensitivity, should have such an encounter. It will be shown how the narrator's contingent life *determines* the possibility of similar encounters. "Chance," remarked Pasteur, "only favours invention for minds which are prepared for discoveries by patient study and persevering efforts."[11] The narrator's preparation will constitute not only study and persever-

8. *Pastiches*, p. 108. See also *Proust: A Selection*, p. 24 n.
9. I, 36; *Swann*, I, 47.   10. I, 34; *Swann*, I, 44.
11. Quoted in Koestler, p. 145.

ance but also the other encounters generated by a life lived with intensity. These facts do not negate, however, the meaning of Proust's argument: for as much as life determines chance, so chance determines life, and the finest preparation may be reduced to nothingness by death.

Proust's entire description of the madeleine episode shows convincingly that one essential difference between involuntary and voluntary memory is that the first takes the form of an encounter while the second does not. Indeed, all of Marcel's encounters are involuntary, and all are, therefore, in one way or another, chance events. As the most spectacular of these events the involuntary memory of Combray is also a perfect example of Rollo May's creative encounter. It is not willed, it produces joy and a heightening of consciousness, it occurs in an area in which the narrator was intensely committed in life, and it results in the union of the self with its world. Above all, once the encounter is initiated, it demands that the narrator *will* to give himself to it in order to bring something new into being. Memory is seen as a process and the work of the mind is shown as an activity in time because both depend on the acts of the will. The madeleine encounter describes a form of memory which is in this respect more "voluntary" than the earlier and false recollection of Combray. The bedroom drama is only remembered; Combray in its entirety is created. In Proust's novel, the more an event is involuntary and, consequently, the more it shocks the mind, the greater are the potential demands it makes on the will for its full meaning to be understood.

Memory and Space

Other encounters of involuntary memory occur at intervals throughout the novel. Most important in the way it foresees Marcel's final discoveries is a sequence of experiences described in *Le Côté de Guermantes*. One Sunday morning in Paris Marcel awakes to find that a cold mist has replaced the fine weather of the preceding days. The centrifugal being he was is transformed into a man "longing for the chimney corner and the nuptial couch." This transformation shows Marcel that "a change in the weather is sufficient to create the world and oneself anew." The harmony of the self and the external world is repeated internally, for the presence of the mist recalls similar days spent at Doncières:

From this point of view the new world in which the mist of this morning had immersed me was a world already known to me (which only made it more real) and forgotten for some time (which restored all its novelty).[12]

Marcel's happiness results neither from the shock of a pure sensation nor from a sudden recovery of the past. It is more the result of sensory associations in which the happiness of the present is completed and given depth by the past. Marcel returns to this idea again, later in the same volume:

> we make little use of our experience, we leave unconsumed in the summer dusk or precocious nights of winter the hours in which it had seemed to us that there might nevertheless be contained some element of tranquillity or pleasure. But those hours are not altogether wasted. When, in their turn, come and sing to us fresh moments of pleasure, which by themselves would pass by equally bare in outline, the others recur, bringing with them the groundwork, the solid consistency of a rich orchestration.[13]

Much of Proust's art directs itself precisely to giving to the thin, linear life of the present the rich orchestration of the past, the full temporal and spatial consistency of a life lived in time. For Proust, the profound reality and truth of any moment lies in the identity or virtuality memory gives to the present. "La réalité, he writes, "ne se forme que dans la mémoire."[14]

During a night of cold fog in Paris, Marcel adds to these same recollections of evenings at Doncières and Rivebelle. He is going out to dinner with Saint-Loup. The fog suddenly takes him back to a similar night at Combray. Although he is unable to identify with certainty the exact year of the past that has been evoked, he does perceive the great differences which separate his past experiences at Combray and at Rivebelle:

> what a world of differences! I felt on perceiving them an enthusiasm which might have borne fruit had I been left alone and would then have saved me the unnecessary round of many wasted years through which I was yet to pass before there was revealed to me that invisible vocation of which these volumes are the history.[15]

12. I, 965; *Guermantes*, II, 346.   13. I, 1002; *Guermantes*, II, 396.
14. I, 141; *Swann*, I, 184.   15. I, 1002; *Guermantes*, II, 397.

If it is not the ultimate revelation of truth, this experience does move him a step closer to that truth by making him question the meaning of the encounter:

> Is it because we live over our past years not in their continuous sequence, day by day, but in a memory that fastens upon the coolness or sun-parched heat of some morning or afternoon, receives the shadow of some solitary place, is enclosed, immovable, arrested, lost, remote from all others, because, therefore, the changes gradually wrought not only in the world outside but in our dreams and our evolving character (changes which have imperceptibly carried us through life from one to another, wholly different time), are of necessity eliminated, that, if we revive another memory taken from a different year, *we find between the two, thanks to lacunae, to vast stretches of oblivion, as it were the gulf of a difference in altitude or the incompatibility of two divers qualities,* that of the air we breathe and the colour of the scene before our eyes? But between one and another of the memories that had now come to me in turn of Combray, of Doncières and of Rivebelle, I was conscious at the moment of more than a distance in time, of the distance that there would be between two separate universes the material elements in which were not the same.[16]

This passage, which is a variant of Proust's explanation of the *intermittences du coeur*, also prefigures the description of the *vases clos* of the past that involuntary memory reveals to Marcel in *Le Temps retrouvé*. His present experience already exposes, however, certain important truths concerning his other encounters with the past.

In the involuntary memory of his grandmother at Balbec, Marcel faces the contradiction of similarity and difference between the present and the past. In his recollections of Doncières, he created a kind of mixed time by associating, through a vague identification of similarities, the past with the present. In the madeleine encounter Proust's interest was directed not so much to showing the difference between past and present or even their similarity, at least as revealed through the existence of a common sensation; rather he emphasized how the mind discovers and regains the past by eliminating the distance which separates it from the present. In the Paris encounter, the resurrection of Combray, however vague, is immediate; but because this recollection was preceded by oth-

16. I, 1002–3; *Guermantes,* II, 397–98.

ers, Marcel can now perceive the differences in essence and in time that separate several mutually exclusive moments of the past. The autonomy and individuality which mere association denied to past time is precisely the core of Marcel's present discovery. Since he now confronts *more than one* moment from his past, Marcel is able to make comparisons and to recognize differences—above all, the differences which exist within himself. In Proust's novel the total recognition and comprehension of difference must precede the discovery of similarity. It is this ultimate discovery that Marcel does not make. He is fascinated by the void or abyss of *oubli,* lying between any two moments of the past, but he does not perceive in these inner distances the continuity of his own existence in time. This discovery emerges at the end of the novel. Here, the recognition of a multiple past does not yet precipitate the movement into unity.

In his conclusion to the essay on Sainte-Beuve, Proust repeats his idea that to discover the essence of an artist's vision one must compare his different works. The "ideal" work exists *in between* the others, not because the ideal is a mixture of two or more works, but because, insofar as it does not exist in any one work, it is evoked by them, in much the same way as the meaning of a metaphor is born from the juxtaposition of its two terms. And Proust concludes:

> Why is reality brought back to us by this coincidence of two impressions? Perhaps because then it is resurrected along with what it *leaves out* [avec ce qu'elle *omet*], while if we apply our reason about it, or tax our memories, we add or take away.[17]

In Proust's novel even the slightest presence can evoke a whole absent world. Marcel's telephone call to his grandmother shows how a voice, isolated from its habitual context, can suggest an entirely new context—that of the absent future. The fragile taste of the madeleine, on the other hand, carries the complete world of Combray, the absent past of its original context which, because it has been forgotten or omitted, can be evoked again. So in Marcel's present experience the isolated moments of the past "leave out" their wider context—the inner space and time or *essence* of his life. Once again loss allows gain, and exclusion makes inclusion possible.

With Saint-Loup and the carriage waiting to take him away from his thoughts, however, Marcel does not complete the temporal and spatial metaphor of his life. Like goddesses standing for a moment in "the

17. *Proust on Art*, p. 267; *Sainte-Beuve*, p. 303. Proust's italics.

frame of a door," whose threshold he will not cross for many years, the ideas that had appeared to him take flight, and he finds himself, no longer alone, thrown back into friendship. For Proust, artists have the "duty" to live for themselves, "and friendship is a dispensation from this duty, an abidication of self."[18] Indeed, there is little difference between the superficial self and the "other" who is a friend, since both are "strangers" to, and exclude, the real self that alone "exists" and whose truths cannot be communicated through conversation. Once again the plunge into the depths has been replaced by a linear movement on the surface of life.

The Instants Profonds: *The Hawthorns*

It is not only the resurrections of the past that produce joy. When in *Le Temps retrouvé* the narrator penetrates more thoroughly the meaning of involuntary memory, he relates his encounters with the past to certain encounters with the beauties of nature he experienced as a child, and which demanded of him the same form of creative activity:

> after having meditated a short while over these resurrections of past memories, I became aware that in another way obscure impressions had sometimes, even as far back as Combray along the Guermantes way, engaged my thoughts after the manner of those subjective recollections, but these others concealed within themselves, not a sensation of bygone days, but a new truth, a priceless image, *which I sought to discover by efforts like those one makes to recall something forgotten,* as if our most beautiful ideas were like musical airs that would come back to us without our ever having heard them and which we would make an effort to seize and transcribe.[19]

One of the earliest of these encounters with a "new" image that solicits the creative activity of the narrator's mind occurs not along the Guermantes way, but in the church at Combray. One Sunday during the "month of Mary," Marcel is enchanted by the living and naturally ornamental beauty of the bouquets of white hawthorns on the altar. His enchantment is increased when, by "imitating" within himself "the action of their blossoming," he imagines the flowers as young girls dressed in white.[20] In this passage the reader is not simply presented with an image, he is shown the creative act which is its genesis. The fusion of

18. II, 998; *Temps retrouvé*, III, 875.   19. II, 1000; *Temps retrouvé*, III, 878.
20. I, 85–86; *Swann*, I, 112.

flower and girl is inseparable from the fusion of Marcel's mind with the hawthorns. By plunging into the life of the flowers, Marcel brings his own imagination to life. By miming their motion within himself, he sets his own mind in motion. He becomes like the flowers, and, in doing so, he converts them into an inner object the *esprit* can penetrate and possess.

The white hawthorns are encountered again during a walk Marcel takes by the park of Swann's residence at Tansonville in the company of his father and grandfather. This time, however, he seems unable to penetrate more deeply into the meaning of the flowers:

> it was in vain that I lingered before the hawthorns, to breathe in, to marshall before my mind (which knew not what to make of it), to lose in order to rediscover their invisible and unchanging odour, to absorb myself in the rhythm which disposed their flowers here and there with the light-heartedness of youth, and at intervals as unexpected as certain intervals of music.[21]

The form of Marcel's creative activity closely resembles the narrator's attempts to discover the meaning of his joy during the madeleine encounter. Here again the repetition of the impression reveals nothing new. Here again he seeks to "refresh" his mind, to allow it a *recul* by turning his attention to other flowers. Looking once more at the white hawthorns he creates both physically and mentally a shelter for his mind, but their secret still eludes him: ". . . in vain did I shape my fingers into a frame, so as to have nothing but the hawthorns before my eyes; the sentiment which they aroused in me remained obscure and vague, struggling and failing to free itself, to float across and become one with the flowers."[22]

Marcel is now faced with a dilemma. On the one hand, because he desires to discover the particular essence of the hawthorns, other flowers are too different to be of use. That is, between the other flowers he sees and the image of the hawthorns he carries in his mind, the distance is too great for any relationship to be established. On the other hand, the white hawthorns, because of their very sameness, cannot reveal anything new. Then suddenly his dilemma is resolved:

> And then, inspiring me with that rapture which we feel on seeing a work by our favourite painter quite different from any of those that we already know, or, better still, when some one has

21. I, 106; *Swann*, I, 138.   22. I, 106–7; *Swann*, I, 139.

taken us and set us down in front of a picture of which we have hitherto seen no more than a pencilled sketch, or when a piece of music which we have heard played over on the piano bursts out again in our ears with all the splendour and fullness of an orchestra, my grandfather called me to him, and, pointing to the hedge of Tansonville, said: "You are fond of hawthorns; just look at this pink one; isn't it pretty?"

And it was indeed a hawthorn, but one whose flowers were pink, and lovelier even than the white.[23]

As the comparisons drawn from the world of art suggest, the pink hawthorn is like a different work by the same artist. It is sufficiently different to reveal something new, yet similar enough for its revelation to have meaning within the particular context of Marcel's search. Or, to state the relationship in another way, it is because the pink flowers are similar to the white ones, that is, still hawthorns, that their difference is experienced as a renewal having the force of a revelation. It is the *memory*, though recent, of the white hawthorns, which makes it possible for Marcel to recognize and identify both the variety and underlying unity of the flowers. The new present is seen and apprehended by means of a known past. Moreover, since memory recognizes difference as well as similarity, the present is not simply reduced to the past, but rather transforms the past and develops its meaning. The sense of fulfillment and completion derives from the way the pink hawthorns clarify the obscurity of Marcel's first impression, sharpening its vague form.

By comparing the flowers to works of art Proust, through his hero, is in fact revealing the presence of certain profound similarities between the methods of creation and criticism. During his first encounter with a work the reader must plunge into its life and repeat within himself the rhythms of the artist's style.[24] This is what Marcel does when he sees the hawthorns in the church. But it is only in subsequent encounters with other works by the same artist that his particular vision can be perceived as the unchanging essence of his creation. The artist's works are then comprehended as *inevitable* expressions of an inner reality. Marcel discovers a similar truth in the hawthorns at Tansonville. The pink flowers appear "more vivid and more natural" and consequently affirm with greater evidence the same value of natural beauty Marcel had indistinctly perceived in the white blossoms:

23. I, 107; *Swann*, I, 139.
24. See *Proust on Art*, p. 265; *Sainte-Beuve*, p. 301.

And, indeed, I had felt at once, as I had felt before the white blossom, but now still more marvelling, that it was in no artificial manner, by no device of human construction, that the festal intention of these flowers was revealed, but that it was Nature herself who had spontaneously expressed it.[25]

Not only here, but throughout Proust's work, the absence of artifice is a mark of both artistic and moral perfection. In *A la Recherche,* Marcel learns this particular aesthetic from his grandmother, who values works like the Combray church and people for their natural grace and lack of pretence. The festive character of the hawthorns has not been imposed from without; it comes from within, and is the *inevitable* expression of their essence revealing itself through all variations in color. Marcel delights in this persistence of a common characteristic, especially when he notices that all the various shades of the pink hawthorns merely affirm "the special, irresistible quality of the hawthorn-tree, which, wherever it budded, wherever it was about to blossom, could bud and blossom in pink flowers alone."[26]

In these encounters, Marcel's discovery of the hawthorn's meaning is directly related to the nature of his mental activity. It is only because he seeks for that meaning within himself that he is able to discover that the essence of the hawthorns also exists within them. Neither he nor they call for any outside help to express themselves. Yet Marcel's discovery has a rather paradoxical nature. Although the hawthorns continue to exist outside of himself, he has succeeded in penetrating their *material* autonomy or strangeness by confronting it with a "spiritual equivalent" of his own making. At the same time this interior equivalent helps him understand what alone can be comprehended by the mind—the *spiritual* autonomy or otherness of the flowers. To use the language of "L'Etranger," Marcel brings forth the individual "soul" of the hawthorns, their unique and irreplaceable essence. Marcel does not yet realize that by such activity he will one day discover his own autonomous identity.

The creation of this spiritual equivalent is ultimately the result of Marcel's ability to bring to the encounter not only his memory of other hawthorns but also of other things. From the beginning, the hawthorns evoke a variety of comparisons drawn from the worlds of religion and art, animal life and foods. The flowers are seen as metamorphosed insects; their hedge is like "a series of chapels"; their movements recall the

25. I, 107; *Swann,* I, 140.   26. I, 107–8; *Swann,* I, 140.

rhythms of music; and their coloring and "taste" are like those of pink biscuits or cheese "à la crème rose." The metaphors Marcel discovers once he finds that other things in life are the "equivalents" of flowers complete the union of subject and object. They reveal as well the far more fundamental and extensive unity that underlies all the "works" of nature and man.

A particularly interesting passage describes what Marcel sees when he turns momentarily away from the white hawthorns in order to refresh his mind:

> My eyes followed up the slope which, outside the hedge, rose steeply to the fields, a poppy that had strayed and been lost by its fellows, or a few cornflowers that had fallen lazily behind, and decorated the ground here and there with their flowers like the border of a tapestry, in which may be seen at intervals hints of the rustic theme which appears triumphant in the panel itself; infrequent still, spaced apart as the scattered houses which warn us that we are approaching a village, they betokened to me the vast expanse of waving corn beneath the fleecy clouds, and the sight of a single poppy hoisting upon its slender rigging and holding against the breeze its scarlet ensign, over the buoy of rich black earth from which it sprang, made my heart beat as does a wayfarer's when he perceives, upon some low-lying ground, an old and broken boat which is being caulked and made seaworthy, and cries out, although he has not yet caught sight of it, "The Sea!"[27]

The imagery of this passage shows clearly how Marcel transforms certain elements of the exterior world into "annunciating signs." Creation for Proust is a "deciphering" of signs, a "translation" of material sensations into their spiritual equivalents.[28] But here again it is not so much the final revelation that counts, but the movement toward it and the activity of the searching mind. As the description indicates, the revelation already takes place in the movement itself. The sea is known by its signs before it is seen, experienced in its virtuality before the encounter with its actuality. Although the hawthorns are experienced in their actuality, they also have a kind of virtual life that attracts Marcel's atten-

27. I, 106; *Swann*, I, 138–39.
28. II, 1000–1001; *Temps retrouvé*, III, 878–79. The importance of "signs" in *A la recherche* is the subject of an excellent study by Gilles Deleuze, *Proust et les signes* (Paris: PUF, 1970).

tion. In other words, the virtual excites the mind when it is on the verge of becoming actual, when it is sensed as a hidden life ready to burst forth. The impression of *immanence* is created when something present announces something absent, or, in this instance, as with the hawthorns, when what is absent is repeatedly evoked by a series of intermittent signs moving in a rising rhythm of expectation. The position of the flowers, hawthorns or others, as well as their perfume, is always *ici et là*, here and there, absent and present, and the mind moves among their spatial and temporal dimensions as through a musical rhythm composed of "unexpected intervals."

The lush and complex imagery of the passages on the hawthorns doubtless reflects the associations generated in Marcel's imagination during his encounters with the flowers. But the problem of expression as such is never posed, and one could certainly not attribute the actual writing of the passages to Marcel. He is still far from having such a command of language. It is, in fact, the failure to go beyond his joy and to express adequately his impressions that often plagues Marcel during his walks at Combray.

One day, for example, he comes upon the little tool shed of M. Vinteuil's gardener built beside a pond. It has just rained, and nature appears as an image of itself having the organic unity of a work of art in which all elements have been suffused by the same light. Brandishing his umbrella Marcel cries out his enthusiasm, but he immediately senses the inadequacy of his response. "The bulk of what appear to be the emotional renderings of our inmost sensations," writes Proust, "do no more than relieve us of the burden of those sensations by allowing them to escape from us in an indistinct form which does not teach us how it should be interpreted." For the first time, and because of his failure, Marcel is struck by the "lack of harmony between our impressions and their normal forms of expression."[29] Much of his development as a writer will depend, as J.-Y. Tadié suggests, on the "invention of a language" capable of giving an intelligible form to his impressions.[30]

The Steeples of Martinville

Marcel does succeed in penetrating and expressing the essence of an impression when, riding in the carriage of Doctor Percepied, he sees the

29. I, 119; *Swann*, I, 154–55.
30. Jean-Yves Tadié, "Invention d'un langage," *NRF*, no. 81 (September 1959), 500–513.

twin steeples of the neighboring town of Martinville and that of Vieux-vicq. What he experiences is a kind of optical illusion. Not only has the setting sun placed the exterior world in a "new light," but the very rapidity of the carriage's movement and its changes in direction have given to the steeples a free, living *mobility* that enables them to negate distances and combine in unexpected ways. Like the narrator in the opening pages of the novel, Marcel also is embarked on a voyage through time and space. What he encounters is not a succession of mutually exclusive moments from his own past, but a present, actual space that he must make his own, and that time has begun to reveal in *all* its dimensions. The steeples in their movement present Marcel with a kind of "objective correlative" of his own mobility. His habitual consciousness of time and space encounters a new world in whose freedom he senses his own liberation. He begins to perceive that time and space are inseparable coordinates of existence, and when the carriage suddenly deposits him in front of the Martinville church that moments before had appeared so distant in time and space, he recognizes as well the illusory nature of his perspective. Illusory but not false, for the whole encounter shows again how truth can be revealed when a new experience exposes the senses to the "illusion" of a unique way of seeing the world.

Although he is struck by the strange movements of the steeples, Marcel realizes that he must do more than simply note what he sees. He senses the presence of something immanent behind the mobility and luminosity of the steeples that they seem "at once to contain and to conceal."[31] For Proust "every impression has two parts, one of them incorporated in the object and the other prolonged within ourselves and therefore knowable only to us."[32] Despite the difficulty of the task, Marcel knows that he must search within himself to discover the reason for his joy. One might say that his effort must include finding the "subjective correlative" of the exterior scene, the interior image containing both subject and object.

After a brief stop at Martinville, the carriage begins the return journey. Marcel glances back to look at the steeples, but now circumstances help him to make the effort his weakness sought to avoid. The coachman is indisposed to conversation, and Marcel is forced to turn to himself and to the *image* of the steeples held in his *memory*. With his at-

31. I, 138; *Swann*, I, 180.   32. II, 1010; *Temps retrouvé*, III, 891.

tention thus firmly committed to the inner world he experiences the exhilarating joy of discovery.

> And presently their outlines and their sunlit surface, as though they had been a sort of rind, were stripped apart; a little of what they had concealed from me became apparent; an idea came into my mind which had not existed for me a moment earlier, framed itself in words in my head; and the pleasure with which the first sight of them, just now, had filled me was so much en-hanced that, overpowered by a sort of intoxication, I could no longer think of anything but them.[33]

In this moment of creative discovery there is no longer any need to pre-serve consciousness from corruption. The truth that is bursting forth is so totally present to the mind that it excludes all alien thoughts. Marcel looks back for a last time at the steeples, now black in the evening sky, and once they have disappeared he asks the doctor for a pencil and paper and composes a short descriptive piece on his experience: "Without ad-mitting to myself that what lay buried within the steeples of Martinville must be something analogous to a charming phrase, since it was in the form of words which gave me pleasure that it had appeared to me."[34] And having written the piece, he feels so happy, that like a hen that has just laid an egg he cries out his joy.

Marcel's encounter with the church steeples gives some answers to questions Proust raises throughout his works, namely, the relationship between impression and expression, sensitivity and intelligence, seeing and knowing. In *Le Temps retrouvé,* Proust writes:

> Only the subjective impression, however inferior the material may seem to be and however improbable the outline, is a cri-terion of truth and for that reason it alone merits being appre-hended by the *mind,* for it alone is able, if the mind can extract this truth, to lead the mind to a greater perfection and impart to it a pure joy. The subjective impression is for the writer what experimentation is for the scientist, but with this difference, that with the scientist the work of the intelligence precedes, and with the writer it comes afterwards.[35]

The impression produced by the steeples lies beyond any "abstract truth" and is as individual and particular as Marcel's effort to seize its meaning.

33. I, 139; *Swann,* I, 180–81.   34. I, 139; *Swann,* I, 181.
35. II, 1001–1002; *Temps retrouvé,* III, 880.

Although in this encounter the impression does precede the "work of the intelligence" the line separating the two is not very clear. Marcel's experience shows that his impression is not complete until it is fully understood, that is, until it has been adequately expressed. Tadié remarks that in Proust "any penetrating perception is already literature, literature is the very condition of that perception, and one cannot know which comes first."[36] The important word here is "penetrating." For Proust, once a thing is perceived it is by that very act rendered "immaterial." As such it takes up a new existence within the memory of the perceiving mind. The perception of the exterior world is then replaced by an effort to perceive the inner world. It would appear that at a certain depth the mind that plunges into its own life succeeds in converting the image into something comparable to itself, that is, into something intelligible. Because the image was originally perceived by that same mind it already contains, *in potentia,* the intelligible form the *act of creation* will bring into being. Seeing in depth is knowing, but at the same time the mind sees in terms of what it already knows. This idea becomes clearer if one considers the images Marcel uses in his written piece to describe the steeples: "three birds perched upon the plain," "three golden pivots," "three flowers painted upon the sky," "three maidens in a legend." As images they are not particularly striking, and rightly so, for they reflect Marcel's literary vocabulary at this early point in his apprenticeship. Since his mind is literary rather than, say, musical, he expresses his experience in a "charming phrase"; and because he is still young and untested in his skill, his impression formulates itself only in the words his mind knows how to use.

It is interesting that these words and images are not discovered until the visible world is first excluded. For Proust the mind is not always free to create if the eye remains fascinated by the actual presence of an object. A similar idea is expressed later in the novel when Proust speaks of "the inexorable law which decrees that only that which is absent can be imagined."[37] "But how can the imagination apply itself to the steeples of Martinville, since the hero has them before him?" asks Tadié. "Because in penetrating his impression, that part of the object which is in him, he frees himself from the visible world, realizes its absence."[38] It is true that Marcel excludes the actual steeples by turning to their virtual presence within him. But since the impression he penetrates is really the

36. Tadié, p. 502.   37. II, 996; *Temps retrouvé,* III, 872.
38. Tadié, p. 511.

memory of an impression, his search involves from the beginning an act of recollection. Once the process of memory has begun the proper conditions exist for discovery. As Proust demonstrates in Marcel's encounter with the hawthorns, the mind's knowledge, and consequently its ability to see the world from within itself, derives from its memory of other things. What truly excites the imagination is what is absent or "left out," what is at once contained and concealed in the impression produced by the steeples—their expressive form. Marcel's search reaffirms, and on more than one level, the old Platonic belief that imagination is memory. It is for this reason that the mental activity initiated by the taste of the madeleine so closely resembles that required by the sight of the flowers and steeples. In all these encounters the mind must seek "to recall something forgotten"—the form of the past, or the images through which the mind can create and reveal the form of the present. Something new is seen and learned each time the mind discovers a common bond uniting the sensations and impressions of the past with those of the present.

Proust does not, of course, fully explore the question of seeing and knowing in the present context. The problem will receive greater attention later, particularly when the narrator discusses the art of Elstir. Proust does insist that what Marcel sees in the steeples is in fact different from what he knows, to the extent that it presents a new vision of the familiar world. The movement of the carriage provides Marcel with a strange and unknown perspective on reality that replaces his habitual knowledge of things. Indeed, his encounters with the steeples and with the hawthorns are just as "involuntary" as his sudden recollection of Combray. "Whether it was subjective memories," writes Proust,

> or those truths recorded with the aid of external objects, the significance of which I sought to find in my head, where, jumbled together, steeples, wild flowers, they made up a complicated, flower-bedecked medley, their first characteristic was that I was not free to choose them but that they came to my mind pell-mell. And I felt that that must surely be the hallmark of their genuineness [authenticité].[39]

It is now evident why for Proust the impression must come first. It is a *pure presence* uncorrupted by habit or by a choice that is generally based on some preconceived notion imprisoning the mind within the narrow limits of the known. The impression must come first in order to provide

39. II, 1001; *Temps retrouvé,* III, 879.

the mind and will with a new basis for choice and action, a new frame of reference beyond whose limits the mind cannot stray without destroying the authenticity not only of the impression but of its necessary expression. An impression creates a given space to which the mind must choose to give itself in order to free eventually both the impression and itself.

Marcel's written text on the steeples includes more than simply the initial impression. He describes the steeples from their first apparition to their final disappearance into the night, and under all the angles and perspectives of his vision. The description reveals an interesting pattern of development that will recur, with important variations, in other encounters. An initial illusion, here produced by distance and movement, is dissipated by a sudden confrontation with the object in proximity. Illusion returns, modified by time and the intervening confrontation, when the object moves away again into the distance. It is interesting to note that the images Marcel presents in his "exercise" occur at the beginning when he describes his first vision of the steeples ("birds"), and at the end, after his abrupt arrival at Martinville, when the steeples are seen again at a distance ("pivots," "flowers," "maidens"). A certain distance is necessary, it would seem, for the world to reveal its potentiality as art. If in this case distance creates an artistic illusion, it is also because it permits the mind to see its object in isolation and separated from its usual context. The steeples are first seen and described as "seuls, s'élevant du niveau de la plaine et comme perdus en rase campagne." Because the steeples alone are seen and not the church to which they belong, they are free to combine with other elements in Marcel's imagination. It is as if the physical independence and mobility of the steeples assured their semantic motion or metaphoric possibilities. Seen in all their individuality and related to each other through images, the steeples are also free to combine with themselves. Marcel signals this ultimate movement into unity at the end of his text when playing on the meanings of the key word *seul* he describes the steeples as fusing themselves into "une seule forme noire."[40] This fusion is finally represented by the text itself, for although the different aspects of the steeples are described as they were seen, that is, successively, Marcel presents them within the frame of a complete, autonomous whole. Succession and multiplicity in time and

---

40. I, 139–40; *Swann,* I, 181–82. In the Moncrieff translation these passages are rendered respectively as "Alone, rising from the level of the plain, and seemingly lost in that expanse of open country," and as "a single dusky form."

space are given identity and unity within a work of art, which itself creates a virtual time and space.

The images Marcel discovers attest to his success in "going beyond the appearance" of the object to discover its essence. And in expressing his impression he liberates himself not only from the visible world, but from the inner world as well. To go beyond the appearance does not mean, however, to do away with it, but to give it "depth." The images perform this function by extending the meaning of the steeples through comparisons, which are themselves presented in the very context of appearances and circumstantial events that evoked them. Marcel does describe, for example, the movement of the carriage to and from Martinville. It is equally true that as an expressive form the entire text is itself placed within the context of the encounter whose culmination it marks. That encounter in turn is a poetic moment set in the much wider context of Marcel's daily existence. Although each new event or form represents a break with its context, its full value or meaning can be understood only in relation to it. Like Japanese boxes set one within the other, the different moments of the encounter create in their totality a complex structuring of spaces. Proust presents, therefore, what Marcel's text "leaves out" —the drama of its creation.[41] Between its origin in illusion and its result in expression Proust follows the *process* of creation itself. He wants to show how the mind in imitating the spontaneous activity of nature succeeds in converting a visual illusion into a verbal fiction expressing truth.

The Trees of Hudimesnil

Marcel's success is not repeated when years later, while riding in another carriage with Mme de Villeparisis and his grandmother along the Balbec coast near Hudimesnil, his attention is drawn to three trees that form a pattern he believes he has seen before. Once again he is suddenly filled with a "profound happiness," perceives a "reality" that transforms his actual surroundings into a merely "fictional" world, and confronts an object whose secret seems at once near and far away.[42] This time, however, his impressions escape elucidation. He cannot decide whether the trees belong to the past or to the present, and it is as if the very similarity of the creative efforts directed toward these two segments of time were

41. For another expression of this idea in the form of an excellent critique of Tadié's article, see Bersani, *Marcel Proust,* pp. 229–30.

42. I, 543–44; *Jeunes filles,* I, 717–18.

the cause of his confusion, for he is unable to discover whether the trees contain a memory or a "new idea."

"The steeples of Martinville and the trees of Hudimesnil," writes Howard Moss, "are not memories . . . but premonitions. They contain a hidden future as memories contain a hidden past."[43] It is perhaps for this reason that Marcel is unable to discover the meaning of the trees either in the past or in the present. Their reality also must be "formed in memory" to be discovered in the future. In this respect even his success with the steeples, which was marked by his ability to see them in the perspective of art, will acquire greater significance and meaning when through the final revelations of *Le Temps retrouvé* the entire past, with its successes and failures, will be seen as the material of art.

What particularly strikes the reader is the care Proust takes to make the encounter at Hudimesnil a kind of résumé of the creative experience. He uses the incident not only to present again the pattern of spiritual activity, but also to reveal the richness and ambiguity of the sources of creation itself. This encounter, like the others in the novel, is perfectly timed. As the last of the important *instants profonds* of his youth, Marcel's experience at Hudimesnil occurs at a significant moment in his life. It is precisely through the influence of Mme de Villeparisis, whom he has just met at Balbec, that Marcel will enter the world of the Guermantes. Thus his artistic failure takes place at the inception of his social success. Unlike Dr. Percepied's carriage, whose movements had revealed to Marcel the full spatial and temporal dimensions of the steeples, the present carriage seems the incarnation of actual time drawing him away from the inner space created by the encounter: "It was bearing me away from what alone I believed to be true, what would have made me truly happy; it was like my life." Marcel's life has indeed taken a new direction, leaving behind the joys of nature and leading him toward the more disconcerting revelations of human psychology—in particular, homosexuality.

Marcel's failure is also a moral one. As the trees move into the distance they seem to speak to him, saying: "What you fail to learn from us today, you will never know. If you allow us to drop back into the hollow of this road from which we sought to raise ourselves up to you, a whole part of yourself which we were bringing to you will fall for ever into the abyss." These words, which in their tone and meaning so closely

43. Moss, *Magic Lantern*, p. 101.

resemble those addressed to Dominique by his disappearing soul, attest to the permanence of Proust's vision. And here again the moral atmosphere of the early years is present: "I was wretched," says the narrator, "as though I had just lost a friend, had died myself, had broken faith with the dead or had denied [a god]."[44]

Instinct and Intellect

Shortly before he began writing *A la Recherche* Proust described in the preface to his *Contre Sainte-Beuve* the important role played by the *moments bienheureux* in his own life. These moments, he writes, revealed to him the limits of the intellect:

> Every day I set less store on intellect. Every day I see more clearly that if the writer is to repossess himself of some part of his impressions, get to something personal, that is, and to the only material of art, he must put it aside. What intellect restores to us under the name of the past, is not the past.[45]

As the last sentence suggests, Proust attacks the intellect in the name of involuntary memory. But his argument also justifies by extension the importance of similar involuntary events that reveal to a writer the essence of his life. Proust notes, however, that it is the intellect itself that learns to acknowledge its own "inferiority," and that decides to give to *instinct* the first rank in "the hierarchy of virtues."[46] While the meaning of this word is not clearly explained, Proust's entire discussion suggests that by "instinct" he is referring to that unique mode of perception which enables an artist to recognize immediately the importance to him of certain sensations and impressions that contain essential truths. He is emphasizing, in other words, what Marcel's joyful encounters repeatedly demonstrate—the primacy of sensitivity.

Proust expresses these same ideas again in *La Fugitive:*

> It is life that, little by little, case by case, enables us to observe that what is most important to our heart, or to our *mind,* is learned not by reasoning but by other powers. And then it is the intellect itself which, taking note of their superiority, abdicates its sway to them upon reasoned grounds and consents to

44. I, 545; *Jeunes filles,* I, 718–19. Moncrieff translates "méconnaître un dieu" as "denied my God."
45. *Proust on Art,* p. 19; *Sainte-Beuve,* p. 53.
46. *Proust on Art,* pp. 25–26; *Sainte-Beuve,* p. 59.

become their collaborator and their servant. It is faith confirmed by experiment.[47]

"Every day," "little by little," "case by case"—these expressions affirm that for Proust the power of instinct and the intellect's knowledge of itself can be developed only in time and particularly through a series of encounters. That is why Marcel at Hudimesnil so quickly recognizes the nature of his experience and what it asks of him, even though he fails to discover the secret of the trees. He has felt that extraordinary pleasure before and knows that it requires "a certain effort on the part of the mind." He also knows that it is a pleasure which he must "create" for himself.

How this pleasure can be given as well as created is explained by the fact that each of Marcel's *moments bienheureux* offers him the *possibility* of experiencing at least three forms or levels of joy. The first is the "delicious pleasure" produced by the pure immediacy of a sensation or impression recognized by instinct. The second, the joy of discovery, rests with the successful completion of the mind's search for truth and the resulting union of subject and object—the only object capable of such possession being the inner world of the self. The third level of joy is reached when the experience finds expression in art. These last two forms of joy, which are created by the activity of the *esprit* and of the imagination, are each given *par surcroît,* as something extra, and can be attained only if the self refuses to be satisfied with the first delight of the senses. A final level, which is not necessarily accompanied by joy, is reached when the general meaning of the experience is discovered, and when the truth it revealed is placed in the wider context of a total work of art. This last elucidation is more properly the function of the intellect.

It will be evident to anyone who has read *A la Recherche* that such distinctions are somewhat arbitrary. These different levels of joy are not always so separate one from the other. On the contrary, they often merge together. The same can be said of the different forms of mental activity. But Proust does distinguish between two kinds of "intelligence." The first, which in the *moments bienheureux* is represented by the *esprit,* is more intuitive. It works, often with the help of imagination, to discover the essence and unity of things through metaphor. The second is far more rational and analytic. Its function is to reduce the experiences of life to general laws of behavior and aesthetics. This form of intelligence

47. II, 678; *Fugitive,* III, 423.

can be found more readily in the narrator's judgments and comments than in the strict limits of Marcel's encounters, at least in the early part of the novel. Proust's novel does reveal, therefore, a kind of scale of functions in which, following the law of analogy, each mode of perception and form of mental activity is directly related to the world that is its object. In Marcel's joyful encounters Proust is showing that between instinct and intellect is the creative *esprit* which is as far removed from pure intuition as it is from abstract reasoning. And it is the *esprit* that will become in time the focus of Marcel's "experimental faith."

4
Disappointment

Desire

Although Marcel's joyful encounters with the exterior world reveal to him the necessity of an inward search for truth, they do not shake his persistent belief that certain people, places, and works of art contain in themselves "the secret of Truth and Beauty." For Marcel the reality he desires to possess seems the attribute of whatever is different from himself. Convinced in his imagination of the exterior world's "real existence," he tends to neglect his own. "Hardly ever does one think of oneself" remarks the narrator, "but only how to escape from oneself [sortir de soi]."[1] It is this centrifugal movement, the opposite of the inward plunge produced by the joyful encounters, that characterizes Marcel's life throughout the greater part of the novel.

Curiously, Marcel's desire to escape from himself reveals to him the fact of his own existence. The image of the enclosed space is used again, this time to describe a prison, for Marcel sees in the "little sentry-box of canvas and matting" in which he reads in the Combray garden a replica of his own mind:

> And then my thoughts, did not they form a similar sort of hiding-hole, in the depths of which I felt that I could bury myself and remain invisible even when I was looking at what went on outside? When I saw any external object, my consciousness that I was seeing it would remain between me and it, enclosing it in a slender, incorporeal outline which prevented me from ever coming directly in contact with the material form; for it would volatilise itself in some way before I could touch it, just as an incandescent body which is moved towards something wet never actually touches moisture, since it is always preceded, itself, by a zone of evaporation.[2]

1. I, 121; *Swann*, I, 157.   2. I, 63; *Swann*, I, 84.

86

Marcel's discovery that his perception is not free from his consciousness of the self that perceives is the same discovery Proust himself described in his early letter to Darlu. In the novel, however, there is no philosopher to teach Marcel that the reality he seeks can be known only in his individual consciousness of it. The more he desires this reality the more consciousness seems an obstacle preventing the encounter and fusion of subject and object. Conscious of his own presence, he remains unconscious of the world present within him.

Paradoxically, his desire for the real world is often aroused by his reading of books that introduce him to a virtual world composed of "immaterial" images of reality that his mind can "assimilate." The intense fictional life of the characters seems more real and meaningful to him than the "mediocre incidents" of his own life in Combray. His imagination itself creates an enclosed space, an inner focusing of attention and desire framed by the surrounding world yet excluding it.

Once it has been awakened in this fashion Marcel's imagination does not exclude certain other desires seemingly unrelated to the book he is reading. If the landscape described in it makes him long for "a land of mountains and rivers," this dream is impregnated by his ever present dream of a woman whom he will love and whom he imagines as an inseparable part of the desired landscape. In fact, his desire to see and to know any person or place is aroused only when his imagination constructs an a priori model of it. These "doubles" in Marcel's imagination, supported by his faith in the exterior world's "absolute perfection," are the motive force behind the centrifugal movement that carries him out of the enclosed and protected world of Combray and of his innocence.

But in this movement he remains in the "prison" of consciousness:

> Had my parents allowed me, when I read a book, to pay a visit to the country it described, I should have felt that I was making an enormous advance towards the ultimate conquest of truth. For even if we have the sensation of being always enveloped in, surrounded by our own soul, still it does not seem a fixed and immovable prison; rather do we seem to be borne away with it, and perpetually struggling to pass beyond it, to break out into the world, with a perpetual discouragement as we hear endlessly, all around us, that unvarying sound which is no echo from without, but the resonance of a vibration from within. We try to discover in things. endeared to us on that account, the spiritual glamour which we ourselves have cast upon them; we

87

are disillusioned, and learn that they are in themselves barren and devoid of the charm which they owed, in our minds, to *the association* [voisinage] *of certain ideas.*[3]

Proust through his narrator clearly presents here the fundamental causes of the disappointment Marcel will experience in his encounters with reality. He cannot escape the presence of his self because it is that very self that imagines and desires the world. The élan by which Marcel seeks in his joyful encounters to go beyond the image reality places in his mind and to discover its essence within himself is here directed outward in a desire to discover in the exterior world the objective equivalent or correlative of what is only a subjective image. Marcel moves toward a material world which will resist once again the projections of the self, and which his mind will be unable to assimilate.

Names and Places

"All action by the *mind* is easy," writes Proust, "if it is not subjected to the test of reality."[4] The workings of free imagination that precede a disappointing encounter are nowhere more carefully described than in Proust's presentation of the way Marcel weaves images around the names of cities he desires to visit. Marcel first begins to dream of Balbec, for example, after hearing Legrandin describe it as "that funereal coast, famed for the number of its wrecks." Although Legrandin's language paints a rather exaggerated and overly poetic picture of Balbec, Marcel never questions the accuracy of the description. What excites his imagination here as elsewhere is a rich image. Indeed, Legrandin's artificial and subjective language makes Marcel desire a genuine and objective reality. He wants to see not so much a beautiful spectacle as "a momentary revelation of the true life of nature." His search is for the same authenticity and individuality he discovered to be the essence of the hawthorns at Tansonville. Just as he believes that truth exists outside of himself, so he desires a completely natural world free of any trace of "human interference." Anything that has been mechanically or artificially produced to give pleasure or to serve a utilitarian purpose is considered a corruption of nature's autonomy and of the free "space" he needs for the "expansion" of his heart. Marcel's dream of Balbec is soon enriched by Swann, who speaks of the remarkable "Persian" quality of its Gothic church. The rugged coast with its fishermen that Marcel had believed "remote from human history" is now seen in a medieval

3. I, 65–66; *Swann*, I, 86–87.   4. II, 39; *Sodome*, II, 650.

setting. A reciprocal exchange of value takes place between the two "neighboring" images of nature and art, and the imaginary "double" of Balbec is complete.[5]

Marcel also dreams of other places—of the towns in Normandy through which the train to Balbec passes, of the great art cities of Italy like Florence and Venice. Each city seems to contain an atmosphere so distinct that in moving from one to another in his imagination he undergoes "a complete change of tone in my sensibility." After a while Marcel is able to evoke at will the charm of these cities simply by pronouncing their names, but this new method of evocation has its own dangers. Unlike words that present only "little pictures, lucid and normal" of things conceived of as similar and as belonging to the same class, names give to cities the same individuality as they do to persons, a unique reality that nevertheless is based on a "confused picture" drawn from the sound of their syllables and limited, like a poster, to a single "color." Although they are the means by which Marcel imagines an unknown and absent reality, as simple autonomous worlds containing a limited time and space these names "are not very comprehensive" and in fact exclude much of the reality he will encounter.[6]

Now completely a part of the "Age of Names" Marcel does not worry himself with "the contradiction that there was in my wishing to look at and to touch with my organs of sense what had been elaborated by the spell of my dreams and not perceived by the senses at all." Although each city seems a "paradise" to be discovered, Marcel does not think of it as "an inaccessible ideal" but as "a real and enveloping substance" filled with a life into which he longs to plunge—a life which is above all *intact and pure*. Although only something absent can be imagined, the desire born of imagination can be satisfied only in the possession of a real object. Once Marcel learns, thanks to his consultation of train schedules, that the cities have a concrete location in time and space, the more present and real do they appear. He attains "the supreme pinnacle of happiness" when his father reminds him to take along a heavy coat to protect him against the cold of the Grand Canal. He is now able to conceive not only the reality of Venice but also of himself in Venice, of the self he will be in Venice.[7] Here again self and world are closely related, for to be somewhere else is to be someone else. Yet even this new "reality" continues to exist only in his imagination. In becoming more like an object

5. I, 293–94; *Swann*, I, 383–85.   6. I, 295–97; *Swann*, I, 386–89.
7. I, 298–300; *Swann*, I, 390–93.

to be possessed the image of a city may increase Marcel's desire, but it also increases thereby the inevitability of his future disappointment. To this paradox is added yet another, for if the mutually exclusive nature of points in space and time delight Marcel by confirming the particular reality of each city, the same particularity of reality becomes a cause of disappointment when he encounters the objects of his dreams.

Such a disappointing encounter occurs when Marcel first arrives at Balbec. He is surprised to learn that there are two Balbecs, one built on the coast and another inland, and that the church standing in the center of the latter does not overlook a stormy sea but is surrounded by houses, streetcar tracks, and a café. Seen in its actual context the church seems to him "an accident, a by-product of this summer afternoon." Although Marcel attempts to hide his disappointment by telling himself that the church and its statues are now present before him in their unique reality, his desire remains unsatisfied:

> my mind, which had exalted the Virgin of the Porch far above the reproductions that I had had before my eyes, *inaccessible* by the vicissitudes which had power to threaten them, *intact* although they were destroyed, *ideal*, endowed with universal value, was astonished to see the statue which it had carved a thousand times, reduced now to its own apparent form in stone.[8]

The reality Marcel imagined as different from all he knew is in fact different from his image of it in which there was no room for cafés and streetcars. He realizes that the church is not only "accessible" *in* time and space, but is also accessible *to* time and space in all the force of their actuality. His mind is unable to possess and assimilate precisely what he had so desired—a world existing outside the self. In his encounter with the Martinville steeples Marcel begins with reality and succeeds in discovering its spiritual equivalent within himself; at Balbec the a priori creation of his imagination is "reduced" to its material reality. He does not feel liberated but imprisoned; he does not act on reality but reacts to a world that seems to act upon him. Above all he seeks to escape from the truth of his experience by accusing circumstances and by imagining a future whose promise can still be realized.

Marcel's faith in the future is inseparable from his belief in the possibility of possessing a world outside of himself. There are moments, how-

8. I, 501; *Jeunes filles,* I, 659.

ever, when his faith is brought into question. When his father finally accepts Marcel's desire to devote himself to a career in literature, he exposes a disconcerting truth:

> when he spoke of my inclinations as no longer liable to change, he awakened in me two terrible suspicions. The first was that (at a time when, every day, I regarded myself as standing upon the threshold of a life which was *still intact* and would not enter upon its course until the following morning) my existence was already begun, and that, furthermore, what was yet to follow would not differ to any extent from what had already elapsed. The second suspicion, which was nothing more, really, than a variant of the first, was that I was not situated somewhere outside the realm of Time, but was subject to its laws.[9]

Marcel's experience at Balbec shows that the reality of time must be encountered in a concrete situation to be truly understood. No amount of "theoretical" knowledge can replace a direct impression on the senses. The objects he sees confront him with evidence of the world's as well as his own subjugation to the laws of time and space, laws that constitute the fundamental nature of the reality he refuses to accept, and that deny him the possession he seeks.

Although Marcel moves toward the future he believes "still intact" and different from his past experience, his dream of Balbec has been irrevocably corrupted by reality:

> but as for Balbec, no sooner had I set foot in it than it was as though I had *broken open a name* which ought to have been kept *hermetically closed,* and into which, seizing at once the opportunity that I had imprudently given them when I expelled all the images that had been living in it until then, a tramway, a Café, people crossing the square, the local branch of a Bank, irresistibly propelled by some *external pressure,* by a pneumatic force, had come crowding into the interior of those two syllables which, closing over them, let them now serve as a border to the porch of the Persian church, and would never henceforward cease to contain them.[10]

This image of a corrupted space can be seen as yet another variation on the model of Dominique's room in "L'Etranger." Here, however, the meaning of the experience is markedly different. The corruption is not

9. I, 369; *Jeunes filles,* I, 482.   10. I, 501–2; *Jeunes filles,* I, 660–61.

the direct result of a moral failure, which is demonstrated rather by Marcel's choice to return to his dreams and to evade thereby the responsibility of knowing himself. The destruction of the imaginary Balbec is not only inevitable and practically automatic given the shock of the encounter, it is also a necessary part of Marcel's spiritual development. Both the world of the imagination and the self tied to it must be destroyed by reality if Marcel is eventually to discover a self formed by a life in time.

The image of an "hermetically closed" world destroyed by the "external pressure" of reality can also be seen as a variation on a related image Proust uses in his description of Marcel's joyful encounters. The outlines and surfaces of the Martinville steeples, for example, are described as "a sort of rind" which at the moment of discovery is "stripped apart" to reveal the secret of their meaning. The joy of discovery is, therefore, most properly an *ex-plosion,* a bursting forth of creation resulting from the internal pressure produced by the mind's centripetal plunge into its world. At Balbec the centrifugal movement of Marcel's imagination ends in a destructive *im-plosion,* the collapse of his dreams when confronted by the "deluge of reality."

But if Marcel begins to know the "country" precisely because it is unlike the "name," it is also true that the reality he sees is as incomplete and deceptive in its way as imagination. When during his stay Marcel visits Elstir's studio, the painter describes to him all the richly detailed beauty of the church that Marcel, in the shock of his encounter, had failed to see. He realizes that the truth he had desired was there all the time, but had found no place in the arbitrary image he had created of a "Persian church." It is less reality that fails Marcel, therefore, than it is his imagination that fails reality and makes it disappointing.

Elstir's remarks do not redeem, however, the lost charm of the imaginary Balbec. The poetic individuality of the "name" punctured by reality is reduced to an ordinary "word" by Brichot's explanation of its etymology. In time, habit transforms the entire region of Balbec into a flat and familiar world of people, places, and *things:*

> So that it was not merely the place-names of this district that had lost their initial mystery, but the places themselves. The names, already half-stripped of a mystery which etymology had replaced by reason, had now come down a stage farther still.[11]

This loss of a sense of mystery as the unknown becomes the known and as imagination is replaced by intellectual reasoning, is one of the funda-

11. II, 362; *Sodome,* II, 1108–9.

mental aspects of Marcel's experience in life. Yet here again the same paradox of a loss that makes possible a gain is in operation. Although he continues to lament over the loss of his faith, Marcel does acquire a knowledge of reality and of the "laws" governing the self and the world. In emptying Balbec of its imaginary mystery reality also fills the void it creates and expands the restricted space of the name. Marcel is now free to make new discoveries. He meets Albertine, Saint-Loup, and Mme de Villeparisis and is able, thanks in part to Elstir, to enjoy the beauties of even the most banal objects and scenes. With these encounters new desires are born or old desires are given new objects. But Marcel does not escape from disappointment. His second stay at Balbec failed as much as his first, says the narrator, to live up to his expectations:

> The images selected by memory are as arbitrary, as narrow, as intangible as those which imagination had formed and reality has destroyed. There is no reason why, existing outside ourselves, a real place should conform to the pictures in our memory rather than to those in our dreams. And besides, a fresh reality will perhaps make us forget, detest even, the desires that led us forth upon our journey.[12]

The reality of Balbec never ceases to change, because it exists, like Marcel's desires, in time. And now time extends not only toward the future but toward the past as well, for if the new Balbec does not duplicate the images in Marcel's memory it is above all because the present is transformed by the suffering born from his involuntary memory of his grandmother. The forgotten reality of the past gives a new depth and form to the present.

Years later when this second Balbec has itself moved into the past, he discovers how limited his knowledge of its reality was. After Albertine's death Aimé informs Marcel in a letter of her secret meetings with young girls in the Balbec baths. It is now the past that is transformed. Balbec is seen retrospectively as an unknown and unknowable "hell" filled with the new and more frightening mystery of Albertine's homosexuality. Although this last, infernal Balbec is also forgotten, Marcel's encounters have created a past which, because it exists outside of time and within himself, is alone "intact" and capable of being possessed in its entirety. With the help of involuntary memory Balbec's multiplicity in time will be given form and unity in a work of art.

12. II, 111; *Sodome*, II, 752.

The Duchess

Just as Marcel dreams of certain cities before encountering them in reality so he dreams of certain persons. Among those who hold a particular fascination for him are the Guermantes. Although he knows that the Duke and Duchess, who are so near yet inaccessible in space, are "real personages," he endows their world with an abstract and ideal existence. He associates them in his imagination not only with their ancestors represented in the Combray church, but also with the whole of the "Guermantes way" and its natural beauties. Marcel does receive more precise information concerning the Duchess's appearance from Dr. Percepied, who also shows him a picture of her in a magazine, but he is no less shocked and disappointed when he suddenly sees her in the church.

Marcel's encounter with Mme de Guermantes is an excellent example of Proust's technique of presenting his characters in the form of "apparitions." The Duchess first attracts Marcel's attention precisely because he does not recognize her. She is a stranger, "a lady with fair hair and a large nose."[13] Marcel succeeds in combining this set of disjointed and isolated traits and in identifying her only by comparing what he sees with the few facts he knows about the Duchess. Here again recognition is based on memory, for it is memory that enables the mind to perceive analogies between the present and the past, the unknown and the known, and in so doing to assemble the fragments provided by vision into a unified whole identifiable by a name. The Duchess comes to birth before Marcel's eyes as her identity is formed within him. He discovers her reality by creating it.

But Marcel finds no pleasure in what he sees. It is as if, in discovering similarities between reality and the model in his imagination, he is able to perceive all the more clearly the differences between the two. His disappointment is so great that in his first efforts to interpret the reasons for it he replaces one misconception of reality by another. On the one hand, it is certainly true that the "real" Duchess differs markedly from the model in his imagination. Having formed her freely, if arbitrarily, and having placed her in "another" world unlike the present one he knows, Marcel now sees the Duchess as formed by time and imprisoned by the "laws of life." To his dismay he is forced to acknowledge that the woman he sees is real to the extent that she does in fact exist outside of himself in a world over which he has no control and in which he cannot

13. I, 134; *Swann,* I, 174.

intervene. He is confronted, that is, by the real "otherness" of this woman who is at once materially present yet far removed from the realm of his desires. On the other hand, the "real" Duchess disappoints Marcel less because she is simply different from the imaginary model than because he judges her as similar to ordinary women like Mme Sazerat. The woman he sees now is no longer the "lady" who first struck his attention with all the mystery of the unknown. She has become just another member of a class, an example of "a certain type of femininity."[14] In moving from the "name" to the "woman," from imagination to intelligence, Marcel remains blind to the true individuality of Mme de Guermantes. He is even unaware of the degree to which this "real" Duchess is in part the creation of his own mind, and he does not realize that the associations made by the intelligence are just as simplified, arbitrary, and limited in truth as those of the imagination.

Faced by a reality that seems to exclude him while revealing the fictional nature of his imaginary world, Marcel refuses to allow this world and the self that created it to die. Here as in his moments of great suffering what reacts within him is the "instinct of self-preservation." Instead of accepting the truth of his disappointment, Marcel convinces himself that the very presence of the Duchess proves that his desires have been satisfied. By omitting from his gaze the features of her face that might have reminded him of the faces of other women, he brings about their absence; and his imagination, which had been paralyzed for a moment, comes to life again. He associates the Duchess once more with the rich images and *idées voisines* that had given so much value to her name but that the shock of the encounter had stripped away. "How lovely she is!" he cries. "What true nobility! it is indeed a proud Guermantes, the descendant of Geneviève de Brabant, that I have before me!"[15] Marcel's reaction, which is another instance of the corruption of consciousness, is also a fine example of what Gilles Deleuze calls "the mechanism of objective disappointment and subjective compensation" in Proust's novel.[16]

At first glance the structure of Marcel's encounter with the Duchess seems clearly dialectical. The imaginary model is destroyed by reality that in turn is replaced by a new synthesis combining elements drawn from imagination and reality, subject and object. Yet as the narrator remarks, this new synthesis is only a "deliberately unfinished sketch" and, therefore, fundamentally false. Although Marcel succeeds in convincing

14. I, 134; *Swann*, I, 174–75.   15. I, 136; *Swann*, I, 176.
16. Deleuze, *Signes*, p. 45.

himself again of the Duchess's qualities, he does so by carefully excluding those elements of her appearance that would obstruct the renewed activity of his imagination. He forgets or ignores what he has seen in order to remember his dreams and to project them once again outside of himself. The truth of the Duchess is lost in a succession of mutually exclusive points of view in time. Unable to combine imagination with intelligence, he seems incapable of understanding that the Duchess can be at once similar to and different from other women. On the one hand, his intelligence acts as an obstacle preventing him from going beyond the Duchess's material appearance toward a discovery of her true uniqueness. On the other hand, his subjective associations hide the truth of her existence in time. Marcel's impression is confused, therefore, by a series of self-conscious half-measures. He remains on the surface of reality as he remains on the surface of his self. Based on associations, the union of subject and object is itself a mere association and not the fusion Marcel achieves in his encounter with the church steeples. All this does not imply that Marcel has only to combine the abstraction supplied by his intelligence with that provided by imagination in order to perceive the truth. The individuality of the Duchess at this particular moment is contained in the total living impression produced by the encounter. It is not simply in the fact of her physical presence, but in the complex *activity* of Marcel's imagination and intelligence when confronted by that presence. In other words, her individuality is revealed through the impression that Proust's description of the encounter produces on the reader. Both Proust and the reader see from a perspective that is denied to Marcel, who is himself too much in time and too close to his object to be able to encompass the totality of his experience.

These problems of time and distance are posed again in Marcel's subsequent encounters with the Duchess. When his parents rent an apartment in the Hôtel de Guermantes in Paris, and Marcel is able to see the Duchess every day, the inescapable reality of her life and his own habit of seeing her destroy the distance required by imagination. But if the magic of the Duchess's name perishes when Marcel moves closer to the woman so does the simplicity of the world it enclosed. The more Marcel encounters the Duchess, the more he becomes conscious of the complexity of her existence in time:

> If the name, Duchesse de Guermantes, was for me a collective name, it was so not merely in history, by the accumulation of all the women who had successively borne it, but also in the course of my own short life, which had already seen, in this single

Duchesse de Guermantes, so many different women superimpose themselves, each one vanishing as soon as the next had acquired sufficient consistency. Words do not change their meaning as much in centuries as names do for us in the space of a few years. Our memory and our heart are not large enough to be able to remain faithful. We have not room enough, in our mental field, to keep the dead there as well as the living.[17]

The multiplicity of the self in time and the successive destruction of the past by the present are, of course, problems that Marcel faces in all the domains of his experience. Yet if he cannot hold in his conscious memory all the incarnations of the Duchess, these different women are stored in his unconscious memory and will be reborn at the end of the novel by the single name that unites them all. While during his first encounter Marcel moves from a simplified fiction to an equally simple reality and back again, in the novel as a whole this pattern is repeated, but with two important differences: the reality he successively encounters is much more complex and is finally seen in its totality from the new distance and inclusive perspective of art.

La Berma

Many of the problems related to perception in time raised by Marcel's encounter with Mme de Guermantes are presented again in Proust's decsription of his hero's encounter with the great actress La Berma. Like the other disappointing encounters, this one also is carefully prepared.

La Berma is at first associated with Marcel's "platonic love" for the theatre, which is also the core of his desire to understand "art itself." She grows in prestige when Marcel hears her praised by Swann and learns that she is Bergotte's favorite actress. The rich imagery of Bergotte's article on La Berma in the role of Phèdre completes the "double" in Marcel's imagination, and the actress is inseparably linked to the grandeur of Racine's tragedy. His desire to see La Berma in *Phèdre* rather than in a new and unfamiliar play is also related to the important problem of aesthetic judgment. He believes that the only way to judge La Berma's unknown and "inconceivable" art in all its purity and strangeness is to separate it from what is already known in order to perceive more clearly what she will add to the play. His intelligence as well as his imagination, therefore, have prepared the ground for his encounter. Both will prove inadequate to his impression.

Marcel's excitement continues to grow during his first moments in the

17. I, 1095; *Guermantes*, II, 531–32.

theatre. The lobby, the stage, and even the farcical curtain-raiser seem part of a truly magical and mysterious world. His pleasure lasts even through the early scenes of *Phèdre*. So well do the actresses playing the roles of Aricie and Oenone correspond to his expectations that he momentarily mistakes them for La Berma. Marcel's reaction ironically reveals the truth of Proust's idea that "one can see only with something analogous to what is seen." He appreciates the art of the two actresses because it "fits into" the pattern of his inner model. He knows what to look for and in fact sees precisely what his imagination and intelligence had constructed a priori. So perfect is the correspondence between inner and outer worlds that he can accept without alteration the total reality he perceives. The two actresses even satisfy his desire for new truths by revealing to his intelligence the meaning of certain verses.

This situation is completely reversed and his pleasure ends abruptly with the sudden entrance of La Berma, whose acting bears no resemblance to that of the other two actresses. Marcel now attempts to bridge the distance between his inner model and this startling new reality, but, writes the narrator,

> in vain might I strain towards Berma [my] eyes, ears, mind, so as not to let one morsel escape me of the reasons which she would furnish for my admiring her, I did not succeed in gathering a single one. I could not even, as I could with her companions, distinguish in her diction and in her playing intelligent intonations, beautiful gestures. I listened to her as though I were reading *Phèdre,* or as though Phaedra herself had at that moment uttered the words that I was hearing, without its appearing that Berma's talent had added anything at all to them. I could have wished, so as to be able to explore them fully, so as to attempt to discover what it was in them that was beautiful, *to arrest, to immobilise* for a time before my senses every intonation of the artist's voice, every expression of her features.[18]

The inner model by means of which Marcel perceived the art of the other actresses now acts as an obstacle preventing his perception of La Berma's talent. He cannot "see" her talent not only because his model is in no way "analogous" to the reality confronting him, but also because that model is the *only* basis for his perception, the sole frame of reference he possesses. Yet it is precisely because he does possess this model that he is

18. I, 344; *Jeunes filles*, I, 449. Moncrieff's translation is obscure here. He rendears "tendre vers la Berma mes yeux" as "strain towards Berma's eyes."

confronted by certain truths whose meaning he will not understand until later. First, by helping him perceive the talent of the other actresses while preventing him from understanding La Berma's, his model makes him more acutely aware of a difference between the former and the latter. Second, by making him believe that he can judge talent only by separating the acting from the text of the play, the model makes him more conscious of La Berma's fusion with the text. Third, insofar as it is static and abstract the model forces upon Marcel's mind the reality of La Berma's mobile existence in time. In all these impressions it helps to produce, the model confuses and renders unintelligible the very truths it reveals. Thus, if La Berma is seen as being different from the other actresses, she is judged as possessing a far smaller talent than they. Even lycée students, Marcel feels, would not have neglected as she does certain dramatic intonations in Phèdre's declaration of love to Hippolyte.

Proust's primary concern is, however, to describe the dilemma posed by perception in time. Marcel has no difficulty judging the art of the other actresses because their intonations and gestures are exaggerated enough to be distinguished successively without any real effort on his part. So well do they correspond to his inner model that he has only to *look at* them in order to perceive their talent. Such is not the case with La Berma. So different is she from his model that he is forced to *look for* the reasons for her greatness, and the more intense his search and the efforts of his attention, the more his object seems to escape him. In attempting to see everything at once he sees little or nothing and in pressing his object too closely he destroys the possibility of an "authentic" impression. Although La Berma's art is in its essence temporal, Marcel himself by his self-conscious search both intensifies his mind's race against time and assures his own defeat. In his efforts to stop and immobilize each intonation of the actress he succeeds only in exposing himself to the anguish of having to experience mutually exclusive moments in time in rapid succession.

Marcel is disappointed, but already he begins to hide the reality of his encounter. The applause of the audience awakens in him a feeling of admiration, and, remarks the narrator, "the more I applauded, the better, it seemed to me, did Berma act." Once home, he turns to M. de Norpois whom he believes much more intelligent than himself and therefore capable of revealing to him the truth of La Berma's art and justifying the desire he had had to see her. Norpois speaks to him of La Berma's intelligent choice of plays, of her taste in costumes, of her admirable voice. Marcel eagerly "absorbs" all these remarks until he is able to say, "No; I have not been disappointed!" Later the same evening Marcel reads a newspaper review of La Berma's performance. The words of elaborate praise he finds there complete what is now an a posteriori model of his experience in the theatre. Marcel's "objective disappointment" has again led to a "subjective compensation." Freed from "the limits of reality," his imagination is once more able to direct itself toward an absent world, now no longer in the future but in the past. Commenting on this encounter René Girard writes: "Proustian desire is each time the triumph of the suggestion over the impression."[19] Marcel's original model was itself composed of the "suggestions" of others that in fact corrupted his impression of La Berma. Now, after the performance, such suggestions hide the impression of disappointment as well. For whether these suggestions are found in his own imagination as when he transforms the Duchess in the Combray church, or whether he receives them directly from others as he does here, they always represent someone else's ideas and remain outside of his individual impression.

Proust, through his narrator, finds in Marcel's escape from reality an important law of human psychology:

> It may doubtless be argued that I was not absolutely sincere. But let us bear in mind, rather, the numberless writers who, dissatisfied with the page which they have just written, if they read some eulogy of the genius of Chateaubriand . . . are so filled with that idea of genius that they add it to their own productions, when they think of them once again, see them no longer in the light in which at first they appeared, and, hazarding an act of faith in the value of their work, say to themselves: "After all!" without taking into account that, into the total which determines their ultimate satisfaction, they have introduced the memory of marvellous pages of Chateaubriand which they assimilate to their own, but of which, in cold fact, they are not the authors . . . and let us then declare whether, in the communal life that is led by our ideas in the enclosure of our minds, there is a single one of those that make us most happy which has not first sought, a very parasite, and *won from an alien but neighbouring idea the greater part of the strength that it originally lacked.*[20]

19. René Girard, *Mensonge romantique et vérité romanesque* (Paris: Grasset, 1961), p. 39.
20. I, 368–69; *Jeunes filles,* I, 481.

These remarks immediately recall the description of Marcel's desires that were born from the *voisinage de certaines idées.* It would appear, therefore, that subjective associations are both the source of desire and the means by which one hides the reality of failure. Disappointed by his encounter with La Berma, Marcel turns to a form of self-deception that is itself the most insidious form of "self-consciousness" as it is a consciousness of a self that is not truly his own. His own consciousness is in this way corrupted by insincerity. He finds it easier to forget an impression he cannot accept than to forget and exclude from his mind the reassuring images and ideas whose accuracy he does not question so long as they justify his desires and beliefs.

The question of sincerity, which for Proust is essentially fidelity to one's true impressions, will be discussed in greater detail in the following chapter. It is important to note that Proust's law of insincerity, or of the *idées voisines,* can also be discovered in other encounters. Dominique's guests are, after all, the incarnations of his self-conscious and subjective beliefs whose presence he requires in order to save himself from the necessity of accepting the truth of his soul. In moments of solitude and suffering Marcel turns to his mother and grandmother to seek in them the strength he lacks. His reliance on Norpois' ideas represents only another variation on this pattern. Either because of his fear of solitude or his refusal to be disappointed, his weakness, or his belief that truth exists only outside of himself, he always seeks to assimilate or to associate himself with some outside source of strength and prestige.[21]

Marcel's "subjective compensation" for his disappointment exposes once again the problem of imagination, that is, the fact that his imagination can operate only outside the limits of reality and when divorced from the actual impression. This dissociation of imagination and sensation is related to the equally acute problem of the dissociation *in time* of intelligence and sensitivity. Marcel recognizes this dilemma when sometime *after* his encounter in the theatre he hears Bergotte compare one of La Berma's gestures to that of an archaic Greek statue:

> But of Berma in that scene all that I retained was a memory which was no longer liable to modification, slender as a picture which lacks that abundant perspective of the present tense where one is free to delve and can always discover something new, a picture to which one cannot retrospectively give a mean-

21. This particular aspect of Marcel's psychology receives careful attention from Leo Bersani, *Marcel Proust,* pp. 33–34.

ing that is not subject to verification and correction from without.[22]

It is not until his second encounter with La Berma some years later that Marcel is able to resolve the dichotomy of intelligence and sensitvity. This time, however, his attitudes have completely changed. He attaches no importance to the possibility of hearing La Berma again, for the art of the theatre now seems to him "a feeble, tawdry thing" containing "no deep-lying soul," and he considers actors to be merely "people of the same substance" as those he knew. But Marcel's indifference does not signify that he has closed his mind to what he will see. It is rather the sign of his liberation from the distorting expectations of the past. The old "double" in his imagination, no longer supported by faith and desire, has been forgotten, carrying with it the naive self that had endowed La Berma and *Phèdre* with an "absolute existence." Whereas in the past he was anxious lest some disturbance in the theatre corrupt the purity of La Berma's acting, it is now rather the inner world of his mind that has been freed of encumbering images and ideas. Instead of looking for something whose value he has decided on in advance, Marcel is able to look at what he sees with an open mind. He does not seek to confront the impression with his expectations, but is prepared to *receive* an impression and to interpret it by means of all the knowledge he has acquired from his past experience.

No longer blinded by an imaginary model, Marcel is able to perceive the faults of the minor actresses whose intelligence does not succeed in giving a truly artistic value either to their voice, which remains unalterably their own "with its material defects or charms," or to their gestures, which instead of expressing the "fine shades of Racinian meaning" merely demonstrate certain "muscular attachments."[23] The art of these actresses is a failure because it is an overly self-conscious art, and just as their self-consciousness separates them from the play by interposing the characteristics of their own contingent life so Marcel's self-conscious imagination during his first encounter had prevented him from making contact with the essence of La Berma's art. If in their willful effort to be supremely artistic the actresses reveal only the insignificance of daily life, so Marcel's limited conceptions of artistic grandeur and his anxious effort to find them in La Berma's acting had made him judge her talent as indistinguishable from common speech. Marcel himself does not discover these analogies between his previous mental attitudes and the art

22. I, 427; *Jeunes filles*, I, 560–61.   23. I, 746; *Guermantes*, II, 46.

of the minor actresses, yet they are obviously implied in Proust's presentation. Here as elsewhere it is part of Proust's genius to lead his reader to the recognition of such analogies linking the inner patterns of Marcel's mind with the exterior world of experience.

With La Berma's entrance Marcel suddenly understands the reasons for his earlier failure to perceive her genius:

> the talent of Berma, which had evaded me when I sought so greedily to seize its essential quality, now, after these years of oblivion, in this hour of indifference, imposed itself, with all the force of a thing directly seen, on my admiration.[24]

The need for a *recul,* the importance of forgetfulness, and the "involuntary" nature of Marcel's impression clearly relate his present encounter with those of involuntary memory. Although Marcel's memory of his past experience helps him to understand his present one, there is, strictly speaking, no resurrection of the past involved here. He does, however, regain or rediscover in a new light La Berma's artistic perfection that he had failed to understand in the past:

> Formerly, in my attempts to isolate the talent, I deducted, so to speak, from what I heard the part itself, a part common to all the actresses who appeared as Phèdre, which I had myself studied beforehand so that I might be capable of subtracting it, of receiving in the strained residue only the talent of Mme. Berma. But this talent which I sought to discover outside the part itself was indissolubly one with it.[25]

Through her art La Berma has "spiritualized" her body and her gestures in a work reflecting her "soul" and composed of "unbroken surfaces" into which all dramatic effects have been completely "absorbed." In her voice, says the narrator, "not one atom of lifeless matter refractory to the *mind* remained undissolved." As for her intelligence, Marcel discovers that La Berma's attitudes on the stage are the result of

> reasonings that had lost their [voluntary origin], and had melted into a sort of radiance in which they sent throbbing, round the person of the heroine, elements rich and complex, but which the fascinated spectator took not as an artistic triumph but as a natural gift.[26]

24. I, 747; *Guermantes,* II, 47.   25. I, 747; *Guermantes,* II, 47.
26. I, 747–48; *Guermantes,* II, 48. Moncrieff translates "origine volontaire" as "original deliberation."

Proust is presenting here some of the essential aspects of his conception of artistic perfection through a characteristic comparison of good and bad art and artistic practices. A complete discussion of his conception will be undertaken at the end of this study, for it revolves precisely around the idea of *fondu*, a blending or fusion of all elements into an autonomous whole, that Marcel will find in the works of other artists. In his present encounter Marcel clearly recognizes the paradox that the highest degree of naturalness is the hallmark of great art. His original judgment of La Berma's talent is completely reversed, and his childhood desire for a world free of all artificiality is satisfied. For just as the artificial self-conscious "art" of the minor actresses resembles the false life of self-deception, so the great art of La Berma represents the perfected and true life of the soul. Marcel is able to assimilate La Berma's art not only because she has rendered it immaterial and therefore analogous to his profound self, but also because he has come to her with a mnd that is, *like her performance,* "a window opening upon a great work of art," a mind analogous to the object of its perception and from which all "refractory," "opaque," and "material" elements have been eliminated. And because the new freedom of his mind allows him to fuse himself with the work, Marcel is no longer confronted by the dilemma of perception in time:

> I had no longer any desire, as on the former occasion, to be able to arrest and perpetuate Berma's attitudes.... I realised ... that that charm which floated over a line as it was spoken, those unstable poses perpetually transformed into others, those successive pictures were the transient result, the momentary object, the changing masterpiece which the art of the theatre undertook to create and which would perish were an attempt made to fix it for all time by a too much enraptured listener.[27]

Marcel now realizes that the essence of theatrical art is precisely its temporal becoming, its virtual life in time. He has been able, in other words, to enter a world existing outside the limits of contingent reality yet capable of being experienced directly.

For Marcel, La Berma's interpretation is, around the work of Racine, "a second work, quickened also by the breath of genius." This "second work" is the *role* of Phèdre, the result of a perfect fusion of subject and object, of La Berma with Racine's play.[28] Whereas the work of the other

27. I, 750; *Guermantes,* II, 52.   28. Deleuze, *Signes,* p. 47.

actresses is merely an association of two different personalities that are easily distinguishable, La Berma's achievement is the creation of a *metaphor* in which opposing personalities have combined to create an impersonal but highly individual work of art revealing at once the essence of each. La Berma's own genius is in no way dependent on the greatness of the play to be interpreted. When during the same evening at the theatre Marcel sees her perform a mediocre modern play, La Berma's acting is still sublime. "I realised then," says the narrator, "that the work of the playwright was for the actress no more than the material, the nature of which was comparatively unimportant, for the creation of her masterpiece of interpretation."[29] La Berma's works of art are roles, but they are roles that *she* creates. Success is measured by genius and not by the materials of creation.

Satisfied with his encounter Marcel does not attempt to penetrate the full meaning of these discoveries and their implications for his own life. He will continue to believe in the objective value of people and places and seek them before he is finally able to view them as "indifferent material" for his creation. It will not be until the end of the novel that he will see in his own past life the "first work" to be interpreted and "redesigned" into a new work of art reflecting the essence of his existence.

The Paradox of Language

It remains to be noted that Marcel's most important discovery during his second encounter with La Berma concerns the very nature of his previous disappointment. The impression produced by a person or work of art is so particular, says the narrator, that it can never correspond to an a priori, abstract, and false idea. Truly beautiful works disappoint us the most, for they contain no "empty space" for our abstractions and confront us with a form for which we possess no "intellectual equivalent" by which to interpret our individual impression. The essence of this experience is presented by Proust in one of the most extensively applicable "laws" in the novel:

> We feel in one world, we think, we give names to things in another; between the two we can establish a certain correspondence, but not bridge the interval. It was quite narrow, this interval, this fault that I had had to cross when, that afternoon on which I went first to hear Berma, having strained my ears to

29. I, 749–50; *Guermantes,* II, 51.

catch every word, I had found some difficulty in correlating my ideas of "nobility of interpretation," of "originality," and had broken out in applause only after a moment of unconsciousness and as if my applause sprang not from my actual impression but was connected in some way with my preconceived ideas, with the pleasure that I found in saying to myself: "At last I am listening to Berma." And the difference that there is between a person, or a work of art which is markedly individual and the idea of beauty, exists just as much between what they make us feel and the idea of love, or of admiration. Wherefore we fail to recognise them.[30]

In all his disappointing encounters Marcel faces this gap or interval separating the abstract "name" belonging to a world of absolutes from the sensation directly produced by a concrete and particular experience. Indeed, whether he approaches them with a "double" formed by his imagination or simply sees them through an image established by habit, almost all the characters and places in the novel—Balbec, the Duchess, La Berma, as well as the grandmother and Venice—strike Marcel at least once, if not several times, as "strangers" confronting him with an unknown presence. Paradoxically, each offers to his senses, at least during the first moments of the encounter, exactly what his imagination sought —"a momentary revelation of real life" uncorrupted by human interference, including his own.

Most often in describing such confrontations Proust favors the technique he admired so much in Dostoevsky and Mme de Sévigné, namely, that of presenting things not in their logical order by beginning with the cause of an impression, but by showing first the effect of an impression, "the illusion that strikes us." It is in this manner that Proust, in a frequently cited passage, describes Marcel's impression of rain:

> A little tap at the window, as though some missile had struck it, followed by a plentiful, falling sound, as light, though, as if a shower of sand were being sprinkled from a window overhead; then the fall spread, took on an order, a rhythm, became liquid, loud, drumming, musical, innumerable, universal. It was the rain.[31]

Another example of the same technique can be found later in the novel

30. I, 749; *Guermantes*, II, 50. 31. I, 77; *Swann*, I, 101–2.

when Proust describes Marcel's encounter with one of the many "in-carnations" of the Baron de Charlus:

> I perceived a tall, stout man in a soft hat and long ulster, whose purplish face made me hesitate whether he was a certain actor or a painter, both of whom had been involved in countless no-torious cases of sodomy. As I was certain in any case that I did not know him, I was greatly surprised when his glance met mine and I noticed a look of embarrassment on his face as he stopped short and came toward me. . . . Just for a second I won-dered who was greeting me—it was M. de Charlus.[32]

A la Recherche contains dozens of such passages. Gaëtan Picon, who has made an extensive and brilliant study of them, remarks that Proust through these descriptions repeatedly shows how "the mechanism of re-duction" or identification always replaces "the movement of the appari-tion."[33] Picon is certainly correct in noting that the identity of things, which is generally based on the knowledge of habit, blinds us to their reality. Marcel's identifications do in fact arrest the "mobility" of others, just as the narrator's habit immobilizes the "kaleidoscope of the darkness" and makes it possible for him to identify his room. That such identifica-tion is often a deadening activity is proved by the truth Proust expresses from the beginning of the novel, that immobility and indifference are the two sides of the same coin, each being the cause of the other.

The problem contains, however, certain complexities. The sound of something striking the window, a man seen walking in the street, or a woman seen in a church may be aspects of reality, but they would leave anyone indifferent unless they revealed a particular reality to a particular person within an equally particular context. A total stranger staring at us in the street might arouse our attention, but his presence and actions would have no real significance for us unless they appeared to reveal something new about him or about our own preconceptions and expec-tations. Such a revelation is prepared, for example, when Marcel notices a man staring at him the day he encounters Gilberte in the park at Tansonville. Later he learns that the man is Charlus. Later still, having discovered the Baron's homosexuality, he finally understands the mean-ing of the original event. Since "reality" in Proust is always and only what is strange, new, unknown, or inhabitual, it must be so in reference

32. II, 918–19; *Temps retrouvé*, III, 763.   33. Picon, *Lecture de Proust*, p. 61.

to something that is already known, that already possesses some form of identity. It is this knowledge, however submerged it may be at times, that makes the revelation of reality possible, that gives it meaning, that allows it quite simply to strike him as "real." Between the first explosion of reality and its final loss in the identity of habit there is the moment, if not the movement, of identification itself, the act of discovery.

This sequence is most clearly present in Marcel's encounter with the Duchess. The exclamation "It was she!" at the beginning of the encounter does not have the same meaning as "It is indeed a proud Guermantes" at the end. The first, which identifies the "lady," recognizes her reality by acknowledging the *difference* that exists between the "double" and the woman. The second hides that reality by establishing an identity that denies this difference. Although Marcel does not confront the Baron with great expectations, or make positive efforts to escape from reality, his encounter with Charlus, as with the other strangers, always contains a moment, however brief, of discovery.

This discussion is directly related to the fundamental problem Proust raises when he speaks of the distance separating sensitivity and intelligence—that of language. Marcel's disappointing encounters pose this problem in a particularly meaningful way because they attract attention to one of the essential functions of language, that of identifying things, of giving them names. They force him to question the value of a language that most often hides reality, that is periodically forced to recognize its own inadequacy, and that is even used to hide its own weaknesses. In his encounter with the Duchess, Marcel first confronts this verbal distance, then he leaps over it.

Although he does the same at his first encounter with La Berma, when he sees the actress a second time he does in fact succeed in bridging the gap between feelings and words. At the end Marcel's ideas are truly his own. Paradoxically however, they are composed of the same words found in his first, abstract conception. He discovers that La Berma's art does indeed reflect a "breadth of style," a "nobility of interpretation," "beauty," and "originality." But now these words no longer inhabit the model created by the imagination, nor are they the supports of a short-circuited and compensatory response to experience prompted by the instinct of self-preservation. They are the end result of Marcel's careful elucidation of his impression, an elucidation made possible through a utilization of all the knowledge gleaned from his total experience with the art of the theatre. It is only by *comparing* his past encounter with his present one, the art of the minor actresses with La Berma's, her performance in *Phèdre* with her performance in another play that Marcel is able to perceive the nature of La Berma's genius and that of his own disappointment and early failure. In other words, it is in memory that he finds the "intellectual equivalents" for his impression. Marcel does not simply "see" the reality of theatrical art, he confronts it with the past, he discovers it.

It can be argued that Marcel's elucidation merely proves the inadequacy of language, for both his past experience as well as his final impression far exceed the meaning of a few words like "beauty" and "originality." Yet these words no longer have, for Marcel and in reference to a particular reality, the meaning they once had. It would be more accurate to say that by its very demonstration of the inadequacy of language Marcel's total experience makes possible a *renewal* of language. This process is described early in the novel when Swann gives Marcel a photograph of the Giotto fresco in which charity is represented by a woman who possesses none of the traits usually associated with that virtue. This "Charity without charity" is so original that it is no longer equivalent to the abstract notion of charity. At the same time this notion is no longer an adequate description of the fresco. The fact that Giotto himself inscribed the word "Caritas" on his work only intensifies the shock of discovery and recognition. What occurs in Marcel's mind is a qualitative shift in the meaning of the word. The abstract notions and images associated with the old word are replaced by the impression produced by the particular and concrete form of Giotto's figure. Although the "new" word that results from this transformation is the same, its meaning has been greatly expanded.[34]

This power to renew language is also an attribute of reality. In this respect art is merely the highest form of reality because it reveals a vision of the world that is perpetually new, particular, and inhabitual. For Proust, both reality and art are active forces that destroy in order to create. As Marcel's encounters amply demonstrate, this destruction is most often resisted by a self which sees in the loss of certain cherished images and beliefs its own death. *But "names" must be reduced to "words" so that words, now free of the abstract particularity of 'names, can acquire the concrete particularity of experience without losing their more universal applicability.* By comprehending the absolute perfection

34. I, 61–62; *Swann*, I, 81–82.

of La Berma's art within the limits of her highly individual genius, Marcel moves closer to comprehending the nature of perfection in all art. He learns that words like "beauty" and "originality" do not exist in themselves but only in relation to an *activity* that reveals or discovers their meaning. These words have a real value only as metaphors created by the union of an inherited vocabulary and a new impression. Artistic creation, like criticism, renews our vision by closing the interval between words and feelings.

Giotto's "Charity" reveals yet another truth that can be applied to these encounters. Looking at it and at the other figures from the Arena Chapel, Marcel notices that each seems not to understand or to be conscious of the particular virtue or vice it is supposed to represent. Surprised at first, he later discovers the cause of this strange effect:

> I understood that the arresting strangness, the special beauty of these frescoes lay in the great part played in each of them by its symbols, while the fact that these were depicted, not as symbols (for the thought symbolised was nowhere expressed), but as real things, actually felt or materially handled, added something more precise and more literal to their meaning, something more concrete and more striking to the lesson they imparted.[35]

So completely has Giotto interiorized in each figure the vice or virtue it represents, that each is in fact the symbol of itself. "Charity" *is* charity. In the same way, so well does La Berma interiorize her role that, unlike the minor actresses who self-consciously play their parts, she *is* Phèdre. It is this total inclusion of identity that excludes and leaves no "empty space" for Marcel's expectations. The same is true of the Duchess and of Balbec. The "newness" that defines reality derives from this autonomy, this refusal of other persons, places, and things to play the roles assigned to them by imagination or habit. Marcel gradually learns that the truths he seeks really are *in* the exterior world, but not for that reason outside of his self. As his encounters with La Berma reveal, the door that opens onto the exterior world exists not beyond but within his own mind and memory. Although the world excludes his habits and desires, it never ceases to fill Marcel with impressions which, as they are stored in memory, gradually enclose his own existence and identity so that he also eventually *becomes what he is.*

Marcel's two encounters with La Berma establish a pattern which is

35. I, 62; *Swann,* I, 82.

that of the novel as a whole. He moves from the enchantment of imagination to the disenchantment of reality and finally to the reenchantment
created by a new perspective on reality. Although disenchantment with
the resulting loss of faith is a vital step in this noetic process, it could
neither exist nor have any value without the first step. Indifference helps
Marcel during his second encounter with La Berma, but indifference
alone can never be the beginning of discovery. "To be sure," writes
Proust, "in order to possess, one must first have desired. We do not possess a line, a surface, a mass unless it is occupied by our love."[36] Desire,
like words, also opens the door it so often closes; and although paradise
must be lost to be regained, it must first have been sought.

36. II, 501; *Prisonnière,* III, 175.

5
Idolatry

Reading

By revealing the inadequacy of the models created by his imagination, Marcel's disappointing encounters also show him that the truths he seeks cannot be simply received from others, no matter how intelligent they may be or appear to be. "Anything we have not had to decipher and clarify by our own personal effort, anything that was clear before we intervened, is not our own," writes Proust reaffirming the lessons of Darlu. "Nothing comes from ourselves but that which we draw out of the obscurity within us and which is unknown to others."[1] Because many of the desires and images that excite Marcel's imagination derive from the reading of books, it would be well to explore Proust's own ideas concerning the value and limits of reading, and by extension, of all active encounters with art.

Proust discusses the question at length in his writings on Ruskin, particularly in the preface and notes to his translation of *Sesame and Lilies*. There he argues against Ruskin's (and Descartes') belief that the reading of good books is like having a conversation with the great men of the past. For Ruskin, books are friends to be prized for the value of the ideas they express. For Proust, however, the superficial and social "exercise" that is conversation cannot be compared to the infinitely more profound "psychological activity" of reading, because "what makes a book and a friend so different, one from another, has nothing whatever to do with the greater or less degree of their wisdom, but with the manner of our communication":[2]

> Our mode of communication with people involves the loss of the soul's active forces which are on the contrary concentrated

1. II, 1002; *Temps retrouvé*, III, 880.
2. *Proust: A Selection*, p. 122; *Pastiches*, pp. 244–45.

and exalted by this marvelous miracle of reading which is communication in the midst of solitude. When one reads, alone, one is totally engaged in the task of thinking, in one's aspirations, in one's own personal activity: one receives the ideas of another, in spirit, that is to say, in truth, so that one can unite oneself with them; one is that other person yet one is in fact developing one's self with greater richness than if one were thinking alone; one is driven by others onto one's own path.[3]

This conception of reading presents yet another variation on the familiar paradox of the loss and discovery of the self. Like Marcel in his relationship with Saint-Loup, Proust associates conversation and friendship with the superficial self whose "egoism" prevents any real communication with another by interposing elements that are "irreducible and refractory" to thought. In the silent communication of reading, the reader discovers his true self and loses this egoism only by becoming like, or "analogous" to, the author. For Proust, this "voluntary servitude" of the reader to the author is the "beginning of liberty." "There is no better way of becoming conscious of what one feels oneself," he writes, "than to try to re-create in one's own mind the feelings of a master."[4] To be at once oneself and another, to have one's sensitivity stimulated while maintaining a high degree of critical intelligence, these are the benefits that make proper reading a "state of grace." If this profound union of reader and author is a friendship at all, writes Proust, it is "a sincere friendship."

The word Proust most often uses to describe the reader's attitude toward the author is "love." In his critical writings, for example, he speaks of the need to "love Balzac" or to "love Baudelaire." To love an author is to open oneself to him, to make oneself fully receptive to his vision. But this love may become a source of disappointment if it turns into adoration and leads the reader to view the author as a kind of "oracle" to be consulted for his opinion on matters of interest. To read a book in this way is tantamount to believing that one can converse with the author. A book gives us only impressions, and the answers we seek can be discovered only in ourselves:

> Indeed, the great, the marvelous power possessed by good books (which makes us realise the part, at once essential yet limited, that reading can play in our mental lives) lies in this, that what

3. *Sésame*, p. 70, n 1.   4. *Proust: A Selection*, p. 95; *Pastiches*, pp. 195–96.

the author may treat as "Conclusions" can, for the reader, be "Incitements." We have a strong feeling that our own wisdom begins just where that of the author finishes, and we want him to give us answers when all he can offer are desires.[5]

Such desires are awakened in Marcel through his reading of Bergotte's works, an author whom he also considers an "oracle." If Marcel's search to find in objective reality the equivalents of Bergotte's images is doomed to disappointment, it is because the reader's love for certain authors makes him attach "a literal significance to matters which, for them, are expressive only of emotions personal to themselves." The same truth applies to our desire to visit the sites painted by an artist:

> What makes them seem to us more beautiful than the rest of the world is that they give, like some vague reflection, the effect that they produced on genius. It would appear to us just as remarkable, just as despotic, no matter what insignificant and submissive corner of the world [he] might have happened to paint. The appearance with which they charm and hallucinate us, and into which we long to penetrate, is the very essence of that something—in a two-dimensional rendering—that mirage caught and fixed upon a piece of canvas—which is what we mean by "vision."[6]

What a work of art shows us is the way the exterior world was "reflected" in the mind of an artist. It presents not objects, but images revealing a particular vision, images detached from actuality and giving only the appearance of reality. The strange beauty and "otherness" of a work of art derive, therefore, from the purely *virtual* nature of its spiritual world. All the writer or artist can do is to teach us to see by partially lifting "the veil of ugliness and insignificance which leaves us incurious before the spectacle of the universe." Reading "stands upon the *threshold* of the life of the spirit"; Proust concludes, "it can show us the way in, but it is not, in itself, that life."[7] The real encounter is always with one's own inner world.

Thinking, doubtless, of himself, Proust finds that this spiritual value of reading may be particularly useful to "certain pathological cases" suf-

5. *Proust: A Selection*, p. 125; *Pastiches*, p. 248.
6. *Proust: A Selection*, p. 126; *Pastiches*, pp. 249–50.
7. *Proust: A Selection*, p. 127; *Pastiches*, p. 250.

fering from a laziness or sickness of the will that keeps them on the surface of their lives and prevents them from descending spontaneously
into the "deepest regions" of the self. Engaged in repeatedly, reading can
become for such persons a kind of therapeutic discipline meant to "reintroduce the mind into the life of the spirit [un esprit paresseux dans la
vie de l'esprit]."[8] But again, reading must not become a substitute for
personal creative activity:

> So long as reading is treated as a guide holding the [magic]
> keys that *open the door* to buried regions of ourselves, into
> which, otherwise, we should never penetrate, the part it can
> play in our lives is salutary. On the contrary, it becomes danger-
> ous when, instead of waking us to the reality of our own mental
> processes [la vie personnelle de l'esprit], it becomes a substitute
> for them: when truth appears to us, not as an ideal which we
> can realise only as a result of our own thinking and our own
> emotional efforts, but as a material *object* which exists between
> the pages of a book.[9]

The reader who expects to find truth waiting for him in a book does
not have as fallacious a conception of reading, however, as the man of
letters who worships a book for itself and makes it into a "immobile
idol," "which, instead of receiving true dignity from the thoughts that
it inspires, communicates an unreal dignity to all around it."[10] Although
Proust admits that this "literary sickness" of book fetishism often strikes
the finest minds, he condemns it no less as a corruption of the spiritual
value of reading.

Ruskin

A great mind who provided Proust himself with the "magic keys" to the
inner world of the *esprit,* but who also succumbed to the sin of idolatry,
was Ruskin. In the preface to his translation of *The Bible of Amiens,*
written shortly before his essay on reading, Proust finds that Ruskin
unwittingly defined the nature of his own idolatry when in his *Lectures
on Art* he described this sin as "the serving with the best of our hearts
and minds, some dear or sad fantasy which we have made for ourselves,

8. *Proust: A Selection,* p. 127; *Pastiches,* p. 250.
9. *Proust: A Selection,* p. 130; *Pastiches,* pp. 253–54.
10. *Proust: A Selection,* p. 132; *Pastiches,* p. 257.

while we disobey the present call of the Master."[11] Whereas Ruskin's definition refers to the false worship of religious art to the detriment of one's moral responsibility, Proust relates the definition to the question of artistic integrity or "sincerity." At the very moment that Ruskin was preaching sincerity, writes Proust, he lacked it himself:

> The doctrines he professed were moral, not aesthetic, yet he chose them for their beauty. And because he did not wish to present them formally as things of beauty, but as statements of truth, he was forced to lie to himself about the reasons that had led him to adopt them. And once the start was made, he found himself involved in a compromise with conscience so continuous, that immoral doctrines sincerely professed would, perhaps, have been less dangerous to his spiritual integrity than moral doctrines enunciated with less sincerity, because they had been dictated by aesthetic considerations which he refused to admit.[12]

Proust's careful analysis of the way Ruskin allowed his consciousness to be corrupted raises several problems intimately connected with Proust's aesthetics. Although he often appears committed in his writings to the familiar idea that "Beauty is Truth, Truth Beauty," Proust's essen-

11. *Proust: A Selection*, p. 83; *Pastiches*, p. 180. Here is the passage on idolatry from Ruskin's *Lectures on Art* that Proust translated: "Such I conceive generally, though indeed with good arising out of it, for every great evil brings some good in its backward eddies–such I conceive to have been the deadly function of art in its ministry to what, whether in heathen or Christian lands, and whether in the pageantry of words, or colours, or fair forms, is truly, and in the deep sense, to be called idolatry—the serving with the best of our hearts and minds, some dear or sad fantasy which we have made for ourselves, while we disobey the present call of the Master, who is not dead, and who is not now fainting under His cross, but requiring us to take up ours." John Ruskin, *Lectures on Art and Aratra Pentelici, 1870*, Vol. XX of *The Works of John Ruskin*, ed. E. T. Cook and Alexander Wedderburn, Library Edition, 39 vols. (London: G. Allen; New York: Longmans, Green, and Co., 1903–12), p. 66.
   Ruskin gives a more complete expression of his conception of idolatry in the lectures of *Aratra Pentelici*, in which he makes a distinction between "the ignoble and false phase of Idolatry" and "the noble and truth-seeking phase" which he calls "Imagination;—that is to say, the invention of material symbols which may lead us to contemplate the character and nature of the gods, spirits, or abstract virtues and powers," p. 242. Although Proust does not mention this aspect of Ruskin's discussion, it is interesting to note that the distinction Proust makes between idolatry and the activity of the *esprit* somewhat resembles the one Ruskin makes between idolatry and imagination. Proust's own conception of idolatry is not, of course, related to religious art.
   12. *Proust: A Selection*, p. 84; *Pastiches*, p. 182.

tial passion is for truth, and particularly for the unknown truth of the inner self. Once this truth is discovered and expressed, everything else, namely beauty and pleasure, is given *par surcroît*. Conversely, beauty and pleasure are only signs of the existence of truth. Ruskin, on the other hand, corrupted his inward search for truth in two ways: first, by an excessive respect accorded to the truths of moral doctrines and, second, by a taste for beautiful images based neither on an accurate knowledge of himself nor of historical fact. When Ruskin calls Egypt the "educator of Moses and the hostess of Christ," writes Proust, he has composed a beautiful sentence, but one that is inaccurate, for the qualities of the Egyptians had little to do with their country's being the hostess of Christ. The form of Ruskin's sentences with their curious mixture of falsified truth and beauty has been imposed from without by his tastes and prejudices. It does not come from within the realm of his deepest thought. He is often not the master but the victim of his style. In fact, the pleasure Ruskin derived from his images was itself corrupted by the self-conscious pride he took in his own knowledge and righteousness. Proust recalls a similar corruption of pleasure he himself experienced when during a visit to the cathedral of Saint Mark in Venice he took pride in his ability to read the Byzantine letters inscribed on the mosaics. "A sort of egotistical turning-inwards on oneself is an inevitable accompaniment of all such pleasures," he writes, "in which art is mixed with erudition, and in which the aesthetic pleasure, sharpened though it may be, loses something of its purity."[13] Here again knowing corrupts seeing and prevents the perfect union of self and art.

Although Proust's conception of idolatry completely eliminates the Christian God, it is in a sense no less "moral" than Ruskin's. For Ruskin, God or Christ calls us to bear our own cross; for Proust, the "master" is the artist who awakens us to the necessity of our own personal creation. Proust had already learned from his early reading of Thomas à Kempis that a good Christian seeks the "image of God" within himself, and attempts to "imitate" Christ through his acts. So the reader must seek out his inner spirit and imitate not the images an artist presents, but his *creative activity*.

While Proust judges Ruskin "in the absolute," he nonetheless sees idolatry as "an infirmity that is part and parcel of the human mind." Relative to Robert de Montesquiou (whom he does not name), Proust

13. *Proust: A Selection*, p. 87; *Pastiches*, p. 186.

discusses certain less complex forms of idolatry. One such form consists in admiring some object in life because it recalls a similar object admired in a work of art. For example, Montesquiou finds the costume of an actress beautiful simply because he recognizes it as a fabric also seen in a painting by Gustave Moreau or described in a novel by Balzac. An inverse form of idolatry, less prevalent among esthetes, consists in admiring in a work of art some object also admired in reality. Once divorced from the context of a work of art, however, an image becomes an object, that is, "a mere sign, stripped of all significance." On the other hand, "the beauty of a picture does not depend upon the objects represented in it."[14] For Proust, an object has value only when it exists as an image in the virtual world of art where it expresses the individual vision of the artist. Although creation implies a preceding abstraction of forms from life and art, these forms are empty until they are assimilated into the inner self where they acquire a new meaning in a new context. Proust restates this idea succinctly when, in reference to Ruskin's veneration for words, he remarks that words are

> at once like works of art whose profound significance we must understand and whose glorious past we must respect, and like simple notes which will acquire value, for us, only by the place we give them and by the relations of reason and feeling that we establish among them.[15]

It is now evident that behind all of Proust's remarks on idolatry and on the fallacies associated with reading there is a criticism of two related weaknesses of the mind—the mind's penchant for letting that which should lead it to truth take the place of truth, and its habit of allowing something contingent and material to take the place of the transcendent and spiritual.[16] Just as the simplest object in nature can be a means of revealing truth once it is "spiritualized" by the creative activity of the artist, so the most illustrious work of art can be reduced to a material object if it is prized for reasons other than for the truth it was meant to

14. *Proust: A Selection,* p. 91; *Pastiches,* p. 191.   15. *Sésame,* p. 103, n 1.

16. The theologian Reinhold Niebuhr writes that man is involved in idolatry whenever he "lifts some finite and contingent element of existence into the eminence of the divine." *The Nature and the Destiny of Man* (New York: Charles Scribner's Sons, 1964), Vol. I, p. 164. This and other passages devoted to idolatry in Niebuhr's book were helpful to the present study. For a general discussion of the history of idolatry and its relation to art, see Edwyn R. Bevan, *Holy Images: An Inquiry into Idolatry and Image-Worship in Ancient Paganism and in Christianity* (London: C. Allen and Unwin, 1940).

reveal. The function of art is to open the door leading to the inner world of the self. It must not become a means of escaping from that world or of forgetting its existence.

Darlu also had insisted on man's moral obligation to remain intellectually sincere with himself, had spoken of the need to reintroduce the *esprit* into its own life, and had warned against judging the superior by the inferior, spirit by matter. He too had condemned those who think in terms of "things" and fail to understand the nature of the activity that perceives them. Proust's attack on idolatry is in fact the natural outgrowth of his early affirmation of the mind's spirituality and freedom. The idols associated with art are merely more complex forms of those "fictions of substance" that prevent the self's encounter with its world.

This is not to belittle Ruskin's contribution to the development of Proust's thought. Certainly, Proust found in the Englishman a great writer who had given expression to many of his own views concerning the role of the artist and the function of art. He readily accepted, for example, Ruskin's belief that the poet is "a sort of scribe imparting, at the dictation of nature, a more or less important part of her secret," and that "the first duty of the artist" is to add "nothing of his own [de son propre cru] to the divine message."[17] Despite his admiration, however, Proust saw that Ruskin himself had not always fulfilled this same "duty" toward his work.

Indeed, what emerges clearly from Proust's remarks on reading, and particularly from his discussion of idolatry, is that he was far less interested in Ruskin's moral and aesthetic theories as such than in the workings of a mind at once similar to, yet markedly different from, his own. In this respect Proust's thought and vision were perhaps more powerfully developed by his critique of Ruskin's sins than by his defense of Ruskin's virtues.[18] If through his analysis of Ruskin's work Proust was able to define with greater precision the nature of good reading and good art, it was because Ruskin's faults made him more conscious of some aspects of bad reading and bad art. As will be shown later, Proust's concept of idolatry provides much of the theoretical ground for his attacks on "realistic" art.

But the value of Proust's *encounter* with Ruskin derives from the

17. *Proust: A Selection*, p. 62; *Pastiches*, p. 156.
18. Ruskin's idolatry was discussed by one of his early critics, J. Milsand, whose work Proust also read, See *L'Esthétique anglaise: Etude sur M. John Ruskin* (Paris: Balliere, 1864).

fact that it led him to examine the workings of his own mind. His conscious *prise de position* against Ruskin's and Montesquiou's idolatry was a kind of intellectual therapy that enabled Proust to free himself from his own idolatry of these two men who had been his "professors of beauty." This auto-criticism was not an easy undertaking, particularly in regard to Ruskin. "I have here, in my effort to push intellectual sincerity to its furthest, its cruellest limits," writes Proust, "to wrestle with my most cherished aesthetic impressions."[19] The refractory matter of idolatry had to be willfully excluded before the experiences of the self could be fully understood. In the end Proust was able to preserve the purity of his mind and reaffirm his independence.

Proust's denunciation of idolatry has an added significance when viewed in relation to his future novel. It seems quite likely that by distinguishing himself from Ruskin and Montesquiou, Proust prepared his mind for discovering with greater clarity the essential difference that separates the hero-narrator of *A la Recherche* from his two alter egos, Swann and Charlus. Critics have seldom failed to note how closely these two characters resemble certain aspects of Proust's own personality. Germaine Brée asks, for example: "Could not Swann and Charlus be personifications of the two forces which for a long time deflected Proust from his path, triumphing in him successively; Swann during the period of his 'social spring,' Charlus in the shadows at first but more and more triumphant?"[20] In Proust's world, where the only true path to success and salvation is the creative activity of art, Swann and Charlus are failures not simply because they yield to the temptations of society and love, but because in so doing they sacrifice the creative potential they possess. Their abdication, which results from a weakness of the will, is marked by their refusal to discover or accept the reality of their lives. And what causes them to remain blind to the truth is idolatry.

Charlus, who is also a fictional avatar of Montesquiou, shares the latter's idolatry of Balzac. Troubled by the thought that the discovery of his homosexuality by Morel's family might prevent him from seeing the young man, the Baron finds some comfort in identifying himself with Balzac's Princesse de Cadignan. At other times he enjoys thinking of himself as another Vautrin-Herrara. So completely does Balzac's world

19. *Proust: A Selection,* p. 88; *Pastiches,* p. 187.
20. Germaine Brée, *Marcel Proust and Deliverance from Time* (New York: Grove Press, 1955), p. 98; Brée, *Du Temps perdu au temps retrouvé* (Paris: Les Belles Lettres, 1950), p. 114.

enclose the Baron's vision of reality, that it often replaces it. "And the death of Lucien!" he exclaims in front of the members of the Verdurin clan. "I forgot who the man of taste was who, when he was asked what event in his life had most distressed him, replied: 'The death of Lucien de Rubempré in *Splendeurs et Misères.*' "[21] The "man of taste" is Oscar Wilde, whose remark on Lucien Proust himself recalls in a letter as an example of "banal aestheticism." Wilde would soon experience during his trial, Proust notes, a much more real suffering.[22] Reality also pierces the Baron's world when Morel and the Verdurins expose him to the bitter anguish of betrayal and humiliation. But Charlus never completely frees his mind from the confusion of art and life, and he persists in his desire to be, like Vautrin, Wilde, and Montesquiou, an "artist of life."

While Swann also enjoys seeing life in terms of Balzac or Saint-Simon, his idolatry is revealed in a more telling fashion in the way he associates the painting of Botticelli, and particularly the music of Vinteuil, with his love for Odette. Swann's idolatry is not more complex than the Baron's, but it is presented far more dramatically. Proust does not simply describe Swann's idols; he shows how they were created through a series of *encounters* with art—encounters that also demonstrate how well Proust was able to combine the fundamental structure he discovered in "L'Etranger" with the lessons derived from his own encounter with Ruskin.

Swann and Vinteuil

Swann as Proust presents him is a man who, like Dominique and like the narrator before the revelations of involuntary memory, has lost and wasted his time in society. He is the very model of the cultivated skeptic and dilettante against whom Darlu preached. He has sacrificed his spirit to the "esprit des Guermantes," the ironic wit of the Duchess and her coterie who see in doubting the highest form of intelligence. Above all, like the pathological cases Proust discussed in his remarks on reading, Swann is the victim of a weak will, a "paresse d'esprit" which, says the narrator, was in him "congenital, intermittent and providential."[23]

These aspects of Swann's character, which will determine the whole course of his development in the novel, are of particular interest to the

21. II, 320; *Sodome*, II, 1050.
22. Marcel Proust, *Correspondance générale,* 6 vols. (Paris: Plon, 1930-36), IV, 234–35.
23. I, 206; *Swann,* I, 268.

narrator, who sees in them certain resemblances with his own character. It is this interest that prompts him to relate in the second section of *Du Côté de chez Swann* the story of the origin, growth, and final decline of Swann's love for the demimondaine Odette de Crécy, an affair that began at the time of the narrator's birth. This section, entitled by Proust "Un Amour de Swann," might well have been called "Deux Amours de Swann" for it relates as well the birth of Swann's love for the music of Vinteuil. As a story of two loves inextricably tied together, "Un Amour de Swann" describes the encounters forming a kind of strange interlude in Swann's wasted life during which he is given a chance to redeem his past and to reenter the world of his spirit through an understanding of the truths proposed by the joy of music and the suffering of jealousy.

Swann's first encounter with Vinteuil's music precedes his encounter with Odette. While at a soirée he hears a work for piano and violin. At first, says the narrator, Swann was attracted only by the material quality of the sounds:

> But at a given moment, without being able to distinguish any clear outline, *or to give a name* to what was pleasing him, suddenly enraptured, he had tried to collect, to treasure in his memory the phrase or harmony—he knew not which—that had just been played, and *had opened and expanded his soul,* just as the fragrance of certain roses, wafted upon the moist air of evening, has the power of dilating our nostrils.[24]

Proust's analogy linking the effect of the music to that of a floral perfume sets the tone of Swann's encounter, for it points to the purely affective and spontaneous nature of the sudden expansion of Swann's being produced by a profound impression of spiritual quality. The narrator even suggests that it is perhaps because Swann does not know music that he is able to experience such a strange and original impression which is "irreducible into any other kind" and which seems *sine materia*. Swann's lack of knowledge assures the primacy of sensitivity over intelligence.

It is true that Swann's confusion and sense of strangeness has its source not only in his lack of knowledge of music in general, but also of the particular work he is hearing for the first time. What is more, the very nature of music presents difficulties owing to the development of its forms in time. Whereas Marcel's perception of La Berma's acting is confused by the existence of a model in his imagination, which makes

24. I, 159; *Swann,* I, 208–9.

him attempt to arrest the flow of time, Swann is confused because he possesses no basis for comparison. The motifs rising from the *fondu* of the music quickly disappear to be replaced by others before the sensations evoked in his mind are sufficiently formed. But it is memory, says the narrator, that comes to Swann's aid by providing him with "facsimiles" of the fugitive phrases so that when they return he is able to seize them by comparing them with those that follow. Swann now possesses "that definite object which was no longer pure music, but rather design, architecture, thought, and which allowed the actual music to be recalled." The knowledge provided by memory makes recognition possible by *spatializing time*. Swann does not immobilize the music. He discovers part of the form of its mobility.

Clearly perceived now as deriving from a musical "phrase," Swann's impression becomes a revelation. He is filled with "a new and strange desire" for this phrase that alone can lead him to an understanding of the "intimate pleasures" it proposes. He follows its developing rhythm, its pauses and sudden changes of direction leading him toward "a state of happiness noble, unintelligible, yet clearly indicated," toward "a vista of joys unknown." And once at home he feels a need for the phrase:

> he was like a man into whose life a woman, whom he has seen for a moment passing by, has brought a new form of beauty, which strengthens and enlarges his own power of perception, without his knowing even whether he is ever to see her again whom he loves already, although he knows nothing of her, not even her name.[25]

By introducing the theme of love (facilitated in the French by the pronoun *elle* referring to the phrase) Proust is preparing the emotional ground on which Swann's inner conflict will be waged. The transcendent love evoked by the phrase, its call to a spiritual unknown, is to be confronted by Swann's love for Odette and his jealous search into the mysteries of her contingent life.

Deeply impressed, Swann does not turn inward to elucidate his impression. Instead, he waits for the phrase to return again. "And reappear it did," says the narrator, "though without speaking to him more clearly, bringing him, indeed, a pleasure less profound." Swann confronts here the same law of diminishing returns that governs the narrator's encounter with his past through the savor of the madeleine dipped in tea. Being

25. I, 160; *Swann*, I, 210.

less lucid than the narrator and plagued by an even greater weakness of will Swann does not seek out the causes of his failure. Nonetheless, he senses that his encounter with the music has brought about a radical and qualitative change in his being, for he finds in himself, in his memory of the phrase,

> the presence of one of those invisible realities in which he had ceased to believe, but to which, as though the music had had upon the moral barrenness from which he was suffering a sort of recreative influence, he was conscious once again of a desire, almost, indeed, of the power to consecrate his life.[26]

If the memory of his past impression holds for Swann the promise of a new future, he does not, unfortunately, act in the present to create that future. Rather, he turns to a future outside of himself in hopes of encountering the sonata again. But time works against him, and the memory of the music fades from his mind. Having failed to discover the name of the work, he finally ceases to think about it.

Despite his initial failure chance works in Swann's favor, for he encounters the *petite phrase* again the following year at the Verdurin's where he has gone in the company of Odette. And now he has no longer to depend on chance, for he learns the name of the unknown phrase—it is the andante from the Sonata for Piano and Violin of Vinteuil. Filled with the joy of possession, Swann immediately asks for information about Vinteuil and his work. He wants to know when Vinteuil composed the sonata, and above all "what meaning the little phrase could have had for him." He dismisses as an impossibility the truth that the Vinteuil in question is the same old man who taught piano at Combray. Although he still desires to learn its "secret," Swann's search for the meaning of the phrase remains directed outward. Indeed, he is already beginning to regard the phrase as a material rather than as a spiritual possession, and the nameless mystery of the music is being reduced to a contingent identity that can be readily known, to a series of facts and details.

In his subsequent hearings Swann continues to be fascinated by the strange beauty of the phrase:

> Deep repose, mysterious refreshment for Swann,—for him whose eyes, although delicate interpreters of painting, whose mind, although an acute observer of manners, must bear for

26. I, 161; *Swann,* I, 211.

ever the indelible imprint of the barrenness of his life,—to feel himself transformed into a creature foreign to humanity, blinded, deprived of his logical faculty, almost a fantastic unicorn, a chimaera-like creature conscious of the world through his two ears alone. And as, notwithstanding, he sought in the little phrase for a meaning to which his intelligence could not descend, with what a strange frenzy of intoxication must he strip bare his innermost soul of the whole armour of reason, and make it pass, unattended, through the straining vessel, down into the dark filter of sound.[27]

Through the strangeness of the music whose sound is its sole mode of expression, and whose transcendent reality excludes the habitual forms of perception, Swann, as Proust so beautifully describes, is brought closer to the "stranger" who is his soul. Nevertheless, Swann remains passive, enjoying the phrase he feels belongs to "another world" but failing to discover within himself forms of vision analogous to those of Vinteuil.

There are also moments when he is disturbed by this otherness and autonomy of the music. Having heard it played each night for him and for Odette by the Verdurin's pianist, Swann associates the phrase so closely with his feelings for Odette that it now seems the "national anthem" of their love. He suffers at the thought that the phrase (like Dominique's soul) is at once "so near and yet so infinitely remote," that while it addresses itself to them, it does not know them, and he almost regrets, says the narrator, that the phrase "had a meaning of its own, an intrinsic and unalterable beauty, foreign to themselves." He refuses to accept, in other words, the very characteristics that make of the music a work of art.

Unable to reconcile the particularity of the music with its indifferent universality that seems to exclude the actuality of his love, Swann refuses as well to accept its meaning:

It seemed to be aware how vain, how hollow was the happiness to which it shewed the way. In its airy grace there was, indeed, *something definitely achieved, and complete in itself,* like the mood of philosophic detachment which follows an outburst of vain regret. But little did that matter to him; he looked upon the sonata less in its own light—as what it might express, had, in fact, expressed to a certain musician, ignorant that any Swann or Odette, anywhere in the world, existed, when he composed it, and would express to all those who should hear it

27. I, 182; *Swann,* I, 237.

played in centuries to come—than as a pledge, a token of his love, which made even the Verdurins and their little pianist think of Odette and, at the same time, of himself—which bound her to him by a lasting tie.[28]

Swann blinds himself to the detachment expressed by Vinteuil's music because he cannot acknowledge the possibility of his own detachment from Odette or of her indifference to him. In fact, it is less such a state of detachment that Swann fears than the suffering that would of necessity precede it. Having reduced the phrase to the needs of his contingent life, and even enjoying the sadness of the music that seems to render more profound and sweet his own happiness, Swann renounces his plans for hearing the entire sonata. Divorced in this way from its larger context that would doubtless reaffirm its meaning and autonomy, the phrase by itself is more surely Swann's possession.

As the months pass the *petite phrase* continues to be associated with Swann's love for Odette, and his life remains a curious mixture of lucidity, desire, and self-deception:

He felt clearly that this love was something to which there were no corresponding external signs, whose meaning could not be proved by any but himself; he realised, too, that Odette's qualities were not such as to justify his setting so high a value on the hours he spent in her company. And often, when the cold government of reason stood unchallenged, he would readily have ceased to sacrifice so many of his intellectual and social interests to this imaginary pleasure. But the little phrase, as soon as it struck his ear, had the power *to liberate in him the room that was needed to contain it; the proportions of Swann's soul were altered; a margin was left* for a form of enjoyment which corresponded no more than his love for Odette to any external object, and yet was not, like his enjoyment of that love, purely individual, but assumed for him an objective reality superior to that of other concrete things. This thirst for an untasted charm, the little phrase would stimulate it anew in him, but without bringing him any definite gratification to assuage it. With the result that those parts of Swann's soul in which the little phrase had obliterated all care for material interests, those human considerations which affect all men alike, *were left bare by it, blank*

28. I, 167; *Swann*, I, 218.

pages on which he was at liberty to inscribe the name of Odette. Moreover, where Odette's affection might seem ever so little abrupt and disappointing, the little phrase would come to supplement it, to amalgamate with it its own mysterious essence.[29]

The structure of Swann's encounter is now complete. The free space created in him by the *petite phrase* required that he fill it through a discovery of his own essential identity, that is, of his own inner self that alone "corresponds" to the transcendent reality of Vinteuil's music. Being weak of will he chooses not to make this effort, and being in love with Odette he is unwilling to acknowledge the limits imposed on that love by its subjective nature. If neither the joy produced by the music nor his love for Odette corresponds to an exterior object, Swann nonetheless needs a *material* presence to save him from his solitude and to satisfy his desire for possession. Odette is such a presence, and his love for her is the *idée voisine* he allows to enter the void left by the phrase. The ideal reality of the music is reduced to the contingent actuality of Swann's life, and if the phrase assures his love by giving a greater value and a "false dignity" to Odette, it does so only by sacrificing the meaning of its own transcendent truth. Although Swann succeeds in possessing the music through Odette and in justifying his need to possess her, he has allowed his consciousness to be corrupted by idolatry. He has interposed between Vinteuil's spirit and his own the insincere and self-conscious desires of his superficial self. Rather than "imitate" the master, he makes him the "friend" of his egoism.

Odette and Botticelli

Although Odette's "name" gives a more precise identity to the strangeness of the music, the *petite phrase* by itself is unable to render intelligible to Swann the strangeness of his love for Odette, whose style of beauty not only leaves him indifferent but even gives him a kind of physical repulsion. Then suddenly one day he is struck by her resemblance to the figure of Zipporah, the daughter of Jethro, in one of Botticelli's Sistine frescoes. Swann's artistic tastes, previously completely divorced from his sensual desires, now act to remove his doubts and to justify his love. "The words 'Florentine painting' were invaluable to Swann," remarks the narrator. "They enabled him (gave him, as it were, a legal title) to

29. I, 181–82; *Swann,* I, 236–37.

introduce the image of Odette into a world of dreams and fancies which, until then, she had been debarred from entering, and where she assumed a new and nobler form."[30]

This particular form of idolatry, which resembles Montesquiou's, is not new to Swann:

> He had always found a peculiar fascination in tracing in the paintings of the Old Masters, not merely the general characteristics of the people whom he encountered in his daily life, but rather what seems least susceptible of generalisation, the individual features of men and women he knew.[31]

It is known that Proust himself often amused friends by comparing certain individuals with figures found in paintings, and several examples of such comparisons can be found in *A la Recherche*. The aging Charlus is seen as resembling a grand inquisitor by El Greco. At a soirée the Duc de Guermantes speaks with the unctuous charm of the burgomaster Six of Rembrandt. Albertine playing the piano recalls, because of the arrangement of her hair, an infanta by Velasquez. And Marcel's desire for the elusive chambermaid of Mme Putbus is excited when her beauty is compared to that of a woman by Giorgione. All these comparisons are, of course, part of a highly effective technique of characterization. If Swann is able to see Odette more clearly when he discovers her resemblance to Zipporah, the same benefit is accorded the reader by Proust, who is, after all, the presiding spirit behind Swann's discovery. It is here, however, that the dangers of idolatry are revealed, for the reader also sees *more* than Swann, because he sees as well an Odette who exists *outside* the image of a Florentine masterpiece. In *A la Recherche* a character's individuality always escapes the limits of any single comparison. In other words, if Proust has Marcel or Swann discover a similarity between an individual and a painting, he himself through the action of the novel reveals the differences between the two. It is this metaphorical *tension* of similarity and difference that exposes and affirms a character's individuality. By comparing Odette with Zipporah Swann attempts to hide her different reality, just as Marcel hides the "real" Duchess beneath the images drawn from his imagination.

Swann's idolatry is habitual, but it cannot be easily explained:

> Perhaps because he had always regretted, in his heart, that he had confined his attention to the social side of life, had talked,

30. I, 172; *Swann*, I, 224.   31. I, 170; *Swann*, I, 222–23.

always, rather than acted, he felt that he might find a sort of indulgence bestowed upon him by those great artists, in his perception of the fact that they also had regarded with pleasure and had admitted into the canon of their works such types of physiognomy as give those works the strongest possible certificate of reality and trueness to life; a modern, almost a topical savour; perhaps, also, he had so far succumbed to the prevailing frivolity of the world of fashion that he felt the necessity of finding in an old masterpiece some such obvious and refreshing allusion to a person about whom jokes could be made and repeated and enjoyed to-day. Perhaps, on the other hand, he had retained enough of the artistic temperament to be able to find a genuine satisfaction in watching these individual features take on a more general significance when he saw them, uprooted and disembodied, in the abstract idea of similarity between an historic portrait and a modern original, whom it was not intended to represent.[32]

Although Swann emerges from this explanation of his idolatry as a dilettante and esthete, it is evident that he does possess a confused sense of the relationship between art and life. When the narrator returns to this question later he remarks that Swann's mania was defensible, "for even what we call individual expression is ... something diffused and general, which can be found existing at different periods."[33]

This idea of the repetition of the general or universal in the individual, that reveals again the lessons of Darlu's idealism, is amply demonstrated in the novel. When during his walks in the environs of Combray Marcel comes upon the church of Saint-André-des-Champs, he is struck by the fact that the simple faith expressed by the sculpture of its portal resembles that of Françoise. Also, the air of simplicity and zeal worn by the little angels in the bas-reliefs recalls to his mind the face of the young shop-assistant, Théodore. He realizes by means of these comparisons that the medieval sculptor had himself chosen the models of his saints and angels from among the peasantry of his time.[34] By recognizing in the humblest objects in life the primary material of art and by revealing their beauty, the sculptor had complied with what Proust early called "a law of life which is to realize the universal or eternal, but only in individuals."[35] The purpose of art is, therefore, to call us back to life and to

32. I, 171; *Swann*, I, 223. 33. I, 408; *Jeunes filles*, I, 535.
34. I, 116; *Swann*, I, 151. 35. *Chroniques*, p. 143.

reveal in life the sources of art. For Proust, the only way to judge the truth of a work of art is to confront it with nature, to give it "the test of reality." Marcel's comprehension of both art and life is enriched by such confrontations, for if life now appears more meaningful, art seems more real and alive.

Here again, however, Proust insists that the discovery of similarity between art and life must be balanced by an understanding of difference, for art is the "spiritualization" of reality and the final expression of an inner creative activity. When during his first stay at Balbec Marcel visits Elstir's studio, he notices that all the painter's portraits of women resemble each other despite the differences among the models used. He realizes that Elstir's artistic genius enabled him to regroup the traits of a woman's face so as to make them satisfy "a certain pictorial ideal of femininity which he carries in his head." "The facts of life have no meaning for the artist," writes Proust, "they are to him merely an opportunity for exposing the naked blaze of his genius."[36] Elstir has reached the age, however, when an artist inclines toward materialism, toward the belief that his ideal can be found realized in the exterior world. Therefore, when Elstir calls his wife "Ma belle Gabrielle," Marcel recognizes that this woman, who had first appeared to him so unattractive, is seen by the artist as the very embodiment of his ideal now "realised outside, apart from himself," so that for the first time he can "extract emotion from it."[37] The equilibrium between life and art, the real and the ideal, has been broken, and life in the form of models become idols, has regained the upper hand. Thus, says the narrator,

> the beauty of life, a phase that has to some extent lost its meaning, a stage beyond the boundaries of art at which I had already seen Swann come to rest, was that also which, by a slackening of the creative ardour, idolatry of the forms which had inspired it, desire to avoid effort, must ultimately arrest an Elstir's progress.[38]

Swann's fault is not that he finds in life the sources of art, but that he replaces art with a life falsely judged as already sufficiently "artistic." This idolatry of life, a "sin" Swann shares with Charlus, will also become the greatest danger confronting Marcel's own search for an artistic vocation.

36. I, 640; *Jeunes filles,* I, 851.   37. I, 639; *Jeunes filles,* I, 850.
38. I, 640; *Jeunes filles,* I, 852.

Behind the idolatry of Swann and Elstir there is the myth of Pygmalion. After having for years transformed the matter of reality into works of art reflecting his ideal, Elstir like Pygmalion has been granted the joy of possessing a *living* model of his work. What repose for Elstir, says the narrator, "to let his lips rest upon that Beauty which hitherto he had been obliged with so great labour to extract from within himself." Swann is not an artist, nor is Odette the incarnation of his ideal of feminine beauty. Once he convinces himself with the help of Botticelli that she is worthy of his love, however, he seeks the same joy and repose in possession as Elstir. But the emotion he experiences is above all suffering, not because Odette does not resemble Zipporah, which she does, but because she *is not* Zipporah but a living woman with an infinitely more complex and mysterious personality. She is less a work of art that has been given life than a life that has been imprisoned and immobilized by an art form imposed from without. Swann not only does not see the difference between art and life, he confuses them to such an extent that his false conception of life is in fact the same as his false conception of art.

What ultimately leads to Swann's suffering is his false conception of love itself. He attempts to create around Odette a "romantic" love story complete with the conventional, and therefore predictable and acceptable, causes of joy and suffering. Then one night when he arrives late at the Verdurin's and discovers that Odette has already left, he suddenly perceives how indispensable she has become to him. Her absence creates a void his habit cannot tolerate, and filled with the anguish caused by separation he searches for her in the darkening streets of Paris like Orpheus in pursuit of Eurydice. Swann's search marks the final "cristallization" of his love, for all that is necessary for love to be born, writes Proust, is that our taste for a person become *exclusive:*

> And that condition is fulfilled so soon as—in the moment when she has failed to meet us—for the pleasure which we were on the point of enjoying in her charming company is abruptly substituted an anxious torturing desire, whose object is the creature herself, an irrational, absurd desire, which the laws of civilised society make it impossible to satisfy and difficult to assuage— the insensate, agonising desire to possess her.[39]

Having forced Odette into his inner world in order to justify what he

39. I, 177; *Swann,* I, 231.

thought to be his possession of her, Swann discovers that she has made that world her own and has carried it off with her.

Although Swann finds Odette that night and makes love to her for the first time, he is doomed, for in his efforts to possess her, and therefore to avoid suffering, he becomes all the more conscious of her unknown and mysterious life to which he has *no access.* He is now transformed by jealousy into a hunter after an elusive prey, and the more intensely he searches the more is he confronted by Odette's multiplicity in time and space, and the less he learns. He begins to understand that this new love for Odette cannot accommodate the romantic story of his dreams, for the essence of his love is now the suffering produced by the very difference he discovers between the fiction he created and the reality he encounters. If in his anguish Swann begins to sense the truth of the subjectivity of his love, he is also forced to recognize the paradoxes posed by its existence in time.

What we believe to be our love or our jealousy, writes Proust, "are, neither of them, single, continuous and individual passions. They are composed of an infinity of successive loves, of different jealousies, each of which is ephemeral."[40] By seeking to possess Odette with such intensity Swann stimulates this destructive-creative action of time, that in turn continually reawakens his suffering by revealing to him the uselessness of his search. By acknowledging the impossibility of ever knowing or possessing Odette, Swann would escape from suffering, for then time would not replace one dying love by another. But because his suffering is inseparable from his love, when Swann contemplates the end of his suffering, he is confronted by the even greater anguish of having to accept the death of his love. Although he can imagine a future when Odette will be indifferent to him and merely a friend, he knows that such a future would imply the death of all that he is at present.

This refusal of the self to die recalls Marcel's own struggle against time in the hotel room at Balbec. What Swann seeks to preserve, however, is not simply a world to which he has become accustomed or even his false myth of love, but rather the whole spiritual life of his sensitivity awakened and enriched by the suffering of love and the beauty of art. During this period of "spiritual superabundance" Swann begins to work again on his study on Vermeer abandoned years earlier, develops a pro-

40. I, 285; *Swann,* I, 372.

found interest in music, and regains his "passion for truth" lost since his youth. In a very real sense, Odette is merely the means for attaining a world beyond her. Yet like a true idolator Swann is unable to separate the means from the end. By her obsessive presence in his mind she limits and corrupts the very world she helps to enlarge. In the period of his love, writes Proust, Swann

> could feel reawakening in himself the inspirations of his boy-hood, which had been dissipated among the frivolities of his later life, but they all bore, now, the reflection, the stamp of a particular being; and during the long hours which he now found a subtle pleasure in spending at home, alone with his convalescent spirit, he became gradually himself again, *but him-self in thraldom to another.*[41]

Odette's presence within him, her "name," encloses his own identity.

The Lost Chance

Despite his struggle against time, Swann's love moves toward indifference. Although he knows that his relationship with Odette has changed, the movement has been so gradual as to prevent him from fathoming the depth of the difference separating his present state from his past one. He thinks about the past but only in an abstract manner as the time when Odette loved him more. Above all, he scrupulously avoids any object or thought that would force his mind to enter the inner space of his suffering.

The situation is completely reversed during a soirée that Swann attends at Mme de Saint-Euverte's. Having returned to the social world he knew before his affair with Odette, he suffers at the thought that the persons around him would consider his love a childish madness and would affirm by their indifference its subjective nature. He longs to escape from this world where Odette is absent and where only the beginning of a concert forces him to remain. "But suddenly it was as though she had entered," writes Proust, "and this apparition tore him with such anguish that his hand rose impulsively to his heart." Swann has heard Vinteuil's *petite phrase;* and its music, singing to him the "forgotten strains of happiness," provokes an involuntary memory of all the past he had attempted so carefully to hide.[42]

Swann now plunges back into all the living and irreplaceable sights,

41. I, 183; *Swann,* I, 239.   42. I, 264–65; *Swann,* I, 345.

sounds, and smells that composed his love. He hears again Odette's words of affection promising him a happiness that was so quickly lost. So completely does he become his past self, that he is filled with pity at the sight of an unhappy stranger standing immobile before him, until he suddenly recognizes that stranger to be his present self. His pity is now replaced by jealousy directed toward that past self whom Odette had loved. But this *dédoublement* of Swann's being, that forces him to perceive the full extent of his loss, is the cause of an unbearable anguish. Tortured by the contradiction of past and present, he does not move on to the joy of understanding the significance of having the past truly present within himself. He regrets his loss and does not realize he has gained a spiritual world he can possess.

Paradoxically, this opportunity to redeem his past offered to Swann by involuntary memory was made possible by the very association of the *petite phrase* with his love that had so corrupted for him the meaning of the music. Although Swann still regards the phrase as "a protective goddess, a confidant of his love," and even feels that his love is no longer unknown to it, he nonetheless questions it more intensely than before. Whereas in the past he had sensed a quality of suffering in the happiness expressed by the phrase, he now finds in it "the charm of a resignation that was almost gay." Wondering at the music's power to transcend human suffering and happiness, Swann's attention turns to the composer who accomplished such a feat. Vinteuil, once the "friend" of Swann's idolatry, becomes a "fraternal stranger," the object of a love free from egoism and, therefore, more truly unifying than Swann's love for Odette. In moving beyond his egoism Swann is also able to see human emotions as Vinteuil saw them, not as something "less serious than the events of everyday life, but, on the contrary, so far superior to everyday life as to be alone worthy of the trouble of expressing it."[43]

Ever since Vinteuil's work had revealed to him, if only for a time, some of the riches of his soul, remarks the narrator,

> Swann had regarded musical *motifs* as actual ideas, of another world, of another order, ideas veiled in shadows, unknown, impenetrable by the human mind, which none the less were perfectly distinct one from another, unequal among themselves in value and in significance.[44]

43. I, 267; *Swann*, I, 348–49.   44. I, 267; *Swann*, I, 349. Moncrieff's italics.

Although Swann had perceived during his first encounter with the sonata that the phrase was based on a structure composed of five notes of which two were repeated, he also knew that this discovery of his intelligence could not account for the mysterious beauty of the phrase that had so awakened his sensitivity. He now realizes that

> the field open to the musician is not a miserable stave of seven notes, but an immeasurable keyboard (still, almost all of it, unknown), on which, here and there only, separated by the gross darkness of its unexplored tracts, some few among the millions of keys, keys of tenderness, of passion, of courage, of serenity, which compose it, each one differing from all the rest as one universe differs from another, have been discovered by certain great artists who do us the service, when they awaken in us the emotion corresponding to the theme which they have found, of shewing us what richness, what variety lies hidden, unknown to us, in that great black impenetrable night, discouraging exploration, of our soul, which we have been content to regard as valueless and waste and void.[45]

It is perhaps more Proust's own thoughts than Swann's that are expressed in these familiar images of an inner darkness penetrated and elucidated by the creative spirit. Swann does sense that Vinteuil through his music has revealed a world at once human and divine, real and ideal, a world "closed against all the rest," completely autonomous, and "other" than contingent actuality. He is also convinced of the "real existence" of the *petite phrase* both outside himself in the music he hears and within, where its undeniable reality is comparable to that of "certain other conceptions without material equivalent, such as our notions of light, of sound, of perspective, of bodily desire."

But Swann goes no further. He does not identify the bonds that link the darkness of his own soul with the mystery of the music, nor does he explore the reasons behind all the complex transformations that have occurred in time within the inner space of his being. Unable to elucidate completely the relationships between the "other world" in which he places the origin of the music and Vinteuil's inner world, he does not see in the richness of his own experience the material for the creation of a new world of art. He fails to realize that art is created by "another

45. I, 268; *Swann,* I, 349–50.

self" which also "really exists" beyond the suffering of love and the easy pleasures of idolatry.

"From that evening," says the narrator, "Swann understood that the feeling which Odette had once had for him would never revive, that his hopes of happiness would not be realised now."[46] This is the final truth Swann extracts from his encounter. Having confused art and life in the idols of his love, he witnesses their destruction but does not turn to the god within himself. The opportunity provided by chance for a new life is lost because of the weakness of his will. The *petite phrase,* remarks the narrator, "may, indeed, have been able to symbolise a call, but it could not have created talents and made of Swann the writer he never was."[47]

After this period of spiritual enrichment Swann falls back into his old habits. With his love dead, he wonders how he could have wasted years of his life for a woman who was not his *genre.* When his love of music also dies, Vinteuil's Sonata becomes just another link in the subjective associations that form his memory of the past. After hearing it played on the piano by Odette, now his wife, Swann remarks to Marcel that the *petite phrase* reminds him of "the Bois de Boulogne plunged in a cataleptic trance." So completely have the sites of his former affair replaced the profound significance he had once sought in Vinteuil's work, that Swann can say with conviction that what music shows to him "is not for a moment 'Free-Will' or 'In Tune with the Infinite,' but shall we say old Verdurin in his frock coat in the palm-house at the Jardin d'Acclimatation."[48]

Ruskin, Swann, and the "I"

In *Jean Santeuil* there is a chapter in which Proust describes how his hero discovers the ties between music and memory. Jean goes to a soirée at which Françoise, for whom his love is all but dead, plays a sonata of Saint-Saëns. Hearing the "phrase" that recalls the time when they were happy, Jean is struck by the way this music transcends human emotions and seems to ignore the history of their love. But when he hears the phrase by chance again ten years later, it suddenly brings back the natural world that had surrounded his meetings with Françoise, and awak-

46. I, 270; *Swann,* I, 353.   47. II, 1000; *Temps retrouvé,* III, 878.
48. I, 407; *Jeunes filles,* I, 533–34.

ens in him the desire to return to the places they had known together —Saint-Germain, Versailles, and the Bois de Boulogne.[49]

The very similarities that exist between this episode and the last stages of Swann's experience with music also reveal some of the differences that separate Proust's early novel from *A la Recherche*. In *Jean Santeuil* music plays a strictly secondary role to love. It is not the cause of a fully developed encounter promising a spiritual revelation. Also, music is never really seen as a way of bridging the distance between love and art, or of transforming suffering into joy. The greater importance accorded to music in the later novel is the direct result of the fact that the activity of art itself is there more completely the center of attention. The sole means of salvation, art is also the standard against which all the actions and events described in the novel are ultimately judged. Unlike *Jean Santeuil* in which Proust, following Emerson, describes such "representative men" as a politician and a philosopher, *A la Recherche* is a novel in which all the "heroes" are artists. While Jean has a sense of his literary "vocation," his experiences also reflect what Maurice Bardèche calls Proust's attempt to forge for himself an "imaginary life." By "imaginary life" Bardèche means Proust's highly self-conscious description of Jean's social successes, and in particular the punishments that are meted out to all those who stand in his way. After *Jean Santeuil* Proust will no longer use the novel as a means of settling accounts or of satisfying his most egotistic desires and fantasies.[50] In *A la Recherche* the story of social success is completely subordinated to, and fully integrated with, the story of artistic success. Consequently, this novel also presents a far more developed study of artistic failure. It is in this context that the importance of music is shown, for it is the only one of the arts which, in the form of Vinteuil's sonata and septet, is *encountered* by both Swann and the narrator. In *Jean Santeuil* the boundaries of success and failure are not so sharply defined. Jean, like Swann, not only suffers from a certain confusion of society and art, he is also the reflection of a youthful Proust who was then experiencing the pleasures of his "social spring" and who could have himself become a failure, that is, another Swann.

Critics have often remarked that the character of Jean is the source of both Swann and the hero-narrator of *A la Recherche*. Additional justifi-

49. *Jean Santeuil,* pp. 659–62; III, 222–27.
50. Maurice Bardèche, *Marcel Proust Romancier,* I (Paris: Les Sept Couleurs, 1971), 68.

cations for this interpretation can be found in Proust's manuscripts, which contain, for example, an early version of what will become "Un Amour de Swann." While the social world Proust describes recalls that of *Jean Santeuil,* he does hesitate in the text between the couple Jean-Françoise and Swann-Odette.[51] A comparison of Proust's two novels is sufficient, however, to reveal the evolution of his characters. In the episode of the sonata, Jean's reaction to the phrase, while it demonstrates some important aspects of the relationship between music, love, and memory, is rather lyrical and inconclusive. On the other hand, Swann's remarks about the Bois de Boulogne are cynical, if not sadly comic. They are a confirmation of his earlier failure and mark the end of a fully developed sequence of experiences.[52] Marcel's own encounters with Vinteuil's music are the basis for a precise and extensive examination of the nature of artistic creation. It is music that helps him to discover the profound meaning of involuntary memory and that makes possible, consequently, the complete elaboration of his aesthetic principles.

This *dédoublement* of Jean's character is also interesting in relation to the fact that in *A la Recherche* Proust abandons the third person for a first person narration except, significantly, in "Un Amour de Swann." One can say with some justification that these two pronouns are themselves present in the "he" of the earlier novel. Because it is so obviously a disguise for the author, the "he" in *Jean Santeuil* is not very stable and seems at times on the verge of becoming an "I," and more seriously, an "I" that is Proust himself. In *A la Recherche* the "he" that is Swann is placed in a more objective and stable perspective, while the "I" is the center of a more completely fictionalized, if highly complex, point of view.

It is in this context that the real importance of Proust's writings on Ruskin can be understood. The long prefaces and notes that Proust wrote for *The Bible of Amiens* and *Sesame and Lilies* represent the first truly extensive use of the "I" in his works. Certainly, Proust is speaking here directly to the reader, but within these writings there is nevertheless a movement toward the "I" of the novel. The greater part of the preface to *The Bible of Amiens,* in which Proust defends and praises Ruskin,

51. Ibid., I, 296. The text of this and other passages from Proust's manuscripts can be found in the Appendixes of Bardèche's book.

52. Pierre Costil has made a detailed study of the literary evolution of this episode of the sonata in "La Construction musicale de la *Recherche du temps perdu,*" *BMP,* no. 8 (1958), 469–89; no. 9 (1959), 83–110.

was published as articles in 1900. It was not until seven months before the publication of the entire volume in February, 1904, that Proust wrote the "Post-Scriptum" to the preface, in which Ruskin's and Montesquiou's idolatry is condemned. By the following year Proust had already written and published separately his "Journées de lecture" which would serve as the preface to *Sesame and Lilies*. It is the first part of this preface that contains Proust's recollections of childhood days spent reading, recollections whose style and tone already closely resemble the "voice" of the narrator. "Journées de lecture" is a kind of prelude to the future novel. It is as if Proust, having finally judged Ruskin's faults, could affirm not only his own ideas on reading, but his own identity as well.

The identity of the "self" is founded in its simplest form on its distinction from the "other." Once Proust was able to free himself from Ruskin and Montesquiou, once he could say of either of them "*He* is an idolator," he could discover at the same moment the truth exposed by the very activity of his criticism—"But *I* am not." In this way the "he" that remains in *A la Recherche* is the sign of a previous rejection and exclusion, the result of that act of purgation and purification by means of which the self was liberated from the corrupting matter of the idolatrous other. And it is interesting that "Un Amour de Swann," the story of a past danger overcome, is set in a time immediately preceding the narrator's birth.

The *dédoublement* of Proust's own personality into a "he" and an "I" was accompanied during this period in his development by a no less interesting split within the "I" itself. Just as the Proust of the "Post-Scriptum" judges his former admiration for Ruskin, so the narrative voice in "Journées de lecture" explores the self he was as a child. Thanks to the autocriticism and autocontemplation induced by his reading of Ruskin, Proust by 1903 was already on the way toward discovering the double point of view of the hero and narrator of *A la Recherche*.

All this does not mean that Proust was in complete command either of his narrative techniques or of his future as a novelist after his writings on Ruskin. The period of the *Contre Sainte-Beuve* was to follow when Proust would refine his narrative voice and reassemble his cast of characters, while still expressing doubts about the possibility of success. Only an exhaustive study of Proust's manuscripts can dissipate the ambiguity surrounding the birth of the "I." Why is it, for example, that Proust wrote at one time two versions of the encounter with the "little band" of girls at the beach, a version in which Swann is the hero, and another, on the facing page, in which the *il* is replaced by *je?* It remains true, however, that the Ruskin period was perhaps the most important in Proust's life. During this time when he rejected his two professors of beauty Proust also lost his parents, so that by the end of 1905 he was alone. There is no need to discuss here the effect that his father's and particularly his mother's death had on Proust. My point is simply that Proust's work on Ruskin represents a truly creative encounter during which he was able, and in more ways than one, to do precisely what he claimed anyone could achieve through the spiritual activity of reading—to bring his true self into being. This is the self which, having been divorced from the more personal "he" of the earlier works, will be expressed by the *impersonal* "I" of *A la Recherche*. It is the self Swann finds in Vinteuil's music, and that Elstir abandons when he embraces his wife—a self existing beyond the emotions of contingent life and freed from the "dear and sad fantasies" of idolatry. Proust will describe it in the *Contre Sainte-Beuve* as *un autre moi* which in each artist is the source of his creations.

Although he accepted the demands of intellectual sincerity, Proust's description of Swann's failure and idolatry, like his critique of Ruskin's, was an often difficult task. In answer to a letter written by his friend Madame Schiff, who had remarked that after reading the first volume of the novel she felt that Swann would cause her even more sorrow in the future, Proust wrote that it had caused him great pain to describe certain ridiculous aspects of Swann's character. Then he added:

> But I am not free to go against the truth and to modify the laws that control the characters. *"Amicus Swann, sed magis amica Veritas."* The nicest people sometimes go through nasty phases. . . . And he is not the principal character in the book. I should have liked him to be. But art is the perpetual sacrificing of inclination to truth.[53]

The emotions Proust must have felt in sacrificing his alter ego to the laws of his novel and to the truth they express are reflected in the tone of sadness and affection he adopts at times when he describes Swann's suffering or his artistic failure. It can be found, for example, in that long sentence in which Proust, giving Swann the benefit of each "perhaps," attempts to define the reasons for his idolatry. It is present again when shortly before his death Swann says to Marcel, writing thereby his own

53. *Letters of Marcel Proust*, p. 328; *Correspondance générale*, III, 10. Proust's italics.

sadly ironic epitaph that might have been Proust's as well: "J'ai beaucoup aimé la vie et . . . j'ai beaucoup aimé les arts."[54]

Swann never crosses the threshold of the inner door opened by Vinteuil's music. He remains one of those "celibates of art" who find in erudition and aestheticism a means of escaping from the true life they haven't the courage to face:

> They are nature's first efforts in the process of evolving the artist; they are as shapeless and lacking in viability as the earliest animals, which preceded the present species and were not so constituted as to be able to survive. These weak-willed, sterile dabblers should arouse our sympathy like those first contrivances which were not able to leave the ground, but in which there was, not yet the means, secret and still to be discovered, but at any rate the desire, to fly.[55]

It is Marcel who will succeed where Swann failed; but before the final revelations of involuntary memory that reveal to him the "secret means" of creation, and before his own encounters with Vinteuil's music, he must himself experience the anguish of love.

54. II. 76; *Sodome,* II, 703.
55. II, 1011; *Temps retrouvé,* III, 892.

6
Love

Gilberte

The pattern of relationships between happiness, suffering, and art established by Swann's love for Odette is developed with some important differences by Marcel's own love affairs. Significantly, his first love encounter is with Gilberte. Marcel begins to dream of meeting young Mlle Swann when he learns from her father that she is a friend of Bergotte and visits with the writer the old cities, cathedrals, and chateaux described in his works.[1] In his imagination Marcel immediately associates Gilberte with the prestige of Bergotte the "oracle" and with his own dreams of visiting these historic sites. His desire to "get out of himself" now has an object, and he is ready to fall in love. "Once we believe that a fellow-creature has a share in some unknown existence to which that creature's love for ourselves can win us admission," writes Proust, "that is, of all the preliminary conditions which Love exacts, the one to which [it] attaches most importance, the one which makes [it] generous or indifferent as to the rest."[2] This "unknown existence" of Gilberte is also enriched by all the mystery Marcel associates with Odette, whom his parents refuse to meet because of her questionable morality, and with Swann's property of Tansonville that, because of Odette, is a kind of forbidden world existing beyond the limits of the family walks in the countryside of Combray.

One day, however, believing that Odette has left with her daughter, Marcel's father and grandfather decide to walk along the park of Tansonville. Entertaining no hopes of encountering Mlle Swann and "of being identified and scorned by this so privileged little girl who had Bergotte for a friend," Marcel is at first indifferent. He turns to con-

---

1. Most critics are in agreement that the character of Bergotte is modeled, at least in part, on John Ruskin.
2. I, 76; *Swann*, I, 100. Moncrieff translates the "il" referring to Love as "he."

template the pink and white hawthorns forming the hedge of the park. These flowers that enchant him with their autonomous beauty and remind him of young girls prepare for the sudden *apparition* of Gilberte:

> Suddenly I stood still, unable to move, as happens when something appears that requires not only our eyes to take it in, but involves a deeper kind of perception and takes possession of the whole of our being. A little girl, with fair, reddish hair, who appeared to be returning from a walk, and held a trowel in her hand, was looking at us, raising towards us a face powdered with pinkish freckles. . . . I gazed at her, at first with that gaze which is not merely a messenger from the eyes, but in whose window all the senses assemble and lean out, petrified and anxious, that gaze which would fain reach, touch, capture, bear off in triumph the body at which it is aimed, and the soul with the body.[3]

A "nameless" apparition, Gilberte is seen as a true *jeune fille en fleur* in all the electrifying mystery of her strangeness.[4] Marcel is so excited by her actual presence outside himself that he does not even think of elucidating his impression. The entire effort of his attention is directed outward in a desire to possess the girl he sees before him. This desire for possession already reveals some of the paradoxical aspects of Proustian love. The Marcel who seeks to "capture" the body and soul of Gilberte is himself completely captivated by her, and despite the effort of his will expressed in the intensity of his gaze, he is paralyzed and "petrified" by what he sees. His desire seems to be to eliminate the very strangeness and otherness that attracts him both by "knowing" her and by forcing her, as he says, "to pay attention to me, to see, to know me." As in the bedroom drama with his mother, this need to be known by the unknown, to have the exterior world enter his own is the paradoxical complement of Marcel's desire to escape himself.

Above all, the very self-conscious nature of his desire and the intensity of his effort to capture Gilberte distort the reality he sees. He believes that her eyes are blue when they are in fact black, and because his imagination has endowed her with so much prestige he interprets her own attitude toward him as one of indifference, disdain, and scorn, and sees

3. I, 108; *Swann*, I, 140–41.
4. Although Proust himself probably had a similar experience, such an encounter with a girl in a garden is, of course, part of a long literary tradition, which is perhaps best expressed in *Le Roman de la rose*.

only an insolent intention in the "indelicate gesture" she makes at the end of their encounter. It is not until many years later, when he has long since lost his love for Gilberte, and when she herself has become Mme de Saint-Loup, that Marcel learns the truth. Gilberte informs him that her gesture was really an invitation to him to participate with her in the clandestine sexual games played by the youth of Combray in the dungeons of Roussainville. Part of the unknown world he desired, Marcel realizes, truly existed outside himself. Not only had the fantasies created by his imagination prevented him from seeing the truth, they had also led him to believe that the world he sought existed only in his imagination and was itself unknown to girls like Gilberte. Both his desire and his doubt had created a false Gilberte that had blinded him to the real one.[5]

All the problems raised by his initial encounter continue to plague Marcel during his subsequent encounters with Gilberte on the Champs-Elysées where they meet daily to play. His desires now far exceed the satisfaction of his sexual fantasies or even his hopes for entering Bergotte's world. It is through Gilberte that he seeks to realize his whole dream of romantic love born from his reading of books. During the period when he loved Gilberte, says the narrator, "I still believed that Love did really exist apart from ourselves; that, allowing us, at the most, to surmount the obstacles in our way, it offered us its blessings in an order in which we were not free to make the least alteration."[6] What Marcel painfully learns, however, is the impossibility of the happiness he seeks, for the obstacles that prevent the realization of his dreams exist not outside but within himself, in the very nature of his desires.

Here as elsewhere in the novel happiness is seen as the result of a perfect union or identification of the subject with the object of his desire. Marcel believes, therefore, that his romance will truly begin only when he exchanges with Gilberte a "mutual confession" of their love. This event never takes place, not simply because Gilberte, to his eyes at least, remains indifferent, but because she herself cannot satisfy the very desire she awakens in him. "[The most exclusive love for a person is always the love of something else]," writes Proust.[7] Gilberte is not so much the object of Marcel's love as she is the contingent *means* by which he hopes to enter the unknown and absolute world of "Love" itself. Like Swann,

---

5. II, 866–68; *Temps retrouvé*, III, 693–97.   6. I, 306; *Swann*, I, 401.
7. I, 627; *Jeunes filles*, I, 833. Moncrieff translates "L'amour le plus exclusif pour une personne est toujours l'amour d'autre chose" as "Our most intensive love for a person is always the love, really, of something else as well."

Marcel confuses the means with the end and believes that by possessing Gilberte he will also possess his dream. What he constantly confronts, however, is evidence of the subjective nature of his love for which he can find no objective equivalent. Yet if Gilberte is only a means to love, she is no less indispensable, for the only way he can attain the world of love is through her. He suffers because in her inability to satisfy him is the proof that the world he seeks does not exist outside himself.

Marcel begins also to wonder if the Gilberte present in his mind exists in reality. At each of his encounters with her on the Champs-Elysées he finds that the vague image of her preserved in his memory since their previous meeting is no longer adequate to the reality confronting him. If he recalls the brilliance of her eyes, he is now struck by the sharpness of her nose, and because his attention is immediately diverted by the games they play, he is continually forced to postpone his efforts to establish a stable image of her in his mind. And later, when days go by without seeing her, he cannot even recall her face. This confusion and distortion of perception, that was already evident in Marcel's first encounter with Gilberte, is for Proust the inevitable consequence of love:

> The questing, anxious, exacting way that we have of looking at the person we love . . . [makes] our observation, in the beloved object's presence, too tremulous to be able to carry away a clear impression of her. Perhaps, also, that activity of all the senses at once which endeavours to learn from the visible aspect alone what lies behind it is over-indulgent to the thousand forms, to the changing fragrance, to the movements of the living person whom as a rule, when we are not in love, we regard as fixed in one permanent position. Whereas the beloved model does not stay still; and our mental photographs of her are always blurred.[8]

Although Marcel does not attempt to immobilize Gilberte in a stable image such as the one Swann creates of Odette with the help of Botticelli's fresco, this law of inner and outer mobility will return to plague him with even greater intensity when he embarks on his jealous search into the secrets of Albertine's life.

If the object of desire never ceases to be a "stranger" because it continually changes in time, the same is true of the subject. When Gilberte addresses him one day by his first name, and Marcel feels that he has

8. I, 375; *Jeunes filles,* I, 489–90.

been completely assimilated by her, he is nonetheless unable to appreciate at that moment the value of these new pleasures:

> They were given, not by the little girl whom I loved, to me who loved her, but by the other, her with whom I used to play, to my other self, who possessed neither the memory of the true Gilberte, nor the fixed heart which alone could have known the value of a happiness for which it alone had longed.[9]

Although in this instance time makes happiness impossible because it prevents the coincidence of past and present, of a particular subject with the equally particular object of his desire, happiness also escapes Marcel in those rare moments when this divergence in time is eliminated and the exterior world does satisfy his expectations. Thus, when he finally realizes his dream of entering Swann's home in Paris and of being considered by Gilberte as her favorite friend he fails to experience the joy of achievement:

> It appears that in a coincidence as perfect as this was, when reality is folded over to cover the ideal of which we have so long been dreaming, it completely hides that ideal, absorbing it in itself, as when two geometrical figures that are congruent are made to coincide, so that there is but one, whereas we would rather, so as to give its full significance to our enjoyment, preserve for all those separate points of our desire, at the very moment in which we succeed in touching them, and so as to be quite certain that they are indeed themselves, the distinction of being intangible. And our thought cannot even reconstruct the old state so as to confront the new with it, for it has no longer a clear field.[10]

The narrator's remarks here are of the greatest importance, for they show that happiness can be experienced only when there exists at once a similarity *and* a difference between past and present. In other words, the present must fulfill the expectations of the past and the dreams of imagination while at the same time appearing as something new and authentic given directly by reality. In this way the present object of perception can continue to be the absent object of imagination.

Confronted by the inadequacy of objective reality and of the present to satisfy his desires, Marcel continues as well to imagine a future "still unshaped" by the disappointments of the past and the limits of the pres-

9. I, 308; *Swann*, I, 404.   10. I, 410; *Jeunes filles*, I, 537.

ent. As has been shown, for Proust this perpetual flight into the future is inseparable from the centrifugal movement that characterizes life in time. Since it is the most demanding of desires and consequently the least amenable to the anguish of failure, love merely intensifies this movement. For these reasons Marcel builds his hopes on a succession of tomorrows, but within him an "unknown weaver" assembles a past completely different from, and indifferent to, the future, a past that carries within itself the overwhelming proof of the subjectivity of his love and, therefore, of the inevitability of suffering. "There is in love," writes Proust, "a permanent strain of suffering which happiness neutralises, makes conditional only, procrastinates, but which may at any moment become what it would long since have been had we not obtained what we were seeking, sheer agony." The flight into the future is a flight from suffering, and because even the happiness one obtains "is never anything but a fresh starting-point for further desires," sooner or later a limit will be reached and suffering exposed.[11]

Marcel finally must acknowledge the futility of his efforts to win Gilberte. Faced by her indifference he decides to make possible his own by detaching himself from her and beginning the "slow and painful suicide of that part of me which was Gilberte's lover."[12] Like Swann, Marcel finds that this new suffering produced by his admission of failure is unbearable. He resolves to make one last attempt to awaken her esteem by offering her gifts. In order to raise the necessary money he sells an antique China vase inherited from his Aunt Léonie. Yet at the very moment of his joy at receiving a large sum for the vase he sees Gilberte walking on the Champs-Elysées with a young man. This new and startling reality confirms again what he had sensed since his first encounter —the impossibility of happiness in love:

> [happiness] can never be realised. If we succeed in overcoming the force of circumstances, nature at once shifts the battle-ground, [from outside to] within ourselves, and effects a gradual change in our heart until it desires something other than what it is going to obtain.[13]

This recognition of truth leads to an interesting reversal of Marcel's desires. He realizes that he no longer wishes to give pleasure to Gilberte, and that to return to her house now would only make him suffer more:

11. I, 442–43; *Jeunes filles,* I, 581–82.   12. I, 464; *Jeunes filles,* I, 610.
13. I, 474; *Jeunes filles,* I, 624. Moncrieff translates "le bonheur" as "the pleasure" and "du dehors au dedans" as "placing it within ourselves."

Even the sight of Gilberte, which would have been so exquisite a pleasure only yesterday, would no longer have sufficed me. For I should have been miserable all the time that I was not actually with her. That is how a woman, by every fresh torture that she inflicts on us, increases, often quite unconsciously, her power over us and at the same time our demands upon her. With each injury that she does us, she encircles us more and more completely, doubles our chains—but halves the strength of those which hitherto we had thought adequate to bind her in order that we might retain our own peace of mind.[14]

Marcel does not imprison Gilberte, nor does he complete the reversal of his struggle against reality "from outside to within." He imagines instead a future free from the memory of his suffering. But the prison that exists beyond the limits of love itself will be eventually constructed to enclose both him and his next tormentor, Albertine.

Albertine

The Albertine who appears to Marcel during his first stay at Balbec is anything but a prisoner. She is only one of the *petite bande* of adolescent girls he sees moving freely and noisily like sea gulls along the shore. Marcel is struck by the "beauty fluid, collective and mobile" of the girls, by their supple health and carefree gaiety. They seem to belong to "another race" obeying laws unknown to the rest of humanity whom they scorn and even torment. Albertine, who is still nameless, seems to express in herself the essence of the band:

For an instant, as I passed the dark one with the fat cheeks who was wheeling a bicycle, I caught her smiling, sidelong glance, aimed from the centre of that inhuman world which enclosed the life of this little tribe, an inaccessible, unknown world to which the idea of what I was could certainly never attain nor find a place in it.[15]

Strength, mystery, inhumanity, an animal impersonality—all these characteristics affirm the marked otherness of the girls. Much more than Gilberte they represent a world completely different from the one Marcel knows, and unlike Gilberte they immediately impress him as being of easy virtue. A collective love for the band is born in him, a love directed toward the strange fusion of land and sea, floral and animal qualities

14. I, 475; *Jeunes filles,* I, 625.   15. I, 599; *Jeunes filles,* I, 793–94.

he finds expressed in their movements. Even later when his attention focuses on Albertine, his desire to possess the unknown life of the band never fades entirely away, so that he doubts at times not only the objective reality of his love for Albertine but its subjective reality as well.[16]

Introduced to her by Elstir, Marcel detaches Albertine from the group, but at the same time his imagination begins to encounter the limits imposed by her material reality. Her name, her relationship with Mme Bontemps, the way she uses the adverb "perfectly" instead of "quite," and even the beauty-spot on her cheek establish before his eyes an Albertine who is different from the girl seen on the beach. "As I drew closer to the girl, and began to know her better," remarks the narrator, "my knowledge of her underwent a process of subtraction, all the factors of imagination and desire giving place to a notion which was worth infinitely less."[17] But this reduction of Albertine to an immobile object for the intelligence is only temporary. As with Gilberte, the more Marcel sees her the more her face and her expressions change. The beauty-spot moves from Albertine's cheek to her upper lip, and her face that one day is comparable to "an opalescent agate cut and polished," is the next colored by "the violet shade of the red cyclamen." "The human face is indeed," writes Proust, "like the face of the God of some Oriental theogony, a whole cluster of faces, crowded together but on different surfaces so that one does not see them all at once."[18]

This impossibility of seeing and knowing all of Albertine at once will become a source of torment for Marcel. Yet it is also the factor that assures his continuing interest in her, for Albertine gives his love what it needs to survive—something that is not possessed, that is inaccessible. Indeed, more than Albertine's visual multiplicity it is her moral multiplicity that ensnares him. When he first sees her on the shore, Marcel decides that she is possibly the mistress of a racing cyclist, but when later he acts on this supposition and finds himself repulsed, he concludes that Albertine is virtuous. This new hypothesis does not survive her visits to him in Paris, for there she gives herself freely to his desires. Although he takes pleasure in her visits, habit, that has already succeeded in stabilizing the features of her face, now begins to empty Albertine of her original mystery. Then one night she fails to arrive at the appointed hour. While waiting for her Marcel senses that the possi-

16. For a concise, penetrating discussion of Marcel's love for Albertine, see Beckett, *Proust*, pp. 30–46. Beckett's remarks were most helpful to this study.
17. I, 656; *Jeunes filles*, I, 873.   18. I, 686; *Jeunes filles*, I, 916–17.

bility of being deprived of a simple physical pleasure is now causing him "an intense mental suffering." He imagines her enjoying herself in some "other place" that he does not know, and where she holds with her one part of himself "which the other part sought to join." Once again he is filled by "this terrible need of a person" that he experienced at Combray during his mother's absence. Albertine phones to explain the reasons for her delay and says that she will not come that evening, but Marcel suspects that her explanations are lies, and now, even more than before, he must see her. Although she does come to him, he realizes that his victory over her, like his earlier victory over his mother at Combray, is an anticipation of future suffering:

> About Albertine, I felt that I should never find out anything, that, out of that tangled mass of details of fact and falsehood, I should never unravel the truth: and that it would always be so, unless I were to shut her up in prison (but prisoners escape) until the end.[19]

For the moment this threat of imprisonment does not materialize. During his second stay at Balbec Albertine again becomes acquiescent. Marcel knows that he can have her at any time he wishes, that he has only to send the "lift" to get her. But now the possibility of a new unknown disturbs the calm of his dying interest. One evening in the Casino at Incarville near Balbec Dr. Cottard sees Albertine dancing with Andrée, another member of the *petite bande,* and notes the homosexual nature of their pleasure. Although Cottard's remarks hurt Marcel, they act like a poison whose full effects are not immediately felt. He does become conscious, however, of a new mystery beneath Albertine's apparent frivolity. She is no longer the same person she was, and, consequently, he also changes. The very sight of her makes him angry, and he speaks of her in the most injurious manner. Above all, he begins to question her every glance and gesture, and when she goes briefly to another town he is agitated by "the painful longing to know what she could have been doing." And now yet another part of the past comes to haunt him and gives depth to his suspicions—the story of Swann's love for Odette, of the way she deceived him all his life, of the suffering caused him by her clandestine relationships with men and with women. Marcel knows that his memory of this story has made of him a person "predisposed" to the new sources of anguish revealed by Cottard's words:

19. II, 97; *Sodome,* II, 734.

These accounts helped my imagination, in after years, to take the line of supposing that Albertine might, instead of being a good girl, have had the same immorality, the same faculty of deception as a reformed prostitute, and I thought of all the sufferings that would in that case have been in store for me had I ever really been her lover.[20]

This last remark is revealing. Despite his already developed relationship with her and despite his new suspicions regarding her sexual tastes, suspicions that have already begun to fade from his mind, Marcel does not yet love Albertine because his need for her has not yet become *exclusive*. In fact, the sensual pleasures of reality have proved boring compared to the dreams of imagination. So, as the summer wears on he grows tired of her, dreams again of beginning a new life with other women in other places, and after having considered the idea of marrying Albertine, definitely decides against it. Precisely at this moment a new and consuming need for her engulfs him.

The Deluge of Reality

"We may have revolved every possible idea in our minds, and yet the truth has never occurred to us," writes Proust, "and it is from without, when we are least expecting it, that it gives us its cruel stab and wounds us for all time." One evening while returning with Albertine in the "little train" from a party at the Verdurin's chateau, La Raspelière, Marcel prepares to announce to her his decision to end their affair. But because the little train (yet another vehicle rendering concrete the passage of time) is already close to Albertine's stop at Parville, Marcel decides to postpone his announcement until the following day. To fill the time remaining he speaks of his desire to visit La Raspelière once more in order to ask Mme Verdurin for information on the works of the composer Vinteuil, whom he greatly admires from having heard his sonata at Swann's house in Paris. Then, to prove her own usefulness to him, Albertine tells him that one of her closest friends, whom she knew for years in Trieste and will meet again shortly in Cherbourg, is the best friend of Mlle Vinteuil. Both girls are to her like "two big sisters." This sudden revelation of a new and startling truth, that transforms Albertine once again into a stranger, totally disrupts the precarious stability of Marcel's world:

20. II, 147; *Sodome,* II, 804.

At the sound of these words, uttered as we were entering the station of Parville, so far from Combray and Montjouvain, so long after the death of Vinteuil, an image stirred in my heart, an image which I had kept in reserve for so many years that even if I had been able to guess, when I stored it up, long ago, that it had a noxious power, I should have supposed that in the course of time it had entirely lost it; preserved alive in the depths of my being—like Orestes whose death the gods had prevented in order that, on the appointed day, he might return to his native land to punish the murderer of Agamemnon—as a punishment, as a retribution (who can tell?) for my having allowed my grandmother to die, perhaps; rising up suddenly from the black night in which it seemed for ever buried, and striking, like an Avenger, in order to inaugurate for me a novel, terrible and merited existence, perhaps also to making dazzlingly clear to my eyes the fatal consequences which evil actions indefinitely engender, not only for those who have committed them, but for those who have done no more, have thought that they were doing no more than look on at a curious and entertaining spectacle, like myself, alas, on that afternoon long ago at Montjouvain, concealed behind a bush where (as when I complacently listened to an account of Swann's love affairs), I had perilously allowed to expand within myself the fatal road, destined to cause me suffering, of Knowledge.[21]

The image of Montjouvain, recalled here by a form of involuntary memory provoked by Albertine's words, is that of the homosexual and sadistic acts Marcel saw performed by Mlle Vinteuil and her friend late one afternoon when he found himself before a window of the composer's house in the countryside of Combray. Vinteuil had recently died after having sacrificed his creative life to the care of his daughter. He had been killed by the suffering endured because of her sapphism. Yet Marcel noticed that part of Vinteuil had, nonetheless, survived in his daughter. Because of her inherited goodness it was not evil that gave her pleasure, but pleasure that seemed to her evil. For this reason the pleasures she experienced with her friend were never free from feelings of guilt, and the evil she did when she persuaded her friend to spit on the photograph of her father was really the inverted reflection of her profound love for him.

The association of sensuality and sacrilege, the feeling of guilt related to the death or "sacrifice" of a "noble" parent because of a child's corrup-

21. II, 366–67; *Sodome*, II, 1114–15.

tion by sexual pleasures, these themes are found, of course, in Proust's early stories like "La Confession d'une jeune fille" in *Les Plaisirs et les jours* and were discussed in relation to the meaning of "L'Etranger." Although Marcel is constantly shown in the novel as causing suffering to his mother and grandmother by his pursuit of a variety of pleasures, it may not seem clear how the image of Montjouvain, if it is considered as an example of the particular suffering caused by a child's homosexuality, is related by Proust to the idea of a punishment Marcel deserves because he let his grandmother die. "Nothing explains his punishment," remarks Germaine Brée, "unless it be the intimate drama that Proust himself lived, and into which he did not want to drag his narrator but which here escapes his control."[22] Certainly, in reading the novel one may have the impression that although it is Albertine who is suspected of sapphism, the suffering this causes Marcel is a punishment for the anguish Proust himself probably caused his mother because of his own homosexuality. And later, when Albertine is imprisoned and Marcel condemns her "vice" in a moral tone he recognizes as being inherited from his mother, who used the same tone to counsel him, it is as if Proust through his narrator and hero were dramatizing his own moral conflict by having the best part of himself (the mother) attempt to exorcise the worst part (Albertine or his homosexuality). Finally, if Proust's guilt is related in the novel to the grandmother's death, it is probably because Marcel's mother, unlike Proust's, does not die.

Although the idea that Proust's sexual problems disturb here the autonomy of the novel can be justified, another interpretation of the connection between the image of Montjouvan and the idea of punishment is also possible. Speaking of Mlle Vinteuil's naive fascination with evil the narrator remarks:

> Perhaps she would not have thought of wickedness as a state so rare, so abnormal, so exotic, one which it was so refreshing to visit, had she been able to distinguish in herself, as in all her fellow-men and women, that indifference to the sufferings which they cause which, whatever names else be given it, is the one true, terrible and lasting form of cruelty.[23]

Marcel is certainly guilty of this indifference when he cruelly chides his grandmother for posing for a photograph in a large hat he believes expresses a vain coquetry when it is really meant to hide from his own

22. Brée, *Marcel Proust*, p. 171; *Du Temps perdu*, p. 193.
23. I, 127; *Swann*, I, 165.

eyes the signs of an illness that will prove fatal. He is guilty when in his pursuit of Albertine he allows the image of his grandmother to die within him after she is reborn through involuntary memory. Indeed, the grandmother will be avenged by that same Albertine whom Marcel by his excessive demands will render indifferent to the suffering she causes him, an indifference that will be ultimately consummated by her own death. Obviously, such indifference to the suffering one causes or to the suffering one sees is by no means limited to homosexuals. Mlle Vinteuil's profanation of her father's image is more than matched by Gilberte's renunciation of Swann when she assumes her stepfather's name "de Forcheville" in order to fulfill her social ambitions. The most brutal actions and remarks of the homosexual Charlus cannot compare with the vicious indifference of Mme Verdurin's snobbery that crushes so many, including the Baron himself. Finally, Marcel repeatedly witnesses the social world's refusal to allow the death of others to disturb its pleasures. The Duc de Guermantes is more concerned, for example, with the color of the shoes his wife is wearing to a ball than by Swann's announcement of his approaching death. The obsessive and inhuman search for pleasure, the flight from suffering, the refusal to accept death, all are forms of an egoism that hides the truth of the world and of the self, and all derive from what is for Proust the root of all evil—the weakness of the will in the face of truth.

Seen in the light of this special moral code Marcel's punishment clearly fits his crime. Whereas in the past he was able to escape from the reality encountered in the exterior world either by imagining something else or by forgetting the truth revealed, now no such escape is possible. The "deluge of reality" that "submerges" him, that seems "enormous" compared to his previous doubts and suppositions, comes from *within*. Marcel cannot escape from his memory of Montjouvain or of the story of Swann's love, nor can he forget the "Knowledge of Evil" they gave him. And Albertine is now so much a part of these memories, so fused with the new and frightening self within Marcel that her words have brought to birth, that when the train approaches her stop at Parville and she opens the door of the compartment to leave, he is forced to retain her:

> But this movement which she was making to alight tore my heart unendurably, just as if, notwithstanding the position independent of my body which Albertine's body seemed to be occupying a yard away from it, this separation in space, which

154

an accurate draughtsman would have been obliged to indicate between us, was only apparent, and anyone who wished to make a fresh drawing of things as they really were would now have had to place Albertine, not at a certain distance from me, but inside me.[24]

Marcel's world has indeed been "redesigned" for he completes here that movement "from outside to within" already suggested at the end of his affair with Gilberte. The struggle against reality is to take place now beyond appearances and within an inner space-time world.

The entire movement of Marcel's life, based on his repeated and sustained anticipation of a "new day" that would bring him an "unknown happiness," has been reversed. Since it is now filled by the past and is no longer merely the empty prelude to an unrealized future, the present must be lived in the full horror of its suffering. In a word, imagination has been transformed into sensitivity. The anguish that Albertine's supposed homosexuality causes Marcel derives precisely from the fact that he cannot even imagine, let alone give her, the pleasures she finds with a rival who is so unlike him. Nor can he imagine behind Albertine the "blue mountains of the sea" at Balbec, for the unknown to which she has initiated him also exists within, in the image of "the room at Montjouvain where she was falling into the arms of Mlle Vinteuil." So particular and obsessive is this new unknown that Marcel's jealousy itself is limited to it. Although he knows that Albertine can satisfy her desires with other women in other places, he is tormented only by the thought that she may escape to meet the friend of Mlle Vinteuil in Trieste or Cherbourg, just as in the past his desire to see a "Persian church" was inseparably tied to his dream of Balbec. Therefore, says the narrator, "imagination, when it changes its nature and turns to sensibility does not for that reason acquire control of a larger number of simultaneous images."[25]

Reflecting Proust's own passion for truth, Marcel acknowledges for a moment that, by confirming his earlier vague intuitions of her homosexuality, Albertine's revelation has given him a certain intellectual benefit:

> It is often simply from want of the creative spirit that we do not go to the full extent of suffering. And the most terrible reality brings us, with our suffering, the joy of a great discovery, be-

24. II, 367; *Sodome,* II, 1116.   25. II, 370; *Sodome,* II, 1120.

cause it merely gives a new and clear form to what we have long been ruminating without suspecting it.[26]

But this joy is in no way comparable to the emotion experienced during the *moments bienheureux* in which discovery is the direct result of personal creative activity. It is the cold, intellectual joy of a discovery that does not liberate him from contingency, but shows him to what extent he has become bound to it. The door opened by Albertine's words closes upon him, for the spectre of imprisonment that haunted the end of his love for Gilberte has become a reality:

> the words: "That friend is Mlle. Vinteuil" had been the *Open sesame* which I should have been incapable of discovering by myself, which had made Albertine penetrate to the depths of my shattered heart. And the door that had closed behind her, I might seek for a hundred years without learning how it might be opened.[27]

The Prison

Imprisoned in Marcel's heart and mind by the image of Montjouvain and the story of Swann's love, Albertine is also the actual prisoner of a man who never allows her to be alone outside the confines of his apartment, who has others spy on her, and who subjects her to all the painful demands of his need for peace and certainty. By her fateful words Albertine, like Marcel, finds that she has become the inhabitant of a "terrible terra incognita" where neither her desires nor his can be satisfied.

The real prisoner is in fact Marcel. Behind the "closed door" he lives in a world which is the very opposite of the ark. The essence of the Stranger's message to Dominique was to become what he is, to become, in other words, his true, profound self freed from the bonds of time. Marcel's prison is the creation of his fear of becoming what he thinks he is—another Swann or Saint-Loup who will be tormented if Albertine is allowed to escape and to become herself another Odette or Rachel. Her imprisonment can be seen as one more example of Marcel's instinct of self-preservation at work. This instinct generally operates as a means of protecting the present against a future that threatens to destroy it by transforming it into the past. But now, although Marcel fears the possibility of Albertine's escape, that future is so inextricably tied to his fear of

26. II, 367; *Sodome*, II, 1115–16.   27. II, 375; *Sodome*, II, 1127–28.

the past that the prison's primary function is to prevent the past from becoming fully present. As long as Albertine remains imprisoned, Marcel cannot become completely like Swann, and therefore cannot suffer the same anguish. Yet the irony of Marcel's situation is that the prison proves that he is already another Swann, for to be imprisoned by love is to have understood its supreme paradox in which the beloved, like the spear of Telephus whose image Beckett uses to characterize Proustian time, "is successively the malady and the remedy that suspends and aggravates it."[28] In his prison Marcel is entrapped in time.

Because the prison exists within him, Marcel does not feel free even when he himself escapes from the apartment. One night at a soirée given by the Verdurins where he has gone without her, he senses obscurely that Albertine is still with him: "I had that vague impression of her that we have of our own limbs, and if I happened to think of her it was as we think, with disgust at being bound to it in complete subjection, of our own body." Albertine has become a permanent and corrupting presence in the "mobile prison" of consciousness Marcel carries with him. Returning home the same night he stops for a moment on the sidewalk to look at the bars of light formed by the shutters of Albertine's room. The treasure these bars enclose for him has been paid for, he knows, by his liberty, solitude, and thought. He returns home now,

> not to find myself alone, and, after taking leave of the friends who furnished me from outside with food for thought, to find myself at any rate compelled to seek it in myself, but to be on the contrary less alone than when I was at the Verdurins', welcomed as I should be by the person to whom I *abdicated,* to whom I handed over most completely my own person, without having for an instant the leisure to think of myself nor even requiring the effort, since she would be by my side, to think of her.[29]

Marcel's imprisonment by his prisoner does indeed represent the abdication of his creative life and will, for by her actual presence Albertine denies him both the suffering that can be one of the sources of spiritual activity and the solitude that is its necessary climate. Marcel's sacrifice is not entirely comparable to Vinteuil's however, because the latter gave himself freely to his daughter in the purity of his love for her. It is Marcel's own selfish needs that prevent him from fulfilling his

28. II, 167; *Sodome*, II, 833.   29. II, 611–12; *Prisonnière*, III, 331.

vocation as an artist. In fact, that element of pure love represented in his own life by his mother has no place in his relationship with Albertine. His mother, who, significantly, now resembles his grandmother, is *excluded* from the apartment, and it is as if Marcel, like Dominique, has allowed the habits of his contingent self to replace the demands of his soul. But here the situation is more complex, for although the mother is actually absent, it is her moral code that Marcel uses in his struggle with Albertine. Now, like Mlle Vinteuil, Marcel feels guilty because of this residual spiritual presence of a parent within him. Like Mlle Vinteuil again, Marcel is involved in "sacrilege" for if Albertine represents a moral outlook completely different from that of his mother, she is nonetheless asked to perform similar functions. It is the old abdication scene at Combray that Marcel repeats each night when he finds peace and security in the moment of "grace" accorded him by Albertine's kiss.

If this strange conjunction of similarity and difference in the ritual of the good-night kiss forms the basis of Marcel's sacrilegious use of Albertine, it is also in this and other instances the object of his fascinated interest. Just as his mother has grown to resemble his grandmother, so he himself, Marcel discovers, has grown to resemble these two women in the often affectionate care he devotes to Albertine, as when he takes off her shoes before she goes to bed. He resembles his father, because he also has developed an interest in the weather. Finally, when he convinces himself that he is obliged to stay in his apartment for reasons of health, he knows that these reasons are not the true ones. His decision has been determined not by Albertine, but by a being who has "migrated" within him—his Aunt Léonie:

> When we have passed a certain age, the soul of the child that we were and the souls of the dead from whom we spring come and bestow upon us in handfuls their treasures and their calamities, asking to be allowed to cooperate in the new sentiments which we are feeling and in which, obliterating their former image, we recast them in an original creation.[30]

It was not his taste, remarks the narrator, but "the chance of a minute of anguish" that chose Albertine for him. But it is now evident that if that minute has been prolonged, as he says, by the weakness of his character, that character in all its aspects has itself been largely determined by the

30. II, 432; *Prisonnière*, III, 79.

past—his own and that of his family. More important than this sense of determinism is Marcel's discovery that a far greater part of the past than he had previously supposed is not completely lost but continues to exist in his present acts. By revealing a past that is now extensive and "deep enough" for him to initiate the exploration of its form by comparing its different moments, this discovery temporarily breaks down the exclusiveness of his obsession with the image of Montjouvain. Through his perception of similarity in difference, or permanence in change, Marcel is beginning to see that time has enabled him to be both himself and others. His increased knowledge of time is helping him to weaken the power of time over him. He is acquiring a new sense of his own individuality by recognizing that if time has formed his life, it has also been formed *in time* by him into an "original creation." But he does not yet see how the past that has been thus redesigned can be redesigned again into a work of art.

During the months of her imprisonment the calm that Albertine procures for Marcel is a "release from suffering rather than a positive joy." This calm continues to have only a negative value so long as she is actually present to his senses, but when she is in her own room or on an automobile excursion with the chauffeur and Andrée, his two spies, when, that is, she is at once absent yet unable to escape, the calm that she offers him acquires a positive value, for it frees his mind and enables him to experience those joys he can find only in solitude and receive from sources other than Albertine. Certain mornings, for example, Marcel is gradually awakened by the activity of the exterior world:

> At daybreak, my face still turned to the wall, and before I had seen above the big inner curtains what tone the first streaks of light assumed, I could already tell what sort of day it was. The first sounds from the street had told me, according to whether they came to my ears dulled and distorted by the moisture of the atmosphere or quivering like arrows in the resonant and empty area of a spacious, crisply frozen, pure morning.[31]

These modifications and variations of light, sound, and temperature filtering through the window and through his sleep set off within him an "inner violin," and he is filled with a sense of renewal and liberation:

> By themselves these modifications (which, albeit coming from without, were internal) refashioned for me the world outside.

31. II, 383; *Prisonnière*, III, 9.

Communicating doors, long barred, opened themselves in my brain. The life of certain towns, the gaiety of certain expeditions resumed their place in my consciousness. All athrob in harmony with the vibrating string, I would have sacrificed my dull life in the past, and all my life to come, erased with the india–rubber of habit, for one of these special unique moments.

By provoking mild forms of involuntary memory and by revealing thereby correspondences between exterior reality and Marcel's own inner world, these sensations reopen the door of the self and transform the prison into an *ark,* a spiritual world freed from the limitations of actuality and composed of those individual images and impressions that alone can be possessed, for they alone are truly his. Because memory has given it the consistency of the past, Marcel can now enjoy the plenitude of the present. His surface calm assures the intense activity of his imagination, and immobile in his bed he embarks on an inner voyage through time and space:

> Françoise came in to light the fire, and to make it draw, threw upon it a handful of twigs, the scent of which, forgotten for a year past, traced round the fireplace a magic circle within which, perceiving myself poring over a book, now at Combray, now at Doncières, I was as joyful, while remaining in my bedroom in Paris, as if I had been on the point of starting for a walk along the Méséglise way, or of going to join Saint-Loup and his friends on the training-ground.

Each of these moments from the past brings back as well the corresponding self that lived it, for these memories, says the narrator,

> recreated in me, of me as a whole, by virtue of an identical sensation, the boy, the youth who had first seen them. There had been not merely a change in the weather outside, or, inside the room, the introduction of a fresh scent, there had been in myself a difference of age, the substitution of another person.[32]

This resurrection of past selves and places experienced in a room at the moment of awakening recalls the opening pages of the novel in which the "kaleidoscope" of memory is first described. Although here again Marcel finds himself "plunged back" into the depths of his past, he maintains a more conscious control over his experience. Not only does he become more fully aware of the existence of his life in time, he

32. II, 395–96; *Prisonnière,* III, 25–27.

discovers as well within himself certain gradations of the "I," that are not so much past selves as they are modes of consciousness. The basic one he calls "the little person inside me, hymning the rising sun," or "the little fellow of the barometer" who is sensitive to the slightest changes in the weather. Superimposed on this "I" is another that he describes as "a certain philosopher who is happy only when he has discovered in two works of art, in two sensations, a common element."[33] It is evident that Proust through his narrator is here restating the relationship between sensitivity and the functions of the *esprit*. Thus, in his present experience Marcel's sensitivity becomes the basis for his discovery of analogies between past and present, as well as between different moments of the past. The real morning outside the room causes him joy because it belongs to a certain type of ideal morning that has been lived intermittently in the past. "This ideal morning," says the narrator, "filled my mind full of a permanent reality, identical with all similar mornings."[34]

If the past Marcel relives is at once *real and ideal* so, curiously, is the present. He never enters directly into contact with the exterior world. Rather, it enters into his world in the form of light and sounds divorced from their actual context. These sensations are now free to evoke precisely what they "omit"—not only the absent world of the past, but also the absent reality outside Marcel's window. By the intermediary of one or two sensations he is able to recreate *in his mind* the entire morning. Commenting on this phenomenon Gaëton Picon remarks: "it is the perceptible absence, or at least the smallest perceptible presence which makes possible a complete mental presence."[35] This complete mental presence of a world that also exists outside the self and can be *felt as well as imagined* is exactly what is denied Marcel in his disappointing encounters with reality. Indeed, the reality he now possesses is not the destroyer of images but a source of imagination.

There are also moments when Albertine herself gives him the very joys she at other times denies him. Such privileged moments occur when Marcel finds her sleeping. Because she is then at once absent from herself yet present, he can both think about her and find comfort in her presence. Her sleep seems to assure his possession of her:

> By shutting her eyes, by losing consciousness, Albertine had stripped off, one after another, the different human characters

33. II, 385; *Prisonnière*, III, 12.   34. III, 395; *Prisonnière*, III, 26.
35. Picon, *Lecture de Proust*, p. 148.

with which she had deceived me ever since the day when I had first made her acquaintance. She was animated now only by the unconscious life of vegetation, of trees, *a life more different from my own, more alien, and yet one that belonged more to me.* Her personality did not escape at every moment, as when we were talking, by the channels of her unacknowledged thoughts and of her gaze. She had called back into herself everything of her that lay outside, *had taken refuge, enclosed, reabsorbed, in her body.* In keeping her before my eyes, in my hands, I had that impression of possessing her altogether, which I never had when she was awake. Her life was submitted to me, exhaled towards me its gentle breath.[36]

As this passage suggests, Albertine's sleep realizes a kind of purification of her being, for by excluding the reality of her life in time that had corrupted the natural essence Marcel sought in her, it makes her conform more closely to that essence. She is for a moment the "something else" that first gave birth to his love for her. She becomes again *une jeune fille en fleur,* and the sound of her breathing seems to Marcel to be that of the waves on the beach at Balbec. If Albertine now seems completely imprisoned within her body, it is, paradoxically, because sleep has freed her from her human individuality. What Marcel possesses is less her life than the world his imagination had placed in her. Reduced to "an unconscious and *unresisting* object," Albertine can more completely satisfy his desires, because she is at once strange and familiar.

Although Marcel is able during these moments to recapture the past mystery associated with Albertine, he also realizes that she now hides from him the far more complex unknown of her possible homosexuality. The ultimate goal of his imprisonment of her is, therefore, the "expulsion" of *all* mystery from her being, a goal to be achieved by the complete elimination of her individuality:

The image for which I sought, upon which I reposed, against which I would have liked to lean and die, was no longer that of Albertine leading a hidden life, it was that of an Albertine as familiar to me as possible ... an Albertine who did not reflect a distant world, but desired nothing else ... than to be with me, a person like myself, an Albertine the embodiment of what belonged to me and not of the unknown.[37]

To be entirely known and possessed Albertine must become, like the mother and grandmother, a mere extension of Marcel's own self. By

36. II, 426; *Prisonnière,* III, 70.   37. II, 430; *Prisonnière,* III, 75.

negating the independent reality of the Albertine existing outside himself, Marcel hopes to alleviate the suffering caused by the Albertine introduced into his being by the revelation of her relationship with the friend of Mlle Vinteuil.

Once again, however, he encounters the dilemma of love. As a refuge against reality and as a barrier preventing both Albertine's escape and the intrusion of mystery, Marcel's prison may at times make possible the peace of mind he so desperately needs. But without anxiety this "peace" has little value, and without mystery his love cannot endure. "We love only what we do not wholly possess," writes Proust.[38] An Albertine completely possessed would no longer be worth possessing, and a prison totally impervious to reality would enclose only a void.

Marcel never succeeds in creating such a prison, for Albertine can never be possessed. Reality continually penetrates his defense bringing with it suffering which, although it fills the void of habit, leads to the more frightening void of the unknown and of his own loneliness.

The Void

Despite her imprisonment Albertine continues to be an *être de fuite* whom Marcel is unable to immobilize. The woman he possesses is only the "envelope" of a being whose thoughts and past remain unknown and unknowable:

> I realised the impossibility against which love is powerless. We imagine that love has as its object a person whom we can see lying down before our eyes, enclosed in a human body. Alas, it is the extension of that person to all the points in space and time which the person has occupied and will occupy. If we do not possess its contact with this or that place, this or that hour, we do not possess it. But we cannot touch all these points. If only they were indicated to us, we might perhaps contrive to reach out to them. But we grope for them without finding them. Hence mistrust, jealousy, persecutions. We waste precious time upon absurd clues and pass by the truth without suspecting it.[39]

Marcel's desire to possess Albertine here assumes a significance that goes beyond the confines of a love story, however extraordinary and bizarre that story may seem, for his relationship with her can be seen as yet another dramatization of the essential theme of the novel—the spirit's fight against time. Albertine herself appears to be "a mighty goddess of Time,"

38. II, 453; *Prisonnière*, III, 106.   39. II, 448; *Prisonnière*, III, 100.

an incarnation of the exterior world's impenetrability. Marcel is wasting his own time and sacrificing his life in an impossible attempt to possess time itself. By describing in *La Prisonnière* and *La Fugitive* the agony of the spirit's defeat Proust is clearly preparing for its triumph at the end of the novel when Marcel will reverse the direction of his pursuit and discover within himself the essence of his own life in time. In fact, Marcel's suffering is itself a preparation for his eventual victory for it allows him to perceive the dimensions of reality whose existence had until now remained unknown. "[*Love is space and time made directly perceptible to the heart.*]"[40]

Marcel's knowledge of the unknown is suddenly and painfully increased when Albertine, victimized by his jealousy, finally succeeds in escaping from her prison. The words of Françoise's cold announcement: "Mademoiselle Albertine has gone," engulf Marcel in a deluge of reality almost as powerful as that provoked by Albertine's words in the little train. Once again he is confronted by an "unimaginable" event whose intensity and strangeness no amount of thought could have foreseen:

> In order to form an idea of an unknown situation our imagination borrows elements that are already familiar and for that reason does not form any idea of it. But our sensibility, even in its most physical form, receives, as it were the brand of the lightning, the original and for long indelible imprint of the novel event.[41]

Although his instinct of self-preservation attempts to belittle its importance, this new shock to his senses disrupts the entire pattern of his habitual world. Suffering, Marcel acknowledges, penetrates farther in psychology than psychology itself. The strange new reality that confronts him forces him to recognize the limits not only of his imagination but of his intelligence as well.

Because it is now complete, Albertine's absence no longer allows him to experience the "joys of solitude." It is rather the other face of his solitude that is revealed, and that her presence helped to hide—his loneliness:

> The bonds that unite another person to ourselves exist only in our mind. Memory as it grows fainter relaxes them, and notwithstanding the illusion by which we would fain be cheated and

40. II, 650; *Prisonnière*, III, 385. Moncrieff translates "L'amour c'est l'espace et le temps rendus sensibles au coeur" as "Love, what is it but space and time rendered perceptible by the heart."
41. II, 679; *Fugitive*, III, 424.

with which, out of love, friendship, politeness, deference, duty, we cheat other people, we exist alone. *Man is the creature that cannot emerge from himself* [sortir de soi], *that knows his fellows only in himself; when he asserts the contrary, he is lying.*[42]

Marcel has arrived at the fundamental truth he already sensed in his first attempts to "get out of himself." That it confronts him now more powerfully than ever before is not surprising, for love and jealousy demonstrate more conclusively than any other psychological phenomenon the inexorable law of inclusion and exclusion that governs Proust's world in which, as Georges Poulet writes, "each creature is exterior to all others, and nevertheless enclosed within himself, without possibility of communication."[43] But this truth, whose full import he will discover at the end of the novel, is still unacceptable, for Marcel soon revolts against the fact that he is a prisoner of his own self. Like Dominique, he refuses to accept his loneliness, and by means of the very jealousy that makes him suffer, he attempts to reunite himself with Albertine and to reopen to her the door of his prison:

> it was just as well, I told myself, that by incessantly asking myself what she could be doing, thinking, longing, at every moment, whether she intended, whether she was going to return, *I should be keeping open that communicating door which love had installed in me,* and feeling another person's mind flood through open sluices the reservoir which must not again become stagnant.[44]

Certainly, Marcel seems to be using Albertine as much now, during her absence, as he had done when she was still his prisoner. His love for her, or rather his jealousy and suffering, are employed as so many *idées voisines* that help him to escape the truth of his solitude. Like Swann, Marcel is attempting also to prevent the "stagnation" of his spiritual life that would result from the end of his suffering.

Whatever the paradoxical benefits Marcel derives from his suffering, time and reality continually confront him with new sources of anguish that reveal his limitations. Albertine dies and is liberated from time, but this does not calm Marcel's jealousy. He continues to be imprisoned by the temporal and spatial multiplicity of the woman who does not cease to exist within him. Like Swann attempting to discover the secrets of Odette's life, the more Marcel learns about Albertine's past and about

42. II, 698; *Fugitive*, III, 450.   43. Poulet, *L'Espace proustien*, pp. 70–71.
44. II, 698; *Fugitive*, III, 451.

her relationships with other women the more he realizes that the truths he seeks can never be known:

> We suppose that we know exactly what things are and what people think, for the simple reason that we do not care about them. But as soon as we feel the desire to know, which the jealous man feels, then it becomes a dizzy kaleidoscope in which we can no longer make out anything.[45]

The void Marcel encounters in his outward search for truth is the guarantee of Albertine's irreducible individuality. Scattered in confusing fragments from which he is unable to construct a stable and complete image of her, protected and enclosed by time, she remains a stranger.

Even more disturbing than the impenetrable world he finds outside himself is the unknown world Marcel discovers within. Forced to think about himself he encounters another void:

> [as the self lives incessantly in thinking about a quantity of things, so that it is only the thought of these things, when by chance instead of having before it these things, it suddenly thinks about itself, it finds only an empty apparatus, something which it does not know, to which in order to give it some reality it adds the memory of a face perceived in the mirror.][46]

This loss of his identity to the "things" of the exterior world is the price he has paid, Marcel realizes, for the entire centrifugal movement of his life:

> Just as, throughout the whole course of our life, our egoism sees before it all the time the objects that are of interest to ourselves, but never takes in that Ego [Je] itself which is incessantly observing them, so the desire which directs our actions descends towards them, but does not reascend to itself, whether because, being unduly utilitarian, it plunges into the action and disdains all knowledge of it, or because we have been looking to the future to compensate for the disappointments of the [present], or because the inertia of our *mind* urges it down the easy slope of imagination, rather than make it reascend the steep slope of introspection.[47]

45. II, 747; *Fugitive*, III, 519.   46. In French only; *Fugitive*, III, 466 n.
47. II, 709; *Fugitive*, III, 465. Moncrieff translates "déceptions du présent" as "disappointments of the past."

Although there are no more extensive examples of introspection in the novel than the long passages in *La Prisonnière* and *La Fugitive,* in which Marcel analyzes the nature of his jealousy and suffering, his thoughts seem to revolve around an empty center. His attention is directed away from the permanent and essential "I" within him to a succession of selves in time.

It is also time which, in the form of forgetfulness, destroys one by one the innumerable Albertines within him, together with each of the correlative selves that time itself had linked to her. One day he encounters Gilberte, whom he does not at first recognize. The sudden sensual desire he feels for her accelerates the process of destruction by driving from his mind "a certain number of miseries, of painful preoccupations," and with them "a whole block of memories, probably long since crumbled and become precarious, with regard to Albertine." Marcel is witnessing the progressive conversion of time wasted into time lost.

Turning inward he is confronted by the same "dizzy kaleidoscope" he found outside himself. It is his own identity, as well as the meaning of the past, which seems lost in the confusion of former times, places, and selves:

> the memory of all events that had followed one another in my life . . . in the course of those last months of Albertine's existence, had made them seem to me much longer than a year, and now this oblivion of so many things, separating me by *gulfs of empty space* from quite recent events which they made me think remote, because I had had what is called "the time" to forget them, by its fragmentary, irregular interpolation in my memory—like a thick fog at sea which obliterates all the landmarks—confused, destroyed my sense of distances in time, contracted in one place, extended in another, and made me suppose myself now farther away from things, now far closer to them than I really was. And as in the fresh spaces, as yet unexplored, which extended before me, there would be no more trace of my love for Albertine than there had been, in the time past which I had just traversed, of my love for my grandmother, my life appeared to me—offering a succession of periods in which, after a certain interval, nothing of what had sustained the previous period survived in that which followed—as something so *devoid of the support of an individual, identical and permanent self,* something so useless in the future and so protracted in the past, that death might just

as well put an end to its course here or there, without in the least concluding it.[48]

Marcel's identity disappears with the things and persons that comprised his life in time because through his desires, and particularly through love, he allowed that identity to become inextricably tied to them. The "something else" Marcel seeks in his pursuit of Gilberte and Albertine is not simply the world of Bergotte, or the mystery of the sea, or even "Love" itself; it is essentially a different existence. His desire to escape himself always has as its ultimate goal the discovery and possession of a new self. To go to Balbec is to become the person who has seen the beauty of its church; to possess Gilberte is to become the person who lives in the world of love. Marcel's desire for something else is, therefore, also a desire to be someone else, and the women he loves act as mediators in a false search for self-renewal. Yet because Gilberte and Albertine are indispensable, they effectively incorporate within themselves whatever lies "beyond" them. The more he pursues them, the more his desired, as well as his actual, identity becomes bound to them, so that the "fictions of substance" he creates and imposes on them in order to arrest their temporal and spatial "mobility" reveal through their destruction the fictional nature of his own existence. Love places Marcel in a kind of Sartrean hell in which the "other," by the very fact that she is another, not only will not, but cannot, reflect for him the image of what he is or wants to be. Being the most "exclusive" of desires, and demanding therefore a total commitment of the self, love constructs a world in which the self remains perpetually alienated. Proust shows love to be a deadly game at impossible odds, whose stakes are nothing less than the lover's identity, and whose inevitable outcome is a form of spiritual suicide. It is in this way that he renews, through his psychology of time and space, the ageless symbolic alliance of love and death.

What Marcel does not yet understand is the relationship between the successive loss of the self through forgetfulness and the resurrection of past selves experienced during his moments of joyful solitude when by means of the sensations received from the world around him he began to reconstruct the world of the past. In other words, Marcel has yet to comprehend the value to him of the paradoxical destructive-creative action of time.

His present situation contains another paradox. He does not know

48. II, 799–800; *Fugitive,* III, 593–94.

that beyond the void his consciousness confronts lies a rich mine of self-knowledge that the suffering of love has formed within him. Unable now to discover this true substance of himself through which he will recreate his identity, feeling stripped of the past and therefore faced by a present and a future devoid of all meaning, he judges his life as being without significance, as merely "the empty frame of a work of art."[49]

This description of the inner and outer void Marcel encounters after the disappearance of Albertine from his conscious memory concludes the major part of Proust's presentation of love in *A la Recherche*. Certainly, no aspect of Proust's concept of love has attracted more attention from critics or disconcerted more readers than his demonstration of its subjectivity. It must be recalled, however, that Proustian love is marked by suffering and is defined as "space and time made directly perceptible to the heart" precisely because it is directed toward and inseparably associated with an external being. Swann and Marcel discover the subjectivity of love only after they fail to find any objective sanctions for their desires, and, when they completely accept the truth of their discovery, they cease to love.

Once he has acknowledged the subjectivity of love Marcel must also acknowledge the impossibility of realizing his dream of perfection in life. For this reason his failure in love prepares for his future success in art. It is because he knows now that a novel or "romance" cannot be lived that he will be able to write a novel later. In fact, his present failure creates the solitude necessary for creation, for by revealing to him the full extent of the exterior world's strangeness and ineluctability love makes Marcel realize that he can never know or possess anything or anyone outside himself. "Love," writes Germaine Brée, "directs the narrator's attention to the discordance of the two worlds, the world of inner consciousness and the world of objective reality in which men move about; consequently it prepares the synthesis which will in the end lead to the narrator's revelation."[50] It is memory that will form this synthesis, and it is in himself that Marcel will discover his "work of art."

49. II, 733; *Fugitive*, III, 499.
50. Brée, *Marcel Proust*, p. 160; *Du Temps perdu*, p. 182.

7
Revelations

Marcel's pessimistic judgment on the value of his life after Albertine's death shows to what extent his dream of becoming a writer is influenced by his conception of the self and by his knowledge of time, for it is his failure to find by means of his intelligence alone any evidence in time or within himself of *un moi individuel identique et permanent* that forces him to question his creative capabilities. A more profound elucidation of the complex ties existing between art, the self, and time is necessary, therefore, if Marcel is to achieve the final and total reevaluation of his life. Since the intelligence acting alone leads to the void of doubt and indifference, such an elucidation must be based on the convincing evidence that can be provided only by direct impressions on the senses. Marcel receives these revelatory impressions from three different sources: Vinteuil's septet, involuntary memory, and the spectacle of age and social change. Although these encounters give him a new conception of art, the self, and time, respectively, each also contains and develops the truths revealed by the others.

Vinteuil and Art

Marcel's encounter with Vinteuil's septet takes place during a visit to the Verdurins where he goes to verify his suspicions concerning Albertine's homosexuality. Like Swann when he first hears the sonata, Marcel finds himself lifted out of the actual world and transported to a "strange land." The known now helps him to identify the unknown, for he suddenly recognizes in the midst of this new music the *petite phrase* of Vinteuil's sonata to which he had first been introduced by Swann himself and had heard played so often by Odette and later by Albertine during the calmer moments of her imprisonment. Although the phrase, once recalled by the composer, immediately disappears and Marcel finds himself again in an "unknown world," its "magical apparition" fills him with an intense joy and leads him to a more profound understanding of artistic creation.[1]

The inconceivable and unpredictable nature of beauty and therefore of happiness is, as has been shown, a fundamental idea in Proust's aesthetics. Yet a certain unpredictability is part of all of Marcel's encounters including those sudden revelations of "new" truths concerning Albertine that impress themselves so powerfully on his senses and cause him so much anguish. Indeed, Proust's constant effort throughout the novel is to show that life cannot escape such encounters precisely because it is lived *in time*. As new events, both Albertine's escape from imprisonment and the performance of Vinteuil's septet enrich Marcel's knowledge of time itself, but they do so in different ways. In his suffering at seeing his habitual world destroyed Marcel is the victim of time's creation that keeps him imprisoned in material reality. In his encounters with Vinteuil's art he witnesses the power of human creation to transcend the limits of time.

Marcel perceives, nevertheless, both in the septet and in Vinteuil's work as a whole, patterns of development in time:

> I began to realise that if, in the body of this septet, different elements presented themselves in turn, to combine at the close, so also Vinteuil's sonata, and, as I was to find later on, his other works as well, had been no more than timid essays, exquisite but very slight, towards the triumphant and complete master-piece which was revealed to me at this moment.[2]

Vinteuil's art leads Marcel back to his own life, for he now discovers analogies between these patterns in the music and those of his loves. Like the septet, his love for Albertine, he realizes, developed out of a succession of different events that took place first at Balbec, then in Paris, then again at Balbec, and finally again in Paris. Also, like Vinteuil's earlier works, his first loves had not been "hermetically sealed" universes, but only "slight and timid essays, experiments, which paved the way to this vaster love: my love for Albertine." It is only now that Marcel possesses the perspective in time enabling him to perceive this development. "The example of Gilberte," remarks the narrator, "would as little have en-

1. II, 554; *Prisonnière*, III, 249.   2. II, 555; *Prisonnière*, III, 252.

abled me to form an idea of Albertine and guess that I should fall in love with her, as the memory of Vinteuil's sonata would have enabled me to imagine his septet."[3]

It is also now that the reader himself begins to distinguish the similarities and differences between Swann's experience with music and Marcel's. Just as Swann hears only the sonata, so he bears the same relationship to Marcel as that earlier work does to the septet. He represents a first effort to understand the meaning of Vinteuil's art, an effort that Marcel alone will bring to fruition. It is precisely in the ways they perceive the relationships between art, love, and time that the two men reveal some of their differences.

Marcel is not completely free of the idolatry that corrupts Swann's understanding of love and art. Both before and after his encounter with the septet there are moments when he associates his dreams of Albertine with works of art—paintings by Elstir or by other artists, Vinteuil's music, or a book by Bergotte:

> And no doubt the book appeared all the more vivid in consequence. But Albertine herself profited just as much by being thus transported out of one of the two worlds to which we have access, and in which we can place alternately the same object, *by escaping thus from the crushing weight of matter to play freely in the fluid space of mind.* I found myself suddenly and for the instant capable of feeling an ardent desire for this irritating girl. She had at that moment the appearance of a work by Elstir or Bergotte, I felt a momentary enthusiasm for her, seeing her in the perspective [recul] of imagination and art.[4]

The reciprocal exchange of value between a woman and a work of art, the desire to escape material reality through a false spiritualization of love, these are the characteristics of Swann's idolatry as well. Yet it is also clear that Marcel's idolatry is far less conscious and deliberate. He is not so much seeking to justify his love for Albertine as he is rediscovering in her with the help of art the charm she once had for his imagination and that habit and reality have destroyed. Above all, the narrator insists that this revalorization of Albertine was very brief. Marcel never loses sight of the fact that as an effort to immobilize time idolatry is futile. Later, when he looks at her playing the pianola in his apartment, he momentarily sees Albertine as a living portrait of Saint Cecilia. She

3. II, 735; *Fugitive*, III, 502.   4. II, 416–17; *Prisonnière*, III, 56.

is, he thinks, in a sense his creation, for it is he who has developed her tastes in art and bought her the elegant clothes she wears. But this illusion does not last long:

> But no, Albertine was in no way to me a work of art. I knew what it meant to admire a woman in an artistic fashion, I had known Swann. For my own part, moreover, I was, no matter who the woman might be, incapable of doing so, having no sort of power of detached observation, never knowing what it was that I beheld. . . . The pleasure and the pain that I derived from Albertine never took, in order to reach me, the line of taste and intellect; indeed, to tell the truth, when I began to regard Albertine as an angel musician glazed with a marvellous patina whom I congratulated myself upon possessing, it was not long before I found her uninteresting; I soon became bored in her company, but these moments were of brief duration; we love only that in which we pursue something inaccessible, we love only what we do not possess, and very soon I returned to the conclusion that I did not possess Albertine.[5]

As will be shown, the narrator's remarks concerning his lack of an *esprit d'observation extérieure* cannot be entirely justified. What he doubtless does possess, and what Swann lacks, is a highly developed *esprit d'introspection*. Marcel's ability as well as his need to go beyond appearances protects him from Swann's form of idolatry precisely because it enables him to grasp the implications of his love's existence in time. The suffering he endures because of his failure to immobilize Albertine is intensified and partially redeemed by his lucidity. Therefore, while the *petite phrase* is used by Swann to justify his love for Odette, the septet makes Marcel all the more conscious of the emptiness of his life with Albertine. Seeing his love in the perspective of time, he can foresee its end. Only for a moment does he indulge his emotions in the kind of subjective associations made by Swann. A "tender phrase, homely and domestic" of the septet, that he believes may have been inspired by the sleep of Vinteuil's daughter, makes him think of his own "little child," Albertine, asleep in his apartment. He soon perceives, however, the inadequacy of such associations to explain the value and meaning of the music: "Something more mysterious than Albertine's love seemed to be promised at the outset of this work, in those first cries of dawn."[6]

5. II, 648–49; *Prisonnière*, III, 383–84.   6. II, 556; *Prisonnière*, III, 253.

Excluding the thought of his love from his mind, Marcel now turns, like Swann at the Sainte-Euverte soirée, to the composer. Although Vinteuil has been dead for several years, Marcel feels that he is still alive and present in his music. He also wonders how the Vinteuil, whom he knew to be so timid and sad, could have expressed such audacity and above all joy in his music—a joy that anyone listening to his works could not help but experience as well. Much of the power of Vinteuil's music derives, he decides, from its marked originality, for it is the result of such personal discoveries that it can never be imitated. Vinteuil is a "constant innovator" because his originality is evident each time one of his works is played. His music therefore transcends time, for although it was composed in time and occupies a definite place in the evolution of music, it has the paradoxical characteristic of "permanent novelty." Unlike the dead, immobile world of habit and, again, unlike the suffering caused by Albertine, Vinteuil's art is for Marcel "life, perpetual and blissful motion."

Yet if the music places at least a part of Vinteuil's life outside of time, is it, Marcel asks, "Of his life as a man merely? If art was indeed but a prolongation of life, was it worth while to sacrifice anything to it, was it not as unreal as life itself?" This fundamental question concerning the respective values of art and life that here occupies Marcel's mind is also raised earlier when Vinteuil's sonata makes him recall his walks along the Guermantes way and his own dreams of becoming an artist. In abandoning that ambition, Marcel wonders, had he renounced the possibility of attaining "something real"? "Could life console me for the loss of art, was there in art a more profound reality, in which our true personality finds an expression that is not afforded it by the activities of life?"[7] Now, listening to the septet and comparing it with the sonata, he is able to reaffirm the value of art by employing as elsewhere in the novel Proust's own critical method based on the recognition of *phrases-types* that reveal the inner unity of an artist's work. Although the musical phrases in the two works are different, they are nonetheless composed of the "same elements" and express the "same prayer."[8]

The unity of Vinteuil's art impresses itself directly on Marcel's mind because the composer also generally succeeded in avoiding the "detours" of the intellect:

> when Vinteuil repeated once and again a single phrase, diversi-
> fied it, amused himself by altering its rhythm, by making it

7. II, 489; *Prisonnière*, III, 158.   8. II, 557–58; *Prisonnière*, III, 255.

reappear in its original form, these deliberate resemblances, the work of the intellect, inevitably superficial, never succeeded in being as striking as those resemblances, concealed, involuntary, which broke out in different colours, between the two separate masterpieces; for then Vinteuil, seeking to do something new, questioned himself, with all the force of his creative effort, reached his own essential nature at those depths, where, whatever be the question asked, it is in the same accent, that is to say its own, that it replies.[9]

These remarks go to the core of Proust's conception of the will, for they show that for the listener and for the composer the will must be directed not outward but inward toward the elucidation of an "involuntary" impression or the expression of one's individual "essence."

Moving beyond Swann who believed only in the "real existence" of the *petite phrase,* Marcel finds in the original and involuntary *accent unique* heard in all of Vinteuil's compositions "a proof of the irreducibly individual existence of the soul." This affirmation does not imply that Marcel denies either to the sonata or to the septet its individual identity or autonomy. Rather, by comparing the two works he is able to view each of them from a temporal and a *spiritual* perspective. By means of his comparison he understands not only the identity of each work but also the more profound identity that unites them, that exists "in between" them, and that is the identity of Vinteuil's "soul," for through his creative efforts Vinteuil has brought his true self into being, and in the diversity of his works he has remained "identical to himself." Lacking the possibility of such a comparison and, above all, the spiritual strength to profit by it, Swann had placed the origin of Vinteuil's music in "another world." For Marcel, the composer's unique "song" comes from *within*. All of Vinteuil's life, he realizes, was an attempt to enter more deeply into this inner spiritual world. The septet is the composer's most complete work because it represents the purest expression of his "inner country."

Listening to the septet Marcel believes that it is also the expression in music of an inner drama. Unlike the sonata that "opened upon a dawn of lilied meadows,"

it was upon continuous, level surfaces like those of the sea that, in the midst of a stormy morning beneath an already lurid sky, there began, in an eery silence, in an infinite void, this new

9. II, 558; *Prisonnière,* III, 256.

masterpiece, and it was into a roseate dawn that, in order to construct itself progressively before me, this unknown universe was drawn from silence and from night.[10]

The "promise" and "mysterious hope" of this dawn is soon lost in a piercing cry that in turn is replaced "at noon" by bright sounds expressing a rustic joy, comparable, Marcel feels, to the pealing of the Combray church bells that Vinteuil himself had heard so often. After other musical phrases have surfaced and disappeared there is an intense "struggle" between two motifs, one expressing joy and the other sadness and suffering. The septet finally ends with the triumph of "an ineffable joy which seemed to come from paradise."

Although Proust's rather precious description of the septet could be classed among other such *transpositions d'art* in vogue during his youth, its relationship to the rest of the novel is immediately evident. *A la Recherche du temps perdu* is also born out of "the silence and the night" and built "progressively" in time through an interweaving of the themes of joy (light) and of suffering (darkness). In the novel also joy triumphs at the end when the "different elements" are "combined" and reveal their underlying unity.[11] Although Marcel does not foresee the ultimate joy that will be the discovery of his artistic vocation, he does see that Vinteuil has given his self a new future by saving his life through art from the void of the past. His life is saved because music spiritualizes it by giving it a *form*. The patterns of temporal development that Marcel discerns in the septet reflect the way time is being formed by music.[12] The "events" that take place in the *virtual time* thus formed are free from the emotions and limits of material reality. The struggle between the motifs of joy and sorrow, says the narrator, is really a struggle of "energies":

> for if these creatures attacked one another, it was rid of their physical bodies, of their appearance, of their names, and finding in me an inward spectator, himself indifferent also to their names and to all details, interested only in their immaterial and dynamic combat and following with passion its sonorous changes.[13]

10. II, 554; *Prisonnière*, III, 250.
11. Germaine Brée discusses this aspect of the narrator's experience in *Marcel Proust*, p. 198; *Du Temps perdu*, p. 228.
12. See Moss, *Magic Lantern*, p. 96.   13. II, 561; *Prisonnière*, III, 260.

Unlike Swann for whom music remains essentially an affair of the *heart* by being tied to the emotions and particularities of his own life, Marcel, through the activity of his *esprit,* perceives the form of the music and moves, like Vinteuil, from the particular to the general.

Marcel also understands the relationship between the particular and the general to which Swann remains blind. For Marcel, Vinteuil is not simply an unknown composer but the real man he knew at Combray. He possesses, therefore, the relatively precise, material details concerning the composer's life that Swann lacks. Marcel knows that one of the most important sources of the music was the intense suffering Vinteuil experienced because of his daughter's sapphism. He learns not only that Vinteuil was able to transmute his suffering into joy through art, but also that Mlle Vinteuil and her friend have redeemed the suffering they caused by transforming Vinteuil's rough notations for the septet, that his death prevented him from completing, into the finished score played at the Verdurin concert.

By discovering beneath their apparent contrast the secret union between genius and vice, Marcel has found, without completely understanding its significance for him, the relationship between his own creative life and the suffering he endures because of his love for Albertine. That suffering also is linked to homosexuality, begins as in a "dawn of sorrow," and is juxtaposed to moments of joy. In fact, during the first night of his torment when Albertine comes to his hotel room at Balbec, Marcel sees her briefly in the perspective of art:

> Two or three times it occurred to me, for a moment, that the world in which this room and these bookshelves were situated and in which Albertine counted for so little, was perhaps an intellectual world, which was the sole reality, and my grief something like what we feel when we read a novel, a thing of which only a madman would make a lasting and permanent grief that prolonged itself through his life; that a tiny movement of my will would suffice, perhaps, to attain to that real world, to re-enter it, passing through my grief, as one breaks through a paper hoop, and to think no more about what Albertine had done than we think about the actions of the imaginary heroine of a novel after we have finished reading it.[14]

A greater effort of the will and much more suffering will be necessary

14. II, 374–75; *Sodome,* II, 1126.

before Marcel not only sees Albertine as the heroine of a novel but makes her a heroine in his own novel. Only then will he be able to give a spiritual form to his suffering and see Albertine in the *recul* not of someone else's art, as in idolatry, but of his own.

Although Marcel will continue to suffer, Vinteuil's music confronts him with the vision of a different future, for the music seems to him "the promise and proof that there existed something other, realisable no doubt by art, than the nullity that I had found in all my pleasures and in love itself, and that if my life seemed to me so empty, at least there were still regions unexplored."[15] Indeed, the triumphant phrase of the septet holds the promise of a kind of joy that no woman had ever made him desire. That phrase, he feels, is "the only Stranger that it has ever been my good fortune to meet." The communion with another person that Marcel does not achieve in his friendship with Saint-Loup or in his love for Albertine, he enjoys in his new love for Vinteuil. Above all, by communicating through the music with the artist's soul Marcel is brought closer to the threshold of his own. Turning inward he discovers in his own past similar moments of joy that revealed to him, like Vinteuil's music, the existence of "some definite spiritual reality":

> nothing resembled more closely than some such phrase of Vinteuil the peculiar pleasure which I had felt at certain moments in my life, when gazing, for instance, at the steeples of Martinville, or at certain trees along a road near Balbec, or, more simply, in the first part of this book, when I tasted a certain cup of tea.[16]

Although Marcel views these joyful impressions of his past life as "starting-points, foundation-stones for the construction of a true life," he does not imitate Vinteuil by recognizing in them the presence of his own soul. At the end of his encounter he is nevertheless convinced of the spiritual value of Vinteuil's music and of its superiority to the "insignificant reality" of life in time.

But later, when he has fallen back into time, even this conviction is brought into question. Hearing the septet played again by Albertine on

15. II, 563; *Prisonnière*, III, 263.
16. II, 642; *Prisonnière*, III, 374. In a marginal note to this passage in his manuscript Proust reminded himself to leave until the end of the novel any mention of the madeleine episode. He was obviously conscious of the fact that the narrator's allusion to this episode would be more fully justified *after* the revelations of involuntary memory in *Le Temps retrouvé*. When the madeleine is recalled later, no mention is made of "this book." See III, 1091, n 2.

the pianola, Marcel notices that the musical phrases that had been indistinct to him at the concert have now become "dazzling architectures," while those phrases that had been distinct can now be identified with phrases from other works by Vinteuil. More significantly, a phrase that he had first disliked he now likes the most, either because he has become accustomed to its ugliness, he thinks, or because he has discovered its beauty. This last change in his judgment awakens his former doubts concerning the value of art in general and of Vinteuil's music in particular:

> This reaction from the disappointment which great works of art cause at first may in fact be attributed to a weakening of the initial impression or to the effort necessary to lay bare the truth. Two hypotheses which suggest themselves in all important questions, questions of the truth of Art, of the truth of the Immortality of the Soul; we must choose between them.[17]

Basing his judgment on the evidence of his sensitivity, Marcel feels that the music surely "symbolizes" a spiritual reality for having given him such an impression of depth and truth. Unlike a literary work that gives only an "intellectual translation" of feelings and explains and analyzes them in the form of ideas, music, being free of the limits of language, "recomposes" the life of the soul and assumes the inflection of one's inner being. Music is a source of "intoxicating" joy precisely because it represents a "return to the unanalysed" and reveals a spiritual world that the intellect cannot explain away.

But Marcel cannot free his mind of the other hypothesis, "the materialist hypothesis, that of there being nothing":

> I began to doubt, I said to myself that after all it might be the case that, if Vinteuil's phrases seemed to be the expression of certain states of the soul analogous to that which I had experienced when I tasted the madeleine that had been dipped in a cup of tea, there was nothing to assure me that the vagueness of such states was a sign of their profundity rather than of our not having learned yet to analyse them, so that there need be nothing more real in them than in other states.[18]

Marcel's judgment on the value of art remains suspended, therefore, between the certainty provided by his sensitivity and the doubts of his intellect. Although he was able during the concert to make intelligence

17. II, 642; *Prisonnière*, III, 373–74. 18. II, 647; *Prisonnière*, III, 381.

the servant of his impression, with that impression weakened by time he is now reduced to "reasoning" in time and outside his impression. Having reached the threshold of his own inner world, he turns away.

If Marcel's encounter with the septet does not result in a definitive revelation of his artistic vocation, it is not simply because he allows his impression to be corrupted. Art cannot provide such a revelation, for just as art itself has its source in life, so must this revelation come from life. The septet can only help Marcel to reflect on the meaning of the joyful sensations produced by the church steeples or by the taste of the madeleine; it cannot become a substitute for them. It is also in this sense that the narrator can speak of Albertine as being of greater value to him than Vinteuil or Elstir, for although she seems to prevent the realization of his dream of becoming an artist, she nonetheless enriches the life that art will redeem. "A woman for whom we have a great longing," writes Proust, "causes us suffering, draws from us long series of feelings far more profound and vital than would an exceptional man who has aroused our interest."[19] If Vinteuil points to the future, Albertine creates a past that the future will reveal as the source of art.

The Age of Things

At the end of his love for Albertine Marcel's future seems to him as empty as his past. He visits Gilberte at Tansonville only to discover that time has reduced the once poetic world of his childhood to a group of lifeless objects. The river Vivonne appears "thin and ugly," and looking at it he finds it impossible to relive the years of the past. Even when Gilberte informs him that the "two ways" of his walks at Combray, that he had imagined as being so separate one from the other, are in fact united, he is surprised but indifferent. Until now, and despite his earlier doubts, his dream of becoming a writer had remained relatively "pure and intact," but this indifference in the face of the very reality that had once been the source of joy seems to prove that his dream can never be realized.

Then, at the end of his stay at Tansonville, it is his belief in the value of art itself that is more profoundly shaken than ever before. He reads a passage from the *Goncourt Journal* in which is described the same Verdurin salon that he himself knew so well. But Goncourt's description presents a reality so different from the one Marcel remembers, that the only way he can reconcile this difference is to believe either that his

19. II, 1021; *Temps retrouvé*, III, 907.

lack of talent had prevented him from appreciating the value of what he saw, or that literature is merely a lie whose prestige derives from the "illusory magic" by which it hides the insignificance of life. It is this last hypothesis that convinces him that his decision to withdraw from social and artistic life is justified. Leaving Paris and the world he knew behind, he retires to a sanatorium.

Several years pass before he decides to return to Parisian society. During the trip back by train his thoughts turn again to his lack of literary talent and to the inexistence of the ideal of art in which he had believed. And now a final encounter with nature reveals the extent of his disenchantment. At a stop in open country Marcel sees from the train a line of trees whose trunks are half lighted by the rays of the setting sun. Their beauty, however, produces no feeling of joy in him, but evokes only an "absolute indifference." Marcel has reached the end of the "Age of Things." Emptied of its mystery and no longer the source of those joyful impressions that had charmed him at Combray, the world appears as a lifeless surface without depth and without a "soul." Marcel must now acknowledge the death of his own artistic soul, for he too has become a "thing" without beliefs or desires, a past or a future, memory or ambition. Above all, he has abandoned all attempts to direct his life willfully toward a goal. With his life wasted and devoid of meaning there is no longer any reason, he feels, to deprive himself of the empty pleasures of society. He decides to attend a matinée given by the Prince and Princesse de Guermantes.

Reading the invitation Marcel realizes that a more positive reason has prompted his decision. The name Guermantes assumes for a moment the charm and significance it once had for him, and beyond it in the depths of his memory he sees reflected the world of his childhood at Combray. A curious transformation has begun to take place within Marcel. Having reached the limit of the "Age of Things" he is rediscovering the mystery of life experienced during the "Age of Names." And just as a name, Guermantes, is reborn with its former prestige, so the next day a place, the Champs-Elysées, regains its lost charm and plunges him again into the strange world of his forgotten past. As his carriage moves through the streets leading to the Champs-Elysées, Marcel finds himself embarked on a voyage through an inner time-space world:

> They were very badly paved at that time, but from the very moment we entered them, I was nevertheless recalled from my deep thought by a sensation of extreme smoothness; the carriage

> suddenly seemed to run more easily, more softly and noiselessly, *as when the gates of an estate open* and you glide over roads covered with fine sand or fallen leaves. Nothing of the sort had actually occurred, but I felt all at once *the removal of external obstacles,* as though I no longer had to make any effort of adjustment or attention, as we do even unconsciously when we come in contact with new objects; the streets through which I was passing were those long-forgotten paths I formerly used to follow when going with Françoise to the Champs-Elysées. The soil knew of itself where it was to go; *its resistance was overcome.* And, like an aviator who has been laboriously rolling along the ground and then suddenly takes off, I rose slowly toward the silent heights of memories past.[20]

Marcel has entered a world other than the one his senses perceive, a world that no longer "resists" him not only because it is spiritual and not material, but also because he himself is free of the desires that provoked resistance. This spiritual world *comes to him,* and because it is composed of his own memories requires no "adjustment." Completely detached from the reality outside himself, Marcel is also detached from the beliefs that had in the past imprisoned him. The centrifugal movement that formerly governed his life has come to an end. He is now oriented toward the past.

Marcel does not attempt, however, to understand the significance of his feeling of liberation. In fact, although it detaches him from the present, his impression gives him no new perspective on his past. The "gates" that open on the inner world of his memories reveal only a past seen as past and composed of "sad and sweet" images that are still relatively uniform. Then, whatever pleasure he experienced during his ride disappears and his discouragement returns when he attempts voluntarily to evoke moments of past time by means of his intelligence alone. Once again everything seems lost. Finding no trace of joy in his present "sterile lucidity" Marcel concludes that Bergotte's praise of "the joys of the spirit" is as empty and meaningless as his own existence stretching out behind him with "no depth, only length."[21]

The Intemporal Self

At Combray Marcel's father always amazes his family by revealing to them the circular form of their walks into the countryside. At the very

20. II, 985–86; *Temps retrouvé,* III, 858.
21. II, 991; *Temps retrouvé,* III, 866.

moment when they believe themselves to be far from their point of departure he demonstrates his "strategic genius" by suddenly asking: "Where are we?"

> And then, as though it had slipped, with his latchkey, from his waistcoat pocket, he would point out to us, where it stood before our eyes, the back-gate of our own garden, which had come, hand-in-hand with the familiar corner of the Rue du Saint-Esprit, to await us, to greet us at the end of our wanderings over paths unknown.[22]

Marcel experiences the same excitement of rediscovery when in the midst of the new and mysterious music of Vinteuil's septet he suddenly recognizes the familiar sonata:

> As, in a stretch of country which we suppose to be strange to us and which as a matter of fact we have approached from a new angle, when after turning out of one road we find ourself emerging suddenly upon another every inch of which is familiar only we have not been in the habit of entering it from that end, we say to ourself immediately: "Why, this is the lane that leads to the garden gate of my friends the X——; I shall be there in a minute."[23]

And now, when he feels farther away from his point of departure than ever before, when he finds himself in a strange world, not of beauty but of total emptiness, when he believes that everything is lost, his judgment on the meaning and value of his life is completely changed. For it is at this moment that Proust, demonstrating thereby his own strategic genius, presents the group of revelations that enable Marcel to fulfill the promise of the *moments bienheureux* of his youth. Unlike the actual Combray to which he had returned to find nothing, the world he now discovers exists within him, and although it is familiar, it is also totally new, for he approaches it from a "new angle," sees it in a perspective so unexpected that his return is in fact the beginning of a second voyage through time and space whose goal is the complete recapturing and redemption of his past through art. And the image to which Proust himself returns is once again that of the door:

> But sometimes it is just at the moment when all appears lost that a signal comes which may save us; after knocking at all the doors that lead nowhere, the only one through which we can

22. I, 88; *Swann*, I, 115.   23. II, 553; *Prisonnière*, III, 249.

enter, one which we might have sought in vain for a hundred years, we stumble against unwittingly, and it opens.[24]

Chance opens this "inner door" in the courtyard of the Guermantes' mansion when a passing carriage forces Marcel to step aside. He places his foot on a paving stone that is "a little lower than the one next to it," and suddenly, the simple sensation caused by the unevenness of the stones gives him an emotional conviction in no way dependent on the sterile lucidity of his intellect:

> immediately all my discouragement vanished before a feeling of happiness which I had experienced at different moments of my life, at the sight of trees I thought I recognised when driving around Balbec, or the church spires of Martinville, or the savour of a madeleine, dipped in herb tea, or from many other sensations I have mentioned, which had seemed to me to be synthesised in the last works of Vinteuil. Just as when I tasted the madeleine, all anxiety as to the future, all intellectual doubt was dispelled. The misgivings that had been harassing me a moment before concerning the reality of my literary gifts, and even of literature itself, were suddenly banished as if by magic.

Turning resolutely inward Marcel seeks to identify the source of the impression of "deep azure," "coolness," and "dazzling light" produced by the sensation of unevenness. As in the episode of the madeleine the material repetition of the sensation proves useless. So, forgetting the matinée, Marcel attempts to recall his original feeling:

> And almost immediately I recognised it; it was Venice, about which my efforts at description and the supposed "snapshots" taken by my memory had never yielded me anything, but which was brought back to me by the sensation I had once felt as I stood on two uneven flagstones in the baptistry of Saint Mark's, *and with that sensation came all the others connected with it that day,* which had been waiting in their proper place in the series of forgotten days.[25]

Now, always by chance for Marcel but carefully planned by Proust, other moments from the past are reborn and regained. In the Prince's library where Marcel waits for the concert in the salon to finish, a domestic lets a spoon clatter upon a plate. Filled again with joy Marcel recognizes in the sensation of heat and the odor of smoke the same line

24. II, 991; *Temps retrouvé,* III, 866.
25. II, 991–92; *Temps retrouvé,* III, 866–67.

of trees that, only a day earlier, he had contemplated with such indifference. This moment has returned, he realizes, because of the similarity between the sound made by the spoon and the noise of a hammer used by a railroad employee to repair a wheel of the train from which he had seen the trees. Next, two different moments of his life at Balbec are recovered: first when the sensation produced by the texture of a napkin he uses to wipe his mouth brings back a similar sensation from the past, and again when the strident noise made by a water pipe recalls the whistles of pleasure-boats off the Balbec shore. Finally, the sight of a book on the shelves of the library, *François le Champi,* resurrects the night of the bedroom drama at Combray and the child Marcel was then.

Although these resurrections of the past owe nothing to his intellect, Marcel realizes from the start that he must seek to elucidate the nature of the "identical pleasures" he has repeatedly experienced and to understand their significance for his life. He knows also that he is in a race against time, for as soon as the concert ends he will be obliged to enter the salon where his attention will be diverted by others and his impressions lost in the empty conversation of society. Taking full advantage of his solitude he confronts the enigma of his joy.

Marcel immediately recognizes the "great difference" that exists between the false impressions of the past provided by voluntary memory and the true impressions accorded him by involuntary memory. This difference in value between the two types of memory is confirmed all the more clearly for Marcel by the very differences he perceives between each of his "real impressions" of the past. The cause of these differences, he decides, is probably the fact that

> the slightest word we have spoken or the most insignificant gesture we have made at a certain moment in our life *was surrounded and illumined by things that logically had no relation to it* and were separated from it by our intelligence, which had no need of them for reasoning purposes; and yet, in the midst of these irrelevant objects ... the most insignificant gesture, the simplest act remain enclosed, as it were, in a thousand sealed jars [vases clos], each filled with things of an absolutely different colour, odour and temperature. Furthermore, these jars, ranged along the topmost levels of our bygone years—years during which we have been constantly changing, if only in our dreams and thoughts—stand at very different altitudes and give us the impression of strangely varied atmospheres.[26]

26. II, 994; *Temps retrouvé,* III, 870.

Unlike the "uniform painting" of the past life he possessed until now, Marcel has regained that life in all its variety, in all the individuality, autonomy, and particularity of its moments in time. Thanks to the successive revelations of involuntary memory, the true temporal dimensions of his life, partially exposed during his carriage ride through Paris, have been rendered more precise, for it is not an existence "all in length" he sees now, but an existence *in depth.*

As Marcel's explanation suggests, the richness and autonomy of each of the *vases clos* containing the past are the result of a peculiar set of paradoxes. If the reality present in each impression is what the intelligence *omitted* in the past, it is evoked in the present by a sensation precisely because of its previous exclusion. The very faults and limits of habitual perception have made possible the discovery of a reality that is no longer limited but complete. The sensation "common" to the present and to the past itself evokes what it omits—the other sensations tied to it in the past. *All* of Venice is "recreated" by the single sensation caused by the unevenness of the stones.

It is important to note that the sensations causing involuntary memory are produced by *things* that are themselves devoid of any value or meaning, at least at the moment when Marcel encounters them. Even the book, *François le Champi,* evokes the past by the mere sight of its title, and not because of all the images once associated with it. In other words, the resurrection of Combray is precipitated by an object and not by a memory. Although this book is an integral part of the bedroom drama it recalls, the other objects Marcel encounters are relatively unimportant to the scenes they help evoke. While a madeleine and tea were in fact consumed at Combray and stones were stepped on in Venice, the presence of these objects in the inner world Marcel regains is rather insignificant. Other objects like the spoon and the water pipe have no part at all in the memory of Balbec. Also, unlike the flowers and church steeples of the *instants profonds,* these objects are not in themselves sources of aesthetic impressions. Marcel directs his attention to the form of the past moment called forth by the sound of the spoon and not to the form of the spoon itself.

All this may simply prove that for involuntary memory it is the sensation produced by a material object and not the object itself that matters. But it is also true that a sensation of this sort could come spontaneously and gratuitously only from a thing without interest, a thing that is not an object of desire or attention, that is free of all associations, that can give only a sensation and nothing else. *The exterior world had to be reduced to "things," had to have its value destroyed by time, so that, no longer an end in itself, it could truly become a means to an end beyond itself, a means for discovering the spiritual world which time, through its very destruction of the falsely autonomous world of "names," has created within Marcel. The "soul" of the exterior world had to die before he could discover that its value and meaning could not be found in it but could come only from the "god" within himself. Disenchantment had to precede reenchantment.*[27]

Marcel knows that things would lose their power of resurrecting the past if he began to associate them with his present desires and impressions. He must stop looking at *François le Champi,* must forget it again, so that it can evoke Combray once more. In fact, Marcel understands the supreme paradox of involuntary memory, namely, that the moments of his past life had to be successively forgotten and lost in order to be regained:

> Yes, if, thanks to our ability to forget, a past recollection has been able to avoid any tie, any link with the present moment, if it has remained in its own place and time, if it has kept its distance, its isolation in the depths of a valley or on the tip of a mountain peak, it suddenly brings us a breath of fresh air—refreshing just because we have breathed it once before—of that purer air which the poets have vainly tried to establish in Paradise, whereas it could not convey that profound sensation of renewal if it had not already been breathed, for the only true paradise is always the paradise we have lost.[28]

The very forgetfulness which caused Marcel so much suffering when it foretold the death of a self, and which each time it was completed revealed to him an inner void, has made possible his present feeling of joy and of plenitude. This forgetfulness which has preserved the past was itself the inevitable result of Marcel's centrifugal movement toward the future during which he had attempted either to find an imaginary paradise or to flee from the hell reality had repeatedly exposed. By creating "distances" between the various past moments and the present, and be-

27. A brilliant interpretation of this fundamental paradox of loss and recovery related to the whole history of language can be found in Owen Barfield, *Saving the Appearances: A Study in Idolatry* (New York: Harcourt, Brace & World, 1965).

28. II, 994; *Temps retrouvé,* III, 870.

187

tween each of those moments, forgetfulness has guaranteed to each its "specific originality" and autonomy. Indeed, thanks to the long years he spent in a sanatorium, Marcel's entire past is "at a distance" from the present.[29] His past now seems "new" not simply because this distance has rendered it different from the present, but above all because it has rendered it *different from itself*. The Venice resurrected by involuntary memory is the same city Marcel visited at a certain time in his life, yet its present reality is not what his senses consciously perceived or what his memory tried to recall voluntarily. Until now his attitude toward the new had been ambiguous, for although he had often desired it, he had also feared it. Also, as a revelation of the unknown the new had often remained unknowable. But because the past Marcel regains through involuntary memory is *at once different from and similar to itself* it gives him something new that can also be fully known since it belongs to him. In other words, it gives him the two related joys of *renewal* and *recognition*.

Despite this already profound elucidation of his experience Marcel feels that he has not yet progressed beyond the degree of knowledge he attained at the time of his encounter with the madeleine and tea. He knows he must search out the cause of his happiness and of the feeling of certainty it has given him. What facilitates his search now is the fact that his past has been resurrected *more than once*. Therefore, *comparing* his present impressions not only with his past ones but also with each other, he discovers that what they have in common is that he has felt them "as if they were occurring simultaneously in the present moment and in some distant past." Once he has discovered this truth "in between" his different impressions, Marcel knows that involuntary memory has given not merely a moment from the past, but something which, *"common to both past and present, is far more essential than either"*:

> How many times in the course of my life had I been disap-
> pointed by reality because, at the time I was observing it, my
> imagination, the only organ with which I could enjoy beauty,
> was not able to function, by virtue of the inexorable law which
> decrees that only that which is absent can be imagined. And
> now suddenly the operation of this harsh law was neutralised,
> suspended, by a miraculous expedient of nature by which a sen-

29. The role of *oubli* in Proust's novel is discussed by Roger Shattuck in *Proust's Binoculars: A Study of Memory, Time, and Recognition in "A la recherche du temps perdu"* (New York: Random House, 1963), pp. 60–68.

sation—the sound of the spoon and that of the hammer, a similar unevenness in two paving stones—was reflected both in the past (which made it possible for my imagination to take pleasure in it) and in the present, the physical stimulus of the sound or the contact with the stones adding to the dreams of the imagination that which they usually lack, *the idea of existence*—and this subterfuge made it possible for the being within me to seize, isolate, immobilise for the duration of a lightning flash what it never apprehends, namely, *a fragment of time in its pure state. The being that was called to life again in me ... draws its sustenance only from the essence of things,* in that alone does it find its nourishment and its delight. It languishes in the contemplation of the present, where the senses cannot furnish this essential substance, or in the study of the past, rendered barren for it by the intelligence, or while awaiting a future which the will constructs out of fragments of the past and the present from which it has withdrawn still more of their reality, retaining only that part of them which is suited to the utilitarian, narrowly human purpose for which it designs them. But let a sound already heard or an odour caught in bygone years be sensed anew, simultaneously in the present and the past, *real without being of the present moment, ideal but not abstract,* and immediately the permanent essence of things, usually concealed, is set free and our *true self,* which had long seemed dead but was not dead in other ways, awakes, takes on fresh life as it receives the celestial nourishment brought to it. A single minute released from the chronological order of time has re-created in us the human being similarly released, in order that he may sense that minute. And one comprehends readily how such a one can be confident in his joy; even though the mere taste of a madeleine does not seem to contain logical justification for this joy, it is easy to understand that the word "death" should have no meaning for him; situated outside the scope of time, what could he fear from the future?[30]

Certainly, this is one of the most important passages in *A la Recherche du temps perdu,* for Marcel here discovers that involuntary memory has solved the many problems posed by his existence in time by miraculously revealing to him a world and a self existing outside of time. This intemporal reality found neither in the past nor in the present has been

30. II, 996; *Temps retrouvé,* III, 872–73.

formed by a kind of *metaphor* uniting these two previously irreconcilable divisions of time. But life had to be lived in time as a succession of mutually exclusive moments, the self had to die many times so that each moment of past time together with the self that lived it, having preserved its own identity, could unite with a present moment by means of an identical sensation.

This unit of intemporal reality can be called a bit of "pure time" because it has been purified or freed of all the imperfections of perception in time. Instead of the suffering and disappointment he experienced whenever the abstractions of his imagination and intelligence encountered the actuality of the exterior world, Marcel now has the joy of possessing a world that is at once *real and ideal,* present and absent, alive to his senses and open to his imagination. It is a *virtual* world in which essence and existence are one. But a time that no longer changes and whose destructive-creative action has been suspended is a time purified of the very characteristics that normally define its essence. The paradox of an intemporal unit of time is no more remarkable, however, than that of a past made present or of a process of memory that gives not a memory of the past but its living reality. In being recaptured, time the destroyer has been destroyed.

The fact that intemporal reality can be "isolated" and "immobilized" also attests to the transformation of time into space, for it is a "pure and intact" space that is contained in each of the *vases clos* resurrected from the past. Indeed, all of Marcel's lost time has been spatialized in the present. Although Venice, Balbec, and Combray have preserved their individual autonomy and identity, they no longer exclude each other successively in time. Thanks to the repeated acts of involuntary memory each city has come to take up its place next to the others. For the first time Marcel can see spread out before him the depth of his existence.

This space whose reality Marcel can now possess and assimilate is, of course, an *inner space* in which all differences revealing essence have been interiorized. And Marcel also has become an inner man, for the world resurrected by involuntary memory has itself brought forth a "being" analogous to it, *a being who also exists outside of time, who is real and ideal.* This simultaneous rebirth of world and self is not surprising since Proust carefully presents throughout the novel how each defines and determines the nature of the other. In fact, each of the selves from the past reborn in the present was formed through its contacts with its own particular world, was imprisoned by it and died with it, and now because of that very imprisonment and death has been liberated together with its world. Although each of these selves at the moment of its apparition also excludes Marcel's actual self, *none of them is equivalent to the "being" who gives him such delight.* When he is disagreeably struck by the sudden resurrection of Combray and becomes briefly the child who suffered alone in his room, his dismay changes to joy when he realizes that this impression, which at first seemed unlike the others, is in fact similar to them because it too is an instance of involuntary memory. The being who discovers something common between two or more impressions, who finds similarity in difference and unity in multiplicity, whose joy is its very activity, is the *creative spirit,* or the "little philosopher" who elucidates his impressions. It is this same *esprit* that Darlu had described as being real and not material, ideal and not abstract, and whose substance Proust while still a student had defined as "liberty." Marcel himself now realizes that he had failed to understand the meaning of Bergotte's praise of the "joys of the spirit," for just as he had confused his true past with the false images existing "outside" of it and recalled by voluntary memory, so his judgment on the value of the "spiritual life" was inaccurate because he had associated that life with the "logical reasoning" of his intellect.

The Marcel who makes these discoveries and becomes his "true self" is no longer the person who throughout most of his life lived in anticipation or fear of the future; nor is he the narrator who until now judged his past with pessimism. He is a man who can focus on a present that is not simply a transitional period between two voids but a moment which, having the consistency of the past, is nonetheless outside of time and, therefore, totally contained within himself. Liberated from time, Marcel is also liberated from his superficial self, from its desires and its search for truth in the exterior world, and from the self-consciousness associated with that search. This self-consciousness, long considered a barrier preventing contact with the exterior world, was also a barrier preventing Marcel from turning inward in order to discover his profound self. His loss of self-consciousness has made possible his new consciousness of his own essence.

Marcel has also lost his doubts concerning the existence within him of a *moi identique et permanent.* Looking back on the *instants profonds* of his youth at Combray and at his more recent experiences with involuntary memory he recognizes in the impressions of joy given him by all these encounters a "fundamental trait" of his nature. It is as if these im-

pressions were the *phrases-types* of his life between which he discovers
the fundamental unity of his existence in time. His life also resembles
those great works of the nineteenth century like Wagner's tetralogy or
Balzac's *Comédie Humaine* that Marcel, obviously expressing Proust's
own ideas, discusses in *La Prisonnière;* works whose unity was discovered by their creators only *after* they had written supposedly unrelated
pieces. Thus Balzac looking at his different novels at once like "a worker
and a judge," or like "a father and a stranger" drew from this "autocontemplation" the genial idea of combining his novels into a cycle in
which the same characters would continually return:

> A unity that was ulterior, not artificial, otherwise it would have
> crumbled into dust like all the other systematisations of medi-
> ocre writers who with the elaborate assistance of titles and sub-
> titles give themselves the appearance of having pursued a single
> and transcendent design. Not fictitious, perhaps indeed all the
> more real for being ulterior, for being born of a moment of en-
> thusiasm when it is discovered to exist among fragments which
> need only to be joined together. A unity that has been unaware
> of itself, therefore vital and not logical, that has not banned
> variety, chilled execution.[31]

It is through a similar process of autocontemplation that Marcel recognizes between the moments from his past now spatialized in the present
the continuity and permanence of his own essential identity. By bringing forth at once the inner world to be perceived and the self capable of
perceiving it, involuntary memory has filled the void or abyss Marcel
discovered whenever he attempted to search out his identity by means
of his intelligence alone. Now he too can look at his own life, whose
unity was formed unconsciously by him, at once like a "father" and like
a "stranger." In other words, because he is at once present in and absent
from his inner world, he can see the real pattern of his past subjective
relations with exterior reality in the objective perspective or *recul* of
an intemporal self. His spirit has encountered its own "inner country"
which, because it *exists,* convinces him of his own *existence.*

Marcel knows, however, that he cannot rely on involuntary memory
alone to solve all the problems of his life in time. Each place resurrected
from the past surrounds him only for a brief moment, and the dining
room by the sea at Balbec or the baptistry of Saint Mark's after having

31. II, 491; *Prisonnière,* III, 161.

overcome the "resistance" of the Guermantes mansion and "forced open its doors," must soon yield to the power of the present scene. Since he has decided to consecrate himself to the study of the essence of things, Marcel's problem now is to discover a means of "fixing" this essence, of rendering it durable. He knows that it would be useless to return to Balbec or Venice for their reality is within him. Indeed, he has learned through bitter experience the principal cause of all his disappointments in the past: "I came to realise clearly that disappointment in a journey and disappointment in a love affair were not different in themselves but merely the different aspects assumed in varying situations by our inability to find our real selves in physical enjoyment or material activity."[32]

All these facts convince Marcel that the only way he can secure his joy is to convert the world revealed to him during his *moments bien-heureux* into its "spiritual equivalent" by trying "to interpret the sensations as the [signs] of corresponding laws and ideas." In other words, the reality "formed" and "redesigned" in memory must now be redesigned again in *the form of a work of art.* Having been created by essences the mind must search out and create the "essential truths" contained in the joyful impressions of the past. Once again the activity of the *espirit* is described as a plunge into darkness and a bringing up into the light of consciousness:

> To read the [inner] book of these strange signs (signs standing out boldly, it seemed, which my conscious mind [attention], as it explored my unconscious self, went searching for, stumbled against and passed around, like a diver groping his way), no one could help me with any rule, for the reading of that book is a creative act in which no one can stand in our stead, or even collaborate with us.[33]

Proust's analogy comparing the act of creation to the reading of an inner book is significant for it represents a restatement of his belief that art must come from life. Because this "essential book" exists in each of us, the duty of a writer is not to "invent" it, but to "translate" it into the language of art.

Despite the importance he gives to his joyful impressions and to the essential truths they reveal, Marcel realizes that they are "too rare for

32. II, 1000; *Temps retrouvé,* III, 877.
33. II, 1001; *Temps retrouvé,* III, 879. Blossom translates "livre intérieur" as "subjective book."

the work of art to be composed wholly of them." These impressions must be "enchased" in truths that the intelligence "draws directly from reality," truths concerning "passions, characters, and customs." Proust is revealing here at least one of the reasons behind his decision to abandon the idea of writing a novel of "poetic moments." Such a novel would have presented a relatively narrow and static world which would have been incapable of showing all the different dimensions of man's existence in time. By providing impressions with a context of "laws" that can reflect and extend their meaning, the "intellectual truths" also provide them with a wider temporal context and make possible, consequently, a novel which can truly reveal the "becoming" of an artist.

This more complete vision of his future work acts as a revelation for Marcel, who now discovers the secret of his own becoming in time. He understands that the materials for literature had been stored up in him without his being able to foresee their final purpose or even their survival: "And so my entire life up to that day could . . . be summed up under the title, A Vocation."[34] Out of the world of relativity and change an absolute and autonomous world has grown within Marcel, formed and finally discovered by means of a series of chance encounters in time.

The Face of Time

Armed with this knowledge of his past, confident of his future, and feeling that "the liberation of the spiritual life" is sufficiently advanced in him for him to continue his thoughts and preserve his solitude even in society, Marcel now leaves the Prince's library and enters the salon. Immediately, however, he is struck by a curious spectacle. One by one he encounters different persons he knew in the past, but they have been so completely metamorphosed by time that he at first fails to recognize them. M. d'Argencourt, whom he knew as a haughty personage has been transformed into a decrepit clown. Gilberte is now a plump matron, and even Oriane de Guermantes, who once occupied the pinnacle of Parisian society, has taken to consorting with actresses and has become another Mme de Villeparisis. Marcel discovers that the entire social world of Paris has undergone profound changes, for the present Princesse de Guermantes is none other than the former Mme Verdurin.

What Marcel finds in the aged faces he sees is the living evidence of time's destructive-creative action revealed to him at the very moment

34. II, 1015–16; *Temps retrouvé*, III, 898–99.

when he was planning to express in a work of art the intemporal realities uncovered by involuntary memory. He has now truly recaptured the world of time and with it the reality of death—above all, the reality of his own impending death that could abruptly put an end to all his plans and in destroying him destroy his work before it was completed. This startling discovery of time's action would have been impossible, he realizes, if he had continued to live in time among the members of his social world. His long absence from Paris has again proved beneficial to him by creating the distance between past and present necessary to produce the shock of revelation. Now, however, that distance is not obliterated but exposed. During his absence time changed the persons Marcel encounters but it did not modify the images of them stored in his memory. Because he must here attempt to identify an unknown present instead of a known, if forgotten past, this difference between memory and reality increases the difficulty of his task.

What helps Marcel to recognize the individuals "disguised" by time is the one element which, despite certain modifications, has remained permanent, the factor which most strikingly reveals the presence of similarity in difference—the name. "A name," writes Proust, "is frequently all that is left to us of a human being, not when he is dead but even while he is still alive."[35] Thanks to the destructive action of time, names now have a function that is the reverse of the one they had during Marcel's youth. As long as they remained surrounded by the arbitrary images drawn from his imagination and projected outside himself by the force of his desires, names *prevented* him from recognizing individuals like the Duchesse de Guermantes and hid the reality of their life in time. With the destruction of Marcel's imaginary world and of his desires, names also have become means to an end. In fact, he now realizes that it is only *after* time has separated him from persons like the Guermantes that they can be truly known by means of their names.[36]

As he begins to identify the guests at the matinée Marcel perceives that names are not the only factors that have remained permanent despite the changes wrought by time. Although each individual, like himself, has undergone a whole series of transformations in time during which each successive self was replaced by another, it is also true that certain "moral cells that compose our being are more durable than it." Just as he had noticed during his imprisonment with Albertine that various

35. II, 1065; *Temps retrouvé*, III, 966.
36. II, 1072; *Temps retrouvé*, III, 975.

habits and character traits of his parents were present in him, so now he realizes, for example, that the vices and courage of the Guermantes could be found in Saint-Loup. Recognizing within himself "a certain feeling of idolatry for the future Gilbertes, Duchesses de Guermantes and Albertines," he must acknowledge again the permanence of his tastes in love that was also revealed during his imprisonment and that Vinteuil's music had helped him to perceive. Indeed, Marcel discovers the presence of similarities not only between the different selves of a single individual or between the different members of a family but also between individuals in one generation and in all generations:

> [by means of culture and fashion, a single wave spreads throughout the whole extent of space the same ways of speaking and of thinking, just as in the whole duration of time great groundswells lift up, from the depths of the ages, the same forms of anger and of sadness, the same exploits and the same fads through superposed generations, so that each section drawn from several of the same series presents *the repetition, like images projected on successive screens, of an identical painting.*][37]

As this vast vision of permanence in change so clearly shows, Marcel has come to realize through his encounter with the living reality of time that permanence is not and cannot be an attribute of the particular but only of the general, and must be expressed not by names, at least as they were used during his youth, but by words:

> I grasped the meaning of death and love, of intellectual pleasures, the value of sorrow or of a vocation. For . . . if names had lost their [individuality] for me, words disclosed to me their full significance. The beauty of an image is to be found behind the object—that of an idea, in front of it. So that the beauty of the former ceases to enrapture us when we have arrived at the object, but we do not understand the beauty of the latter until we have gone beyond the object.[38]

The new "Age of Words" Marcel has entered is now no longer as it was in the past a period of disintegration when language acts as a mediator between names and the empty reality of things by drawing pessimistic conclusions concerning the destruction of an imaginary world.

37. In French only: *Temps retrouvé*, III, 944.
38. II, 1039–40; *Temps retrouvé*, III, 932, n 1. Blossom translates "individualité" as "meaning."

He has discovered the true domain of the writer, for only words can give form to "ideas" and can incorporate and reflect in their permanence all the differences and variations of life in time. Just as involuntary memory demonstrated the real value of things and the spectacle of age revealed the true significance of names, so now has language itself been "renewed." Having ceased to be the expression of the narrator's reactions to life, it has become the instrument for the creation of a novel.

If the persons Marcel encounters destroy his abstract notions of the meaning of certain words, they also give him a more concrete vision of the different phases of his life. Seeing for the first time Gilberte's daughter, he realizes that in this Mlle de Saint-Loup all the "mysterious threads" of his past have combined in a rich web of memories. She appears to him as a living metaphor in which have been "fused" the two ways of his walks at Combray and with them all his dreams and experiences of love, friendship, society, and art. Neither the matter nor the energy that animated his life has been destroyed but only recreated in a new individual.

Thinking of her and of the past she incarnates, Marcel discovers the essential key to the form of his future novel:

> We could not recount our relations even with someone we have known only slightly without bringing in, one after the other, the most diverse settings of our life. Thus, every individual—and I was myself one of these individuals—measured the duration of time for me by the revolution he had accomplished, not only on his own axis, but about other individuals and notably by the successive positions he had occupied with relation to myself. And in truth, all these different planes on which Time, since I had come to grasp its meaning again at this reception, was arranging the different periods of my life, thereby bringing me to realise that in a book which aimed to recount a human life one would have to use, in contrast to the "plane" psychology ordinarily employed, a sort of three-dimensional, "solid" psychology [psychologie dans l'espace], added a fresh beauty to the resurrections of the past which my memory had evoked as I sat musing alone in the library, because memory, by bringing the past into the present unmodified, just as it appeared when it was itself the present, eliminates precisely that great dimension of Time which governs the fullest realisation of our lives.[39]

39. II, 1111; *Temps retrouvé*, III, 1031.

All the various laws of inner and outer mobility Marcel discovered in suffering and joy, in jealousy and imagination, in the bedrooms at Combray and Balbec and in the shifting perspectives formed by the steeples of Martinville, have acquired a new dimension through this vision of a "psychology in space." Marcel has realized that he must give his reader precisely what he himself gained through his encounters—"an optical view of the years" in which the multiplicity of places in space and the successive incarnations of an individual in time will be incorporated. In his novel the intemporal must be placed in the context of the temporal that led to its discovery, the whole complex pattern of becoming must be revealed in order to express not simply the poetry of certain privileged moments but the poetry of life in time, *its movement into unity*. The function of the creative *espirit* has been expanded. Whereas its task had been to discover unity in the multiple experiences of actual time, it must now reestablish distances so as to create the conditions whereby unity can be discovered within the virtual time of a novel. It must, as Coleridge said of the imagination, "dissolve, diffuse, dissipate in order to recreate." For Proust unity would cease to have meaning if it became the negation of the multiplicity that gave it birth. Unity is not just a state; it is the goal and result of an activity which discovers relationships between things which for that very reason must "omit" or "exclude" the identity of what unites them. Marcel conceives of a novel which, like Proust's, will always leave room for discovery.

Although the spectacle of age forces Marcel back into time, from which involuntary memory had briefly liberated him, it also demonstrates once again the supreme value of a life truly lived in time, complete with its failures and disappointments. Marcel can now fully understand the meaning of the eloquent moral lesson Elstir teaches him at Balbec when, in order to justify "all the fatuous or unwholesome incarnations" of his own self in time, he remarks: "We are not provided with wisdom, we must discover it for ourselves, after a journey through the wilderness which no one else can take for us, an effort which no one can spare us, for our wisdom is the point of view from which we come at last to regard the world." This point of view is evidence, concludes Elstir, not only that we have lived "in accordance with the laws of life and of the mind," but also that we have "extracted something that goes beyond them."[40] Such a transcendent point of view toward his world is what

40. I, 649; *Jeunes filles*, I, 864.

Marcel gains in *Le Temps retrouvé,* for it exists both in the vision of that equally transcendent "being" who delights in the discovery of new analogies and in the vision of the novelist who sees in the "psychology of space" the essential structure of his work. Forced to live in time, Marcel transcends it precisely because his discovery of the way time has formed his life reveals to him the artistic necessity of using time itself to form a new life in a novel. He realizes that time, like words, can be an instrument of creation.

8
Art

The revelations provided by Vinteuil's music, the miracles of involuntary memory, and finally the spectacle of man's existence in time do indeed mark the end of Marcel's long quest for a "vocation." It is, however, Marcel's encounter with the painter Elstir that most clearly and dramatically reveals the fundamental aspects of Proust's aesthetics. Marcel's observations on painting and impressionism are used by Proust to support not only his conception of literature but also of art in general. Nowhere else in the novel is there a more complete presentation of relationships which exist between the reader or spectator and a work of art, between the artist and reality. Above all, it is in his description of this encounter that Proust relates the theme of the enclosed, autonomous space to his vision of the nature of art.

The Virtual World

Marcel's encounter with Elstir's art takes place during his first visit to Balbec. Hoping to meet the girls of the *petite bande* he has no desire to waste his time with a painter, and if he decides finally to see Elstir, it is only in order to obey his grandmother's wishes. But once he enters the artist's studio his boredom and indifference are suddenly replaced by a feeling of joyful anticipation:

> I felt perfectly happy, for, with the help of all the sketches and studies that surrounded me, I foresaw the possibility of raising myself to a poetical understanding, rich in delights, of many forms which I had not, hitherto, isolated from the general spectacle of reality. And Elstir's studio appeared to me as the laboratory of a sort of new creation of the world in which, from the chaos that is all the things we see, he had extracted, by painting them on various rectangles of canvas that were hung every-

where about the room, here a wave of the sea crushing angrily
on the sand its lilac foam, there a young man in a suit of white
linen, leaning upon the rail of a vessel.

The important word is "poetical," for Marcel immediately senses that
Elstir is a maker, the creator of a new world drawn from reality yet
different from it. The painter has consciously "extracted" certain elements or motifs from the confusion and chaos of actuality, and it is
only when they have been thus "isolated" and formed by a creative act
that these elements can be fully *seen*. Marcel is discovering that the only
way to know the world is to see it through the eyes of an artist.

At the same time that he perceives this fundamental distinction between the opaqueness of life and the clarity of art, Marcel also begins
to understand the nature of images and their essential difference from
actual things:

> [The young man's jacket] and the spattering wave had ac-
> quired [a new] dignity from the fact that they continued to
> exist, even though they were deprived of those qualities in
> which they might be supposed to consist, the wave being no
> longer able to splash nor the jacket to clothe anyone.[1]

This observation seems at first glance very simple. Marcel is noticing
what anyone who has looked at a painting has noticed, namely, that
the objects represented are not real things or persons but only images in
paint. Despite its apparent simplicity, however, Marcel's observation is
the key to Proust's conception of art. For Proust the creative act results
in the "spiritualization of reality," and this spiritualization implies the
transformation of the actual into the virtual. Elstir extracts not a wave
but the appearance of a wave from material reality. Whereas in the
context of the actual world the function of a wave is to splash, in the
context of the painting its "new dignity" derives from its new function—
that of a pictorial motif expressing a particular vision of reality. The
extraction (or abstraction) of motifs from the actual world necessarily
implies the *exclusion* of that world together with its confusing appeal
to all the senses. Just as Vinteuil's works are composed only of sounds,
so Elstir creates a world that can be seen *because it is given only to vision*.
In other words, the reality of the world can be known and seen only by
*image*s that by definition determine their own modes of perception,

1. I, 627–28; *Jeunes filles*, I, 834. Moncrieff translates "une dignité nouvelle" as
"fresh dignity."

and that exist only within the limits of the virtual and *purified* space of a work of art.[2]

These same ideas can be applied with equal validity to literature. In *Du Côté de chez Swann* the narrator remarks that a novelist gives his reader a powerful sense of reality precisely because his characters are not "real" people:

> none of the feelings which the joys or misfortunes of a "real" person awaken in us can be awakened except through [an image] of those joys or misfortunes; and the ingenuity of the first novelist lay in his understanding that, as the [image] was the one essential element in the complicated structure of our emotions, so that simplification of it which consisted in the suppression, pure and simple, of "real" people would be a decided improvement. A "real" person, profoundly as we may sympathise with him, is in a great measure perceptible only through our senses, that is to say, he remains opaque, offers a dead weight which our sensibilities have not the strength to lift. If some misfortune comes to him, it is only in one small section of the complete idea we have of him that we are capable of feeling any emotion; indeed it is only in one small section of the complete idea he has of himself that he is capable of feeling any emotion either. The novelist's happy discovery was to think of substituting for those opaque sections, impenetrable by the human spirit, their equivalent in immaterial sections, things, that is, which the spirit can assimilate to itself. . . . [The novelist] sets free within us all the joys and sorrows of the world, a few of which, only, we should have to spend years of our actual life in getting to know, and the keenest, the most intense of which would never have been revealed to us because the slow course of their development stops our perception of them.[3]

Although the narrator's remarks accurately describe what is the discovery of any novelist, they are particularly relevant to his own experience and to the type of novel Proust himself wrote. As was shown, Marcel is continually forced to acknowledge his inability to possess the world outside himself. And when the reality of the exterior world is revealed, it often causes him intense suffering or diappointment. To use the

2. These ideas concerning the virtuality of art are treated by Susanne K. Langer in her book, *Feeling and Form: A Theory of Art Developed from "Philosophy in a New Key"* (New York: Charles Scribner's Sons, 1953).

3. I, 64–65; *Swann*, I, 85–86. Moncrieff translates "image" as "mental picture."

example provided by Elstir's painting, Marcel often begins with an image of a wave in his mind only to discover that in reality a wave splashes. His sole escape from the anguish he must endure each time the "deluge of reality" strikes him seems to lie in habit and forgetfulness. But if forgetfulness protects him from suffering, it also destroys his sense of time and change by creating a succession of selves. *A la Recherche* describes, therefore, *precisely those conflicts and difficulties of life in time and reality that, according to the narrator, it is the novelist's task to overcome, and that Proust in writing his novel did overcome by replacing the strangeness and otherness of the things of life by the strangeness and otherness of the images of art.*

The narrator's definition of the particular form reality takes in a novel adds new significance to Proust's metaphor of the "inner book" revealed by involuntary memory. It explains also why the act of autocontemplation is equated to the "reading" of one's own life. The book of memory gives a "new dignity" to Marcel's existence by revealing a past that has already been spiritualized. He discovers that in this virtual world all events, persons, places, and things "continue to exist" in their reality as images which can be fully possessed or assimilated by the mind. He can therefore see them because they have lost their opacity and know them without having to endure the pain of their actuality. Above all, because of the virtual existence of this world within him, Marcel is able to perceive the true forms of time and space.

The very words that Proust uses to describe the world revealed by involuntary memory apply as well to the world of art. Both are real and ideal without being actual and abstract. In both, persons and places are present as images but absent as actual things. Finally, because both worlds are virtual, they affirm the true existence of reality while at the same time revealing its essence. The world redesigned and rendered virtual by memory must, of course, be redesigned again by art, for art alone can order and give an expressive form to the images that memory has extracted from life. The past that is recovered through involuntary memory must be fully "read" and "translated" by art into the spiritual equivalents of language. Just as a painter gives a form to space by means of paint, so the novelist must form the time and space of his novel by means of words.

It is important to recall that the virtual world Proust presents is for Marcel an actual world until he discovers his vocation and begins to write his own novel. The reader, who can "possess" Albertine despite all her mystery because she is a character, reads the story of a man who cannot possess her as long as she remains for him a "real" person. In other words, the reader is given "ideas" of suffering created by Proust, but Marcel truly suffers. In his encounter with Vinteuil's music Marcel himself learns, of course, that for the artist suffering becomes joy once it is transformed into images or sounds and given form. As early as 1892 Proust expressed the same idea concerning this transforming power of art:

> Its lies are the only realities we know, and as soon as one begins to love them with a true love, the existence of those things that surround us and subjugate us diminishes little by little. The power of making us happy or unhappy is withdrawn from them so that it may grow in our soul where we convert sorrow into beauty. It is there that we find happiness and true liberty.[4]

The function of art is to liberate us from the prison of the actual world by converting things into images. This conversion can take place only within the "soul" because it results from the creative activity of the *esprit,* that Proust also defined as "liberty." Art alone can disarm reality without disfiguring it. Unlike habit and forgetfulness that allow us to escape suffering but blind us to its truth, art gives us knowledge of suffering and of the real world. For both the artist and the reader this knowledge is a source of joy. By means of art both are liberated not only from the subjugation of things but also from the egoism of the superficial self, which, because it is tied to the actual world, can alone by subjugated by it. The spirit of the artist, which is itself real and ideal, creates a world analogous to it, that in turn can be assimilated by the spirit of the reader.

The joy Marcel feels when he enters Elstir's studio is, for Proust, like the joy of the reader who enters the virtual world of art. In fact, the painter's studio seems a concrete symbol of the inner space of the creative spirit:

> The shutters were closed almost everywhere round the studio, which was fairly cool and, except in one place where daylight laid against the wall its brilliant but fleeting decoration, dark; there was open only one little rectangular window embowered in honeysuckle, which, over a strip of garden, gave on an avenue; so that the atmosphere of the greater part of the studio was dusky, transparent and compact in the mass, but liquid and

4. *Chroniques,* p. 129.

sparkling at the rifts where the golden clasp of sunlight banded it, like a lump of rock crystal of which one surface, already cut and polished, here and there, gleams like a mirror with iridescent rays.[5]

This description immediately recalls the works of Proust's favorite painter, Vermeer, which so often represent a room in which all the objects and figures are bathed in the light coming from a single window—a light that is also remarkably fresh and cool. Even more striking are the similarities between Elstir's studio and other such privileged places in the novel. It is cool and dusky like the bedroom in which the narrator first awakes to find "a darkness pleasant and restful for the eyes." It resembles the bedroom at Combray filled with an *obscure fraîcheur* where Marcel reads in the filtered sunlight. The painter's studio is also like Marcel's room in Paris in which he experiences the joys of solitude that transform his prison into an ark. In the clair-obscure, "in-between" atmosphere of these rooms the exterior world enters the space of the *esprit* in the form of images or "reflections" that are at once real and ideal. Proust's art in describing Marcel's room reveals some of the qualities he found in the domestic scenes painted by Chardin, an artist Proust admired for his ability to combine

> things and people in those rooms which are more than a thing and perhaps even more than a person, rooms which are the scene of their joint lives, the law of their affinities or contrarieties, the pervasive secreted scent of their charm, the confidant, mute yet [indiscreet], of their soul, the shrine of their past.

Like Chardin's paintings the privileged rooms of the novel express the "friendship" or "marriage" that exists "between warmth and materials, between beings and things, between past and present, between light and shade."[6] Both beauty and happiness are created by the same conditions of harmony.

One understands now why Proust wrote in 1904 to the Comtesse de Noailles that in a perfect work of art all elements are "bathed in the same atmosphere":

> For if one tries to discover what constitutes the absolute beauty of certain things . . . one sees that it is not profundity, or this or

5. I, 628; *Jeunes filles*, I, 834–35.
6. *Proust on Art*, pp. 332–33; *Sainte-Beuve*, pp. 372–74. Warner translates "indiscret" as "a blabber."

that other virtue that seems eminent. No, it is a kind of fusion [fondu], of transparent unity, where all things, losing their original aspect as things, have come to arrange themselves each next to the other in a kind of order, penetrated by the same light, seen each in the other, without a single word remaining outside, remaining refractory to this assimilation. . . . I suppose that it is what one calls the Polish [Vernis] of the Masters.[7]

Later, in his *Contre Sainte-Beuve,* Proust discovered the same perfection in Flaubert's style:

In Flaubert's style . . . all the elements of reality are converted into one uniform substance, composed of vast unvaryingly polished surfaces. No impurity remains. The surfaces have become like reflecting mirrors. All things are shown there, but only by reflection, without affecting its homogeneous substance. Everything that was at variance with it has been converted and absorbed.[8]

Fondu, vastes surfaces unies, transparence, assimilation, lumière, reflet— these are words that can be found in all of Proust's descriptions of artistic perfection both in his critical works and in the novel. Marcel uses them when he elucidates the qualities of La Berma's acting and Vinteuil's music, and they are implicit in Bergotte's judgment of that supreme example of artistic excellence, the "little patch of yellow wall" in the *View of Delft* by Vermeer.

The word *fondu,* which can be translated as "fusion" or "blending," is at once the most important and ambiguous of these expressions. Since Proust associates it with "assimilation" and "absorption" into a "uniform substance," it may be thought that this fusion of all elements implies the loss of their particularity and consequently of a real multiplicity. This is certainly not the case in *A la Recherche,* whose structure is based on a series of separate and distinct incarnations, apparitions, impressions, and events. However, when Proust speaks of *fondu,* he is really pointing to the difference that exists between the chaotic multiplicity of the actual world and the ordered multiplicity of the artistic components in a work of art. As Marcel learns when he looks at Elstir's paintings, the "uniform substance" of the artist's style and vision does not exclude the presence of a "multiform and powerful unity."[9] *Fondu* describes, there-

7. *Correspondance générale,* II, 86–87.
8. *Sainte-Beuve,* p. 207. Also translated in *Proust on Art,* p. 170.
9. I, 629; *Jeunes filles,* I, 835–36.

fore, the organic unity and autonomy of a work of art that an artist guarantees only by creating a purely virtual world in which things have lost their "original aspect as things" to become images or reflections of reality.

Here again the relationship between art and involuntary memory can be seen, for in the autonomous *vases clos* that Marcel discovers within himself the things of the past exist as virtual components of a distinct "atmosphere." In a work of art, as in the *vases clos,* the barriers between things that the intelligence creates for the needs of practical living are destroyed. Freed from the real world, the things of life are able to blend together so that *each reflects the others.* These analogies that reflections express are examples of the same "law" that governs the activity of the creative spirit as it seeks to discover similarity in difference and unity in multiplicity. The world enters the artist's mind in the same way that it enters Elstir's studio or Marcel's room in Paris—as reflections or images of reality that reveal the presence of hidden analogies.

Seeing and Knowing

Looking at the seascapes in Elstir's studio, Marcel discovers that such analogies are expressed by the artist in the form of "metaphors." By painting the land and sea as if one were the other, Elstir achieves a "metamorphosis" of reality and creates an

> unusual [image] of a familiar object, an [image] different from those that we are accustomed to see, unusual and yet true to nature, and for that reason doubly impressive to us because it startles us, makes us emerge from our habits and at the same time brings us back to ourselves by recalling to us an earlier impression.[10]

Marcel does indeed recall having experienced similar impressions when in the mornings at Balbec some effect of sunlight caused him to confuse the land with the sea or sky: "But presently my reason would re-establish between the elements that distinction which in my first impression I had overlooked."[11]

Proust is describing here, as he does so often in the novel, the fundamental problem of the conflict between sensitivity and intelligence. An impression that excludes the habitual world and the familiar identity of

10. I, 630; *Jeunes filles,* I, 838. Moncrieff translates "image" as "picture."
11. I, 628; *Jeunes filles,* I, 835.

objects is in turn excluded by the intelligence that restores to objects their accepted names. "The names which denote things," writes Proust, "correspond invariably to an intellectual notion, alien to our true impressions, and compelling us to eliminate from them everything that is not in keeping with itself." Elstir can capture and preserve these fleeting impressions in his paintings because, although he possesses an exceptionally cultivated intelligence, he is able "to strip himself, when face to face with reality, of every intellectual concept." Elstir paints what he sees and not what he knows. This idea of the incompatibility of seeing and knowing was an essential part of the aesthetic of impressionism. Proust himself found the idea expressed by Ruskin in reference to the work of Turner. Also, it must be recalled that Proust admired in Mme de Sévigné and employed in his own descriptions the method of presenting things or persons "in the order of our perception of them, instead of first having to explain them in relation to their several causes." There are, however, certain ambiguities present in this particular conception of seeing.

In his remarks on Elstir, Proust condemns as false what can be called our habitual vision. Only those impressions that destroy the abstract notions formed by our habits and intelligence can restore to us our "first vision," which, according to Proust, is composed of "optical illusions." Certainly, Proust does not mean to suggest that all art derives from such illusions. What matters is that the vision of the artist be free of habitual modes of seeing the world. Yet these optical illusions serve a useful purpose in Proust's demonstration, for they most strikingly reveal the existence of analogies or metaphors in nature. It is partly for this reason that Elstir's painting can be said to reflect "the rare moments in which we see nature as she is, with poetic vision." But to see nature "poetically" also means to see it with the eyes of an artist. If Elstir succeeds in preserving these rare moments that are so quickly lost by Marcel, it is not simply because the painter excludes from his mind the abstract notions of his intelligence. He *knows* what Marcel does not know—how to recreate the illusions he sees in art.[12] Marcel himself demonstrates the importance of having a knowledge of expression when he succeeds in writing his descriptive piece on the illusion created by the steeples of Martinville. The artist does not copy the metaphors he finds in nature; he is the *maker* of metaphors. The revelations of his "first vision" can

12. This is the principal argument of Gombrich's book *Art and Illusion*.

supply him only with the motifs for a work of art. It is his conscious, intellectual vision of his art that creates the work.

Marcel's own careful analysis of Elstir's art shows that it is indeed the result of a conscious and deliberate creative act. Looking at a picture representing the port of Carquehuit, Marcel admits that Elstir's metaphoric technique of painting the land and the sea in terms of each other creates an illusion in which no real differences seem to exist between the two elements. When he looks more closely at the painting, however, Marcel's intelligence does succeed in distinguishing those parts which represent the sea from the others which represent the land. By separating the two terms of Elstir's metaphor, he is able to perceive all the more clearly the variety of forms that the sea or the land can take. In other words, by distinguishng the multiplicity of forms that compose the painting, he *discovers* the sources of its unity. Both for the critic and for the artist an impression must be elucidated by the intelligence if it is to be understood or recreated in a work of art.

One can readily accept Proust's idea that an artist recreates things by taking away their names or by giving them other names. Elstir does this when he paints the land as if it were the sea. But he does not forget that land and sea are separate elements. As Marcel's elucidation demonstrates, it is precisely because the painter does know that they are separate that he is able to combine them so skillfully together. The new names Elstir gives to things would be meaningless if the knowledge of their old names were lost. "The words which are fused into a poem," writes W. K. Wimsatt, Jr., "have their new value not by losing their first or ordinary meanings but only by retaining these."[13] Elstir's painting would not impress Marcel as the revelation of a new truth if *he* did not know that land and sea are separate. And when he recognizes the identity of these elements in the painting, he does not destroy the impression it produced; he understands how it was created. He realizes that the painter succeeds in preserving the fleeting impressions he receives from nature because he is able to recreate the unknown out of the known.

It is interesting that Marcel's elucidations reveal as much about Proust's novel as do Elstir's paintings. Although *A la Recherche* contains "moments" and "illusions" comparable to those Elstir captures in his works, it also presents the stages of the creative process Marcel attempts to discover behind the paintings. Since *A la Recherche* describes both

13. W. K. Wimsatt, Jr., *The Verbal Icon: Studies in the Meaning of Poetry* (New York: The Noonday Press, 1964), pp. 129–30.

the *sources* of its own unity and the way certain illusions are *destroyed,* the "old names" of things are retained within the text itself as are the "lines of demarcation" separating one element from another. But the great lesson Marcel learns from Elstir and that Proust repeats throughout his work is the necessity of artistic integrity. Therefore, when Proust writes that Elstir paints what he sees and not what he knows, he means that the painter does not allow his habitual vision to corrupt his artistic vision of reality. Elstir's refusal to allow his consciousness to be corrupted represents, nevertheless, an intellectual choice. He possesses an "experimental faith" in the value of his sensitivity and of his artistic "instinct." Elstir has learned what Marcel also learns "little by little" through his encounters with reality, that sensitivity alone reveals the truths intelligence elucidates.

Inner Reality

Marcel's discovery that Elstir paints reality "as it is" exposes another aspect of Proust's aesthetics that calls for clarification. Proust is intent on demonstrating in the first part of his description of Marcel's encounter that art does in fact correspond to exterior reality. By recalling his own impressions of optical illusions Marcel not only shows that Elstir's art comes from life, he also tests and proves the truthfulness of the painter's vision. The fact that others have had impressions similar to those of an artist does not diminish the value of art. By perpetuating his impressions he helps others to see them more clearly. For Proust the artist is like an "optician" who by lifting us out of our habitual selves enables us to perceive new aspects of reality.

He expresses these ideas more explicitly at the end of the novel:

> It is only by a habit acquired in the insincere language of prefaces and dedications that the writer says "my readers." In reality, each reader reads only what is already within himself. The book is only a sort of optical instrument which the writer offers to the reader to enable the latter to discover in himself what he would not have found but for the aid of the book. It is this reading within himself what is also in the book which constitutes the proof of the accuracy of the latter and *vice versa*—at least to a certain extent, for any discrepancy between the two texts should often be laid to the blame of the reader, not the author.[14]

14. II, 1024; *Temps retrouvé*, III, 911.

Although in this passage Proust is primarily interested in showing that art corresponds to an *inner* reality, no contradiction exists in his views on its value. Novels and paintings reveal truths about the exterior world, but they do so only by forcing the reader or spectator to "read himself." If Elstir's paintings strike Marcel as revelations about the world, it is because they immediately recall to his mind his own past impressions. His memory then helps him to perceive how the artist created his work. In this way, the impressions produced by Elstir's paintings become his own and he truly sees the world with the eyes of an artist. Walter Pater once wrote:

> "To see the object as in itself it really is," has been justly said to be the aim of all true criticism whatever; and in aesthetic criticism the first step toward seeing one's object as it really is, is to know one's own impression as it really is, to discriminate it, to realize it distinctly.[15]

The purpose and method of Marcel's and Proust's criticism is clearly stated here. Marcel sees the world "as it really is" because he sees Elstir's painting "as it really is" by elucidating his impression. This elucidation completes the liberating action of art, which, by lifting him out of his superficial self and plunging him into his inner self, destroys the barriers that habit created between the reality of the exterior world and reality of the interior world.

Marcel soon discovers that art also corresponds to the inner reality of the artist. Looking at different portraits of women painted by Elstir he notices that they all resemble each other. Alhough this "ideal type" becomes near the end of Elstir's life an idol when he finds it already realized for him by his wife, throughout most of his creative life it exists within him as part of his "inner country" and can be fully expressed only in art. In order to express his ideal Elstir often completely transforms the features of a model's face. "Artistic genius in its reactions," writes Proust, "is like those extremely high temperatures which have the power to disintegrate combinations of atoms which they proceed to combine afresh in a diametrically opposite order, following another type."[16]

Although here again Proust is showing that art is a metamorphosis

15. Walter Pater, *The Renaissance: Studies in Art and Poetry* (New York: The New American Library, 1959), p. xii. The relation between the aesthetics of Pater and Proust has been studied by Joseph E. Baker, "Ivory Tower as Laboratory: Pater and Proust," *Accent,* XIX, no. 4 (Autumn 1959), 204–16.

16. I, 647; *Jeunes filles,* I, 861.

of reality, it can be argued that such transformations hardly reveal the world as it really is. In one sense this is true, for despite the fact that Elstir eventually finds in his wife a perfect realization of his ideal, this ideal was never seen by anyone else before he painted it. Marcel's recognition of Elstir's ideal is based on his memory of other portraits by the artist, not on his memory of any impressions directly received from the exterior world. Yet it is also true that all of Elstir's seascapes resemble each other and reflect, therefore, the presence of a certain inner ideal.

This apparent problem is resolved later in the novel during one of Marcel's visits to the Verdurin salon. The Patronne shows him an aquarelle by Elstir representing roses that she herself chose and arranged for the painter. Marcel immediately perceives that Elstir's roses only half resemble the real ones of the past. So clearly does their image reveal the painter's unique vision that these roses are in fact members of a "new variety" which without Elstir one would have never known. Marcel concludes that the painter's work is truly original and creative because "Elstir was unable to look at a flower without first transplanting it to that inner garden in which we are obliged always to remain."[17] Whether an artist receives from nature impressions containing his ideal, or must seek it by breaking through surface appearances, he sees the world only within the inner space of his creative mind. By interiorizing the exterior world and expressing his vision in a work of art, the artist literally and figuratively *makes* the world his own. He makes it real in the only sense that anything can be real, by creating something new. The artist does not represent objects or persons so much as he gives expression to his impressions, and these impressions are truly his own when they show forth his ideal.

For Proust the "reality" of an original artist's inner world is proven by the fact that it is eventually recognized by others in the exterior world. At first people refused to recognize Renoir as a great painter. But in time his vision recreated theirs, and now "women pass in the street, different from what they used to be, because they are Renoirs."[18] An original artist always sees the world as it really is because he always reveals previously unseen or unknown aspects of reality. Unlike others he does not see things *sous la catégorie du temps,* that is, according to the particular habits of thought and conventions of beauty that exist at a certain time. Rather, he sees the world *sous un aspect d'éternité,* in the light of his

17. II, 244; *Sodome,* II, 943.   18. I, 950; *Guermantes,* II, 327.

own inner reality, which, although it was discovered by him only through repeated encounters in time, is intemporal. The work of such an artist appears strange and shockingly new until in time others, through their encounters with his works, learn to see the world as it really was for him.

"Each artist," writes Proust, "seems . . . to be the native of an unknown country, which he himself has forgotten, different from that from which will emerge, making for the earth, another great artist."[19] Just as Elstir's paintings awaken Marcel's memory of similar impressions, so the impressions the painter receives from the exterior world recall his "forgotten country." His talent is "like a kind of memory" which helps him to *recognize* in his impressions the existence of his ideal. Escaping from the prison of habitual vision the artist's creative spirit plunges into its own world, for the true "artistic sense," writes Proust, is this "submission to inner reality." And because self and world are inseparable at this depth, when an artist shows forth his inner reality in his works, he also reveals to others the elements composing his "soul":

> But is it not the fact then that from those elements, all the *real residuum* which we are obliged to keep to ourselves, which cannot be transmitted in talk, even by friend to friend, by master to disciple, by lover to mistress, that ineffable something which makes a *difference in quality* between what each of us has felt and what he is obliged to leave behind at the threshold of the phrases in which he can communicate with his fellows only by limiting himself to external points common to us all and of no interest, art, the art of a Vinteuil like that of an Elstir, *makes the man himself apparent,* rendering externally visible in the colours of the spectrum that intimate composition of those worlds which we call individual persons and which, without the aid of art, we should never know?[20]

Through art Elstir brings his true self into being and reveals himself to others as *he* really is.

The True Life

When in *Le Temps retrouvé* Proust through his narrator presents more directly his conception of art, his remarks reflect the lessons Marcel learns from Elstir and Vinteuil. "The grandeur of real art," he writes,

> is to rediscover, grasp again and lay before us that reality from which we live so far removed and from which we become more

19. II, 558; *Prisonnière*, III, 257.   20. II, 559; *Prisonnière*, III, 257–58.

and more separated as the formal knowledge which we substitute for it grows in thickness and imperviousness—that reality which there is grave danger we might die without ever having known and yet *which is simply our life. Life as it really is, life disclosed at last and made clear, consequently the only life that is really lived, [is literature]*.[21]

Not only do most men fail to discover this true life within themselves but many artists and writers as well. At the same time that he expresses his views on the greatness of art, Proust repeatedly attacks "the falseness of the art that calls itself 'realist'" and that copies only the surface reality seen by habitual vision. Instead of penetrating the crust of the familiar and conventional, this "realism" merely presents a "cinematographic parade" of things. So uncompromising is Proust's attack on this particular form of artistic failure, that an investigation of its nature is essential if the remaining aspects of Proust's aesthetics are to be understood.

Certainly, the best example of "realist" art in *A la Recherche* is Proust's pastiche of the *Goncourt Journal*. In fact, of all the "works of art" that Marcel encounters, it is the only one that actually exists in the novel and, therefore, the only one the reader can directly appreciate. For eight full pages Proust has Goncourt describe his visit to the Verdurin's house in Paris where he meets Cottard, Swann, and other members of the "little clan." Not only does Goncourt describe part of the very world of *A la Recherche,* he also reveals in his style almost all the faults Proust condemned and sought himself to avoid. The Goncourt pastiche is really an anti-Proustian novel. For this reason, when Marcel at the end of the "Age of Things" reads the *Journal* and decides that literature reveals no profound truth, the reader who has just read most of Proust's novel cannot agree.

What immediately strikes the reader about Goncourt's style is that it is extraordinarily self-conscious and self-indulgent. He describes everything he sees or hears—the flowers, the dinner plates, the anecdotes of the guests—and just as each object is considered a "masterpiece" worthy of his attention, so each guest is presented as being remarkable or admirable. The result of this boundless curiosity for the world outside himself is a rather comic paradox. By talking so much about the things

21. II, 1013; *Temps retrouvé,* III, 895. Blossom's translation does not include the words "c'est la littérature." I have changed punctuation in accord with the original.

he sees and by exaggerating their value he ends by destroying their reality and value for the reader. Indeed, the reader feels crushed and finally excluded by a style that seems little more than an endless pouring forth of words, a kind of verbal equivalent of the Verdurin's house filled with the *disjecta membra* of history. Above all, there is the overpowering presence of Goncourt himself who never misses an opportunity to demonstrate his knowledge and culture. His "realism" is simply a tiresome *bavardage artiste* composed of "those remarks that come from the lips rather than the *mind.*"

Goncourt is a victim of the worst type of idolatry, for he believes that he has only to reproduce the beautiful objects and interesting anecdotes he finds in life in order to create a work of art. For Proust, however, it is not *what* the artist sees that matters, but *how* he sees it:

> the men who produce works of genius are not those who live in the most delicate atmosphere, whose conversation is most brilliant or their culture broadest, but those who have had the power, ceasing in a moment to live only for themselves, to make use of their personality as of a mirror, in such a way that their life, however unimportant it may be socially, and even, in a sense, intellectually speaking, is reflected by it, *genius consisting in the reflective power of the writer and not in the intrinsic quality of the scene reflected.*[22]

It is true that Proust himself not only lived for many years in a brilliant social world, but also possessed a highly developed intelligence and a remarkably extensive culture. His experience and knowledge are demonstrated in the novel and shared by his narrator. But in *A la Recherche* this type of "knowing" does not corrupt "seeing"; it becomes the servant of vision. Whereas Goncourt's style is encumbered by the "opaque and refractory material" of his superficial self, in Proust's novel all this material has been "assimilated" and "spiritualized." Goncourt presents not the "reflections of things" but as it were, things themselves such as they exist in the actual world. His is a "literature of notations" that fails to show that things "have no meaning if one does not extract it from them."

These peculiarities of Goncourt's writing add still another dimension to the conflict between seeing and knowing. Any distinction in his case between habitual and artistic vision is meaningless, because what has become habitual for him is a way of seeing the world that is completely

22. I, 423; *Jeunes filles,* I, 554–55.

determined by his knowledge of certain stylistic tricks and techniques. Like habit, his "art" is flat, repetitive, and totally predictable. But an art that is habit, that imprisons the mind and prevents it from truly seeing the world is of course no art at all. As Proust insists throughout the novel, great works are always unpredictable, surprising, and new, because artistic creation is an exercise in freedom—freedom not only from habitual modes of vision or from the idolatry of culture, but also from the limits imposed by any particular set of techniques. In his encounters with La Berma, Vinteuil, and Elstir, Marcel notes that while each is a master of his craft, there is nothing artificial or pretentious about their art. The way they express themselves, the artistic means they employ, never corrupt or obscure the purity and directness of the impression their works present. For this reason their techniques and vision seem to others and are for themselves "involuntary." What is both voluntary and highly conscious is their desire to express and the act of expression itself. In Goncourt the very idea of expression loses its meaning, for what is completely absent from his world is the experience of a creative encounter. It would seem that no truly original impression had ever led him to question his habits of thought. Those superficial "impressions" he does describe remain tied to the exterior world and show no evidence of ever having had a "personal root" within him. "The human plagiarism which it is most difficult to avoid," writes Proust, "is the plagiarism of ourselves."[23] Goncourt's art is a prime example of this plagiarism, which explains why his works resemble each other in such an uninspiring manner. The similarities that exist between the works of a great artist are revealed through an act of discovery, for they are found in the unique vision that fuses all the elements of his art and that lies beneath surface particularities. In Goncourt it is not the conscious expression of an impression that the reader finds but the self-conscious demonstration of "talent." His art is like that of the minor actresses who appear with La Berma in *Phèdre*—a virtuoso performance without depth.

This absence in Goncourt of any vision that transcends the contingent world and transforms its reality signifies for Proust the absence of a true style:

> for style is for the writer, as for the painter, a question, not of technique but of vision. It is the revelation—impossible by direct and conscious means—of the qualitative differences in the

23. II, 687; *Fugitive*, III, 436.

way the world appears to us, differences which, but for art, would remain the eternal secret of each of us.[24]

As the revelation of a qualitatively different vision of reality, style is most effective when it discovers and expresses the hidden relationships that exist between objects. In other words, style is fundamentally related to metaphor:

> An hour is not merely an hour. It is a vase filled with perfumes, sounds, plans and climates. What we call reality is a certain relationship between these sensations and the memories which surround us at the same time . . . , the only true relationship, which the writer must recapture so that he may forever link together in his phrase its two distinct elements. One may list in an interminable description the objects that figured in the place described, but truth will begin only when the writer takes two different objects, establishes their relationship—analogous in the world of art to the sole relationship in the world of science, the law of cause and effect—and encloses them in the necessary rings of a beautiful style, or even when, like life itself, comparing similar qualities in two sensations, he makes their essential nature stand out clearly by joining them in a metaphor. . . . From this point of view regarding the true path of art, was not nature herself a beginning of art, she who had often allowed me to know the beauty of something only a long time afterwards and only through something else—midday at Combray through the sound of its bells, the mornings at Doncières through the hiccoughs of our hot-water furnace? The relationship may be uninteresting, the objects mediocre and the style bad, but without that relationship there is nothing.[25]

This passage is remarkable not only because it shows the importance Proust attributes to metaphor, but also because it reveals how extensive his conception of metaphor is. The purely literary metaphor which is the conscious creation of the artist is related by Proust to the metaphors of time and space revealed by involuntary memory and to those metaphoric transformations of nature he experiences in the solitude of rooms. As Marcel learns, these "natural" metaphors also help to explain the particular quality of Elstir's art. Although Proust repeatedly demonstrates in the novel his mastery of literary metaphor, it is evident that he

24. II, 1013; *Temps retrouvé*, III, 895.
25. II, 1008–9; *Temps retrouvé*, III, 889–90.

considers it to be only the most striking example of a far more comprehensive form of perception which is the ability of the creative spirit to discover similarity in difference, or the "common essence" that unites two objects. It is his possession of this particular ability that "reassures" Marcel when after reading the *Goncourt Journal* he feels discouraged because of his lack of talent for "observing" society:

> Like a geometrician who, stripping things of their perceptible qualities, sees only their linear substratum, what people said escaped me because what interested me was not what they wanted to say, but the way they said it in so far as it revealed their characters or their ludicrous traits; or, rather, there was one thing which had always been the object of my investigation because it gave me a very special pleasure, and that was the point that two human beings had in common.[26]

Given the many detailed descriptions in *A la Recherche* it would be difficult to accept Marcel's (or Proust's) claim that he is a poor observer of the exterior world. Nevertheless, these descriptions are never presented as ends in themselves but as means for revealing a more profound reality existing beyond the surface of things, a reality that finds expression in metaphor or in some general "law" of individual or social behavior. Such laws can be discovered only in time for they depend on the mind's ability to perceive relationships between the sensations of the present and the memories of the past. By describing only the things of the present, "realism" destroys "all communication of our present self with the past, the essence of which was preserved in those objects, or with the future, in which they stimulate us to enjoy the past anew."[27]

During one of his own visits to the Verdurin's house on the Quai Conti in Paris, Marcel discovers, unlike Goncourt, that the identity of their drawing room is situated "halfway down, [beyond surface appearances], in a zone somewhat recessed."[28] Brichot tells him that the present room can give him some idea of the room of twenty-five years ago, when the Verdurins lived on the Rue Montalivet. His own memories of La Raspelière now help Marcel to recognize "a certain common air of family life, a permanent identity" in the arrangement of the furniture. He realizes that beyond the physical reality of the present room Brichot sees that "unreal part" of it existing in the substance of his soul, and of

26. II, 888; *Temps retrouvé*, III, 718.   27. II, 1005; *Temps retrouvé*, III, 885.
28. II, 888; *Temps retrouvé*, III, 718. Blossom translates "au-delà de l'apparence elle-même" as "below the range of vision."

which the external, actual part is only a prolongation. By giving a history to things memory spiritualizes matter. A continuity is established between inner and outer worlds with the result that each, by becoming an extension of the other, gains a new and purely spiritual value. This existence of the past in the present creates an "hallucination," an optical illusion in time, and the objects in the room seem at once actual and virtual. Marcel sees objects which,

> for Brichot, an old frequenter of the Verdurin parties, had that *patina,* that *velvety bloom* of things to which, giving them *a sort of profundity,* an astral body [leur double spirituel] has been added; all these things scattered before him, sounded in his ear like so many resonant keys which awakened cherished likenesses in his heart, confused reminiscences which, here in this drawing-room of the present day that was littered with them, cut out, defined, *as on a fine day a shaft of sunlight cuts a section in the atmosphere,* the furniture and carpets, and pursuing it from a cushion to a flower-stand, from a footstool to a lingering scent, from the lighting arrangements to the colour scheme, carved, evoked, spiritualised, called to life a form which might be called *the ideal aspect,* immanent in each of their successive homes, of the Verdurin drawing-room.[29]

The light of memory not only transforms the room into a privileged space for the mind, it also changes it into a momentary work of art by covering the objects with a *patine* or *velouté* that is comparable to the *vernis* or *fondu* of a masterpiece in which things reflect each other. The artistic promise expressed at the beginning of the novel in the "kaleidoscope of the darkness" with its whirling furniture and in the projections of the magic lantern has here been partially realized. Through its own projections memory creates a metaphor which unites the present with the past, the objects of the exterior world with their "spiritual equivalent." The self no longer excludes this world, nor is it excluded by it. By revealing the common traits that relate the objects the mind sees to the images of them the mind already possesses, memory makes it possible for the self to find itself in the exterior world, to accept that world and to assimilate it.[30]

29. II, 579; *Prisonnière,* III, 286.
30. An excellent discussion of the passages on the *Goncourt Journal* and the Verdurin salon can be found in Leo Bersani, *Marcel Proust,* pp. 150–54. My own analysis coincides with his on several points.

It is now possible to recognize behind *all* of Marcel's discoveries the same fundamental "method" Proust described in his preface to *The Bible of Amiens:*

> To read one book of an author is [to have only one encounter with him]. Now, one conversation with a person may reveal in him a number of singular traits. But it is only their repetition in particular circumstances that will ensure one's recognition of them as characteristic and essential features of his personality.[31]

The general laws of human behavior, the fundamental traits of an individual's character, the ideal form of a place, and the *phrases-types* of an artist's work that reveal his inner country are all discovered by Marcel through his repeated encounters with reality that form his memory and consequently give form to his world by enabling him to recognize similarity in difference, unity in multiplicity, and the identical in the successive. In this way Marcel moves from the particular to the general or essential, which, although it is immanent in each individual manifestation, ultimately exists beyond them and within himself. Through the metaphoric action of memory Marcel internalizes the exterior world and makes it his own.

In his description of Marcel's encounters and, therefore, of the "actual" world in which they take place, Proust shows that his interest is not only in the general laws or essences his hero discovers, but also in the way they are discovered. It has been noted repeatedly that these encounters are creative because they are also in varying degrees destructive. Marcel must lose his false notions about the real world in order to discover what determines its form. Indeed, *Proust's own realism derives from his ability to describe both these aspects of an encounter.* On the one hand, he gives the reader and Marcel a sense of reality by exposing the falsity of abstract notions and the limits of pure imagination. In this sense reality is the world of the particular or actual that destroys Marcel's dreams, disrupts his habits, and disappoints his desires. On the other hand, Proust has his hero move beyond the particular or actual to the general or ideal that reenforces the reality of the novel's world by giving it depth. By describing the *process of discovery* that encounters initiate and sustain, Proust reflects in his novel the ultimate reality of man's existence in the destructive-creative movement of time.

31. *Proust: A Selection*, p. 23, n 1; *Pastiches*, p. 107 n. Hopkins translates "n'avoir avec cet auteur qu'une rencontre" as "but to make his acquaintance."

Death, Art, and the Self

Proust himself certainly lived with this ultimate reality in the one privileged place he does not describe in his novel, but whose presence is felt
throughout—the famous cork-lined bedroom of his apartment on the
Boulevard Haussmann in which he wrote most of his great work. Despite
the physical and emotional torment he endured in the last years of his
life, despite the fumigations, nocturnal visits, and prisoners, this room,
like Elstir's studio, was Proust's "laboratory" for the recreation of reality,
the "ark" from which he viewed the world, the protected, autonomous
space whose solitude enabled him to plunge into his "inner country"
and to elucidate its form and meaning in art. It was here also that his
esprit, confronted by the spectre of death, engaged itself in its last and
most intense race against time:

> I knew very well that my brain was a rich mineral basin where
> there was a vast area of extremely varied precious deposits. But
> would I have time to exploit them? I was the only person able
> to do this, for two reasons: with my death there would disap-
> pear, not only the one miner able to extract the minerals but
> the deposit itself; now, when I returned home presently, a colli-
> sion between the auto I took and another would suffice to de-
> stroy my body and force my *mind*, from which the life would
> be withdrawn, to abandon forever the [new] ideas it was at this
> moment clasping to its bosom and shielding anxiously with its
> quivering flesh, not yet having had time to put them out of
> harm's way in a book.[32]

In this as in most of the passages on art and death that follow Marcel's discovery of his vocation, Proust seems to be speaking directly to
his readers. He is, in fact, bringing together all the rich images associated with the *esprit*, its activity, and its existence in time. The *esprit*,
writes Proust, "has its landscapes which it is allowed to contemplate only
for a moment";

> And having a body constitutes the principal danger that threat-
> ens the *mind*, the life of the thinking human being. . . . The
> body imprisons the *mind* in a fortress; soon the fortress is be-
> sieged on all sides and in the end the *mind* must capitulate.[33]

32. The first part of this passage through the words "force my mind" is found
in the translation in II, 1116; the rest in II, 1115. In the French edition the entire
passage under this form is in *Le Temps retrouvé*, III, 1037.

33. II, 1114–15; *Temps retrouvé*, III, 1035–36.

These images of the spirit that contemplates its own inner "landscape," that extracts the wealth of its "mine" recall Proust's account of the madeleine episode at the beginning of the novel in which the *esprit* is described as being at once "the seeker" and "the dark region through which it must go seeking." Even more remarkable for the consistency of vision it reveals is Proust's description of the mind's dependence on the body, for it contains the very ideas he first expressed while still a student in his dissertation on the "spirituality of the soul."

It is not surprising that the presence of death evokes at the end of the novel thoughts concerning the life of the spirit. Throughout *A la Recherche* Proust shows that life is composed of a series of deaths—not only the death of individuals like the grandmother, Swann, or Albertine, but also the death of dreams, memories, and of the successive selves in time. Since death is often the cause or the result of an encounter, it exposes the reality of time and forces Marcel to reexamine his life and to question the existence of his self. In *Le Temps retrouvé*, however, Proust is no longer describing how a particular contingent self attempts to resist the movement of time in order to preserve itself from death. The force that is opposed to death is not habit or the blind instinct of self-preservation that hides the reality of time, but the conscious activity of the spirit which seeks to liberate its world from the doomed prison of the body in order to preserve it in the protected space of a book.

Paradoxically, the activity of the spirit which struggles against the destructive action of time must itself destroy in order to create:

> This work of the artist, to seek to discern something different underneath material, experience, words, is exactly the reverse of the process which, during every minute that we live with our attention diverted from ourselves, is being carried on within us by pride, passion, intelligence and also by our habits, when they hide our true impressions from us by burying them under the mass of nomenclatures and practical aims which we erroneously call life. After all, that art, although so complicated, is actually the only living art.[34]

To destroy reality in order to recreate it, to replace the centrifugal movement of life by a centripetal return to the depths of the self is not an easy task. It requires "courage of every sort—even sentimental—for it means, first of all, giving up our dearest illusions, ceasing to believe in the ob-

34. II, 1013–14; *Temps retrouvé,* III, 896.

jectivity of what we have ourselves built up." Throughout these final pages of the novel Proust returns again and again to the lesson he learned so well during his encounter with Ruskin—that art demands the destruction of idols, the perpetual sacrifice of sentiment to truth. "It means doing away with all that we clung to most strongly," he writes; and adds later: "One cannot reproduce what one loves without abandoning it." Even death, now reflected in "the great mirror of the *mind*," must be viewed in the perspective of the biblical parable of the seed that must die. It is in these acts of sacrifice to the "inconsiderate demands of the work" that Proust's particular morality is most completely fused with his aesthetics. Artistic creation, even more than the suffering of love, is seen as an act of "expiation," a means of atoning for the sins of the past. It is the "duty" of an artist, writes Proust, to obey the dictates of his creative instinct and to exclude from his mind the pretexts for evasion furnished by intelligence: "But in art excuses count for nothing; good intentions are of no avail; the artist must at every instant heed his instinct; so that art is the most real of all things, the sternest school in life and truly the Last Judgment."[35] One must imagine that during the long years Proust spent working on his novel, art was for him *askesis*.

The destruction of the "false life" also means that the artist must replace his worldly self by that "other self" which alone creates a work of art. It was Sainte-Beuve's failure to understand this essential difference between the selves of an artist that led to Proust's famous attack on his critical method:

> Sainte-Beuve's great work does not go very deep. The celebrated method . . . which consists of not separating the man and his work . . . ignores what a very slight degree of self-acquaintance teaches us: that a book is the product of a different *self* [un autre *moi*] from the self we manifest in our habits, in our social life, in our vices. If we would try to understand that particular self, it is by searching [in the depths of ourselves], and by trying to reconstruct it there, that we may arrive at it.[36]

What this study has shown, I hope, is that this different or "other self" is really the creative *esprit* which is indeed free of the habits and vices of daily existence. It was also noted, however, that in his own criti-

35. II, 1001; *Temps retrouvé*, III, 880.
36. *Proust on Art*, pp. 99–100; *Sainte-Beuve*, pp. 136–37. Warner translates "au fond de nous-même" as "our own bosoms."

cism Proust by no means neglects the contingent life of an artist, and that in the novel Marcel's understanding of Vinteuil's music, for example, is partly based on his knowledge of the composer's life at Combray. Significantly, Proust states in the preface to *Jean Santeuil* that his primary reason for writing that novel was to discover

> the secret relations, the necessary metamorphoses, which exist between a writer's life and his work, between reality and art, or, rather, as we then thought, between appearance and reality—a reality which underlay all things and could be disengaged only by art.[37]

It is precisely these secret relations and metamorphoses that form the essential theme of becoming in *A la Recherche,* and that are revealed most clearly in Marcel's creative encounters. Sainte-Beuve's critical method was a failure, and his judgments of the works of his great contemporaries—Nerval, Baudelaire, Balzac, Stendhal—were false, not because he asked questions concerning their lives, but because he did not understand the metamorphic process of creation. "According to Proust," writes Germaine Brée,

> Sainte-Beuve did not find the solution to the problem he had raised; he did not know how to find the link between the man and the work, the path that connects one to the other. His criticism, in fact, follows two parallel paths which do not converge. He observes the man from the outside and judges him according to social norms; and when he turns to the work, he evaluates it according to more or less traditional standards of taste and style.[38]

Behind Proust's attack on Sainte-Beuve the basic principles of Darlu's philosophy are again visible, for Darlu had repeatedly warned his students of the dangers inherent in any preconceived system which led the mind to judge the superior by the inferior, reality by appearances. The only way to avoid these dangers was to seek to know the world or a work of art by understanding one's own impressions. It is this same idea that Proust expresses when he remarks that a reader must recreate the work of art within himself. *Sainte-Beuve was not "profound" because his judgments were not based on any real encounters with art.* For Proust, if

37. *Jean Santeuil*, p. 18; I, 54.
38. Germaine Brée, "Le 'Moi oeuvrant' de Proust," *MLR,* LXI, no. 4 (October 1966), 611.

Sainte-Beuve had experienced such encounters, he would have been able to discover within himself and in the work evidence of that creative activity of the *esprit* which alone can reveal the secret relations that exist between art and life. The irony of Sainte-Beuve's failure, as Germaine Brée suggests, was that he remained imprisoned by his own method. His inability to discover the real similarities between a work and the life of its author was the fundamental cause of his failure to comprehend the essential difference between the two.

Because of his own profound knowledge of the creative process Proust never forgot this difference between art and life. At one point in the novel, for example, the narrator criticizes the mania some people have of exhibiting works of art together with the objects that surrounded them in the real world and thereby suppressing "the essential thing, the act of the *mind* which isolated them" from reality. It would be preferable, he thinks, to hang a masterpiece in a museum whose bare walls symbolize far better "those innermost spaces into which the artist withdrew to create it."[39] The logic of this belief led Proust to criticize Balzac, a novelist whom he loved, for his failure to "withdraw" himself from his personal life. In Balzac's mind, writes Proust, "there was no dividing line between real life (which as . . . I think, is not real) and the life of his novels (which for the writer is the only true life)."[40] Balzac's penchant for explanatory digressions, his tendency to consider his characters as real persons, corrupted the artistic autonomy of his novels and prevented that "fusion" of all elements Proust admired in the works of Flaubert.

"The writer of first rank," notes Proust in his translation of *Sesame and Lilies,* "is he who employs only those words dictated to him by an inner necessity, by the vision of his thought in which he can change nothing." In the work of a great writer there is never any "argument where he says: 'I.' *He* is only the place where his thoughts form themselves, where they choose themselves at every moment, where they create and perfect the necessary and unique form in which they will be embodied."[41] This may seem a curious statement for an author who wrote his great work in the first person singular; as curious as Proust's famous remark to Gide: "You can tell everything, provided that you never say: *I.*"[42] But to understand the meaning of Proust's position one must recog-

39. I, 490; *Jeunes filles,* I, 645.   40. *Proust on Art,* p. 161; *Sainte-Beuve,* p. 198.
41. *Sésame,* p. 85 n. Proust's italics.
42. André Gide, *Journal,* entry for 14 May 1921. Gide's italics.

nize that the artistic autonomy of a work depends on a more profound point of view than is represented by the use of any single pronoun. Proust immediately sensed behind the apparent objectivity of Balzac's novels the presence of a man who was speaking in his own voice, who was "explaining" his ideas and "conversing" directly with the reader. He also realized that Flaubert's own objectivity was more apparent than real, but for a different reason. In discussing Flaubert's works Proust analyzes the different elements that create the "grammatical beauty" of his style. He speaks of Flaubert's masterful use of the imperfect tense, the art with which he places an adverb in a sentence, and the special value he gives to the conjunction "et" which instead of simply connecting clauses marks a pause in the musical rhythm of his sentences. In other words, Proust discovers in Flaubert's novels the presence of a deeply personal, and in that sense "subjective," vision which is reflected *in the style itself*.[43] One can now comprehend why Proust could say of Balzac: "Style is so largely a record of the transformation imposed on reality by the writer's mind that Balzac's style, properly speaking, does not exist."[44]

As I have already noted, the very questions Proust raised concerning the works of Balzac and Flaubert are posed directly in his own novel, for *A la Recherche* is the story of a man who asks himself how he can transform the reality of his experience in life into a work of art. Marcel's future contains not only the secret of his vocation or of his identity as a novelist, but also the secret of his vision and, consequently, of the means by which he will create this new identity. Although the metamorphosis of man into novelist is also the subject of *Jean Santeuil*, the questions raised there remain essentially unanswered with regard to Jean's own life. Proust's early novel is unfinished because his life was at that time unfinished. His failure was the direct result of the fact that he was forced to give a form to his novel before he had discovered the form of his own existence. How could a "he," a point of view that implies a complete, determined, and finished world, reflect an *inner becoming in time*, and what is more difficult, reflect this becoming in a novel whose time was not set, whose direction was still uncharted, whose own world was still open-ended? This is why the "he" of *Jean Santeuil* is so unstable, and why one so often has the impression of hearing Proust's own voice. Although all the fundamental characteristics of his literary style are present

43. *Chroniques*, pp. 193–211. Translated in *Pleasures and Days*, pp. 223–40.
44. *Proust on Art*, pp. 169–70; *Sainte-Beuve*, p. 207.

in this work, Proust must have judged that in *Jean Santeuil* his true "style," properly speaking, did not exist.

In order to present an inner becoming in time, Proust had to use not only an "I," but an "I" that could reflect on itself. A becoming which involves coming to terms with the past so as to create a future cannot have its meaning revealed unless part of the past and future is already known. The function of the narrator is to establish these temporal dimensions. He cannot, on the other hand, know all the past and future, for then the becoming itself would cease to have a real movement and existence. Therefore, just as the narrator sees the hero in a temporal perspective, he himself is placed in time and at a distance. As Picon remarks, "Only the *I* allowed [Proust] to make of the present the moment of a future already in the past."[45]

Through this double "I" of the hero and narrator Proust's novel itself has a kind of double identity, for it is both a spiritual autobiography and a work of fiction. It is at once the result of that long activity of autocontemplation by which Proust explored his inner world, and a story which, because its narrator is not Proust and therefore detached from him, must be considered as being consciously created, or more accurately, invented by its author. In fact it was only by inventing a narrator different from himself that Proust could write a *novel* and not simply an autobiography. Readers of *A la Recherche* have always noted that the narrator, unlike Proust, is not, for example, a homosexual. While Proust certainly had psychological or moral reasons for changing the sexual identity of his narrator, it is just as certain that this change was a creative necessity. Given the particular artistic problems that confronted Proust, a novel with a homosexual narrator might run the risk of losing its own identity. The expression of a life redesigned by art, *A la Recherche* gives a new meaning to the very situation that causes so much suffering to its hero, for Proust, now the master and not the victim of time, is through the "I" of his novel present at his own absence.

The Proustian "I" is, of course, more complex than this analysis would suggest. In a penetrating study of the subject, Marcel Muller has discovered a variety of identities for the narrative voices in *A la Recherche*. The protagonist of the novel includes not only the hero who is the "I" engaged in his own story and whose future is unknown to him, and

45. *Lecture de Proust*, pp. 32–33. Picon's italics.

the narrator who is the "I" judging and contemplating his past, but also the "intermediary subject" identified as the "I" through which the narrator recalls the hero. Muller also discovers other voices. There is the novelist who is the presence of the story's omniscient inventor, the writer who is the artist of the novel's language, the author who is Marcel Proust revealed in his creative self, and the man who is Marcel Proust's worldly self. These last two voices might be thought to corrupt the autonomy of the novel, and I myself have treated Proust's remarks in *Le Temps retrouvé* as coming directly from him. Such an interpretation is justified because Proust is in fact "explaining" his own aesthetics and "discussing" his life, and because by the end of the novel the narrator has closed the distance separating him from the author. But Muller carefully notes that this presence of the author and man is highly ambiguous, if not false. The Marcel Proust who at times *seems* to speak directly to the reader must also be considered a consciously *invented* voice of the real Proust. Muller's conclusion is that the "I" of *A la Recherche* is as unknown and unknowable as the face of the artist who is viewed from behind in Vermeer's "Allegory of Painting"—a work whose mystery fascinated Proust and led him to remark: "This artist whose back is turned, who does not care to be seen by posterity, and who will not know what it thinks of him, is an admirable and poignant idea."[46]

The "I" of Proust's novel in all its complex forms is, therefore, an autonomous, impersonal "I" which, because it is divorced from the "real" life of the man, can express the essential spiritual reality of his existence in time. This "I" is not simply the expressive form Proust gave to his "other self." It is the voice of a being whose identity, existing beyond all distinctions, is, like that of a work of art, truly "other." At once the creator and the creation of the novel which is its world, the "I" is the space that encloses this world and the mirror in which it is reflected. Like the *esprit* the "I" is also real and ideal, and like Dominique's mysterious visitor it addresses the reader in a voice that seems at once near and far away. Indeed, this voice is *for the reader* the first and most extraordinary Stranger he encounters in the novel.

When enclosed in a room an artist expresses his deepest thoughts, writes Proust, "at that moment he exchanges his soul for the soul of the universe. This great transference is accomplished inside him."[47] This

46. Marcel Muller, *Les Voix narratives dans la "Recherche du temps perdu"* (Genève: Droz, 1965).

47. *Sainte-Beuve,* p. 352. Also translated in *Proust on Art,* p. 311.

"universal soul" that Proust also described while a student is what he finally revealed through the "I" of his novel and through the very activity of creation. By means of art and the final detachment from the self it offered, Proust was able to conquer death and free his mind from the prison of the body:

> *Only by art can we get outside ourselves* [sortir de nous], know what another sees of his universe, which is not the same as ours and the different views of which would otherwise have remained as unknown to us as those there may be on the moon. Thanks to art, instead of seeing only one world, our own, we see it under multiple forms, and as many as there are original artists, just so many worlds have we at our disposal, differing more widely from one another than those that roll through infinite space, and years after the glowing center from which they emanated has been extinguished, be it called Rembrandt or Vermeer, they continue to send us their own rays of light.[48]

The reader of *A la Recherche du temps perdu* enjoys the same experience of liberation whenever he sees, through the world of the novel, his own world in a new light.

48. II, 1013; *Temps retrouvé*, III, 895–96.

Conclusion

In a recently published study on the French New Novel, John Sturrock describes the way three of these novelists have discovered different objective correlatives for the reflective consciousness which is the scene of the novel's composition:

> For Claude Simon . . . this is a study or other room shuttered, not entirely successfully, against the sunlight—the artificial light is a clue to the equation he wants to establish with consciousness; for Michel Butor, in *La Modification*, the same scene becomes a railway compartment in a train—the train being a reminder that we are still carried along in time even when we reflect; for Robbe-Grillet, in *Dans le labyrinthe*, consciousness is figured as a bedroom at the top of a house . . . a hint at the erotic nature of literary creation which this novelist stresses.[1]

Although he is not a New Novelist, Samuel Beckett could be added to this list, for he often describes, as in *Molloy*, a man writing his life in a room which represents at once the space of consciousness and the womb/tomb of existence.

For each of these writers the room also serves as a kind of replica or *mise en abîme* of the novel's form, since their works can be called, despite many differences, novels of mental space. From the first sentence the reader enters a world whose spatial and temporal dimensions are defined by the point of view of an individual mind, and enclosed within this mind he participates in its activity. All characters and events, objects and milieux have no real expressive or dramatic function of their own. They have been reduced to the role of "props" or *supports* of this essential

1. John Sturrock, *The French New Novel* (London: Oxford University Press, 1969), p. 34.

inner drama. Confronted by a public that has grown "suspicious" of any novel written by an omniscient author who hides behind the "truth" of his characters, these writers have realized that the only way to satisfy the reader's curiosity and desire for authenticity is to place him on the novelist's own ground, to force him to view the novel's world from within. They have understood, in other words, the law of modern fiction that Nathalie Sarraute describes in her "L'Ere du soupçon"—namely, that a writer cannot express and dramatize the inner world of psychological reality and draw his reader's attention to it unless he at the same time undramatizes the outer world of action by eliminating the well-constructed characters and plots of the traditional novel.[2]

There are many aspects of the contemporary novel that recall some of the essential characteristics of *A la Recherche du temps perdu*.[3] All these novelists have readily acknowledged Proust's right to be placed in that pantheon of great artists like Joyce, Kafka, and Faulkner who questioned the fundamental preconceptions of the traditional novel and destroyed its form. Proust himself recognized in Flaubert's work the first signs of this metamorphosis of the novel, for he writes: "what, until the time of Flaubert, was action, becomes impression."[4] He defines in this way Flaubert's efforts to undramatize the world of the novel by concentrating less on objective events than on the reactions of the characters.

Building on the work of his predecessor, Proust transformed the novel even more. The characters in *A la Recherche* are not ends in themselves, nor are they creatures in a fictional world whose structure is solely determined by their interactions and conflicts. The world in which they exist does not belong to them but to the "I." It is the means by which the hero-narrator discovers and explores the dimensions of his own intellectual, moral, and creative life. Their conflicts become meaningless when considered apart from the effect they have on him, and their personalities acquire importance insofar as they complete the outline of that image of himself Marcel contemplates in the mirror of his mind. In this

2. Nathalie Sarraute, *The Age of Suspicion* (New York: Braziller, 1963), pp. 68–69; Sarraute, *L'Ere du soupçon* (Paris: Gallimard, 1956), pp. 87–88.
3. Several studies have been written on Proust and the New Novel. See, for example, the last chapter of Picon's *Lecture de Proust,* and the excellent article by Jessie L. Hornsby, "Le 'Nouveau Roman' de Proust," *L'Esprit créateur,* III, no. 2 (Summer 1967), pp. 67–80. The position of Proust within the whole development of the modern novel is treated by Michel Raimond in *La Crise du Roman* (Paris: José Corti, 1967).
4. *Chroniques,* p. 106. Also translated in *Pleasures and Days,* p. 226.

231

sense Proust's characters do tend to be reflections of an inner world of experience. Their "authenticity" is revealed less by their identity as characters than in the impressions they produce, and is inseparable, consequently, from the mental activity which seeks to capture their identity. *A la Recherche* can in fact be called the story of its hero's impressions. Its action is essentially the activity of his mind, its events are his encounters, and the reader identifies himself less with the characters than with the creative process these encounters dramatize.

But *A la Recherche* is not a New Novel. While praising Proust's achievement, Sarraute is careful to note that he, like the traditional novelist, still gives his readers a collection of character types—a rich man of the world, a kept woman, a gullible doctor, a snobbish lady, and others. Also, all of Proust's characters are not as elusive in form as the mother and the grandmother who exist so close to the center of Marcel's world that they are never fully seen by the reader. Swann has greater autonomy, Françoise even more, and Charlus, who dominates the stage when he appears, often seems the reincarnation of one of those Balzacian heroes he so admires. Indeed, there is the whole *comédie humaine* aspect of *A la Recherche* which I have not discussed since it falls outside the limits of this study, but which is, nevertheless, an essential part of Proust's novel.

Again, unlike many contemporary writers, Proust through his narrator explains and analyzes at length all that happens in the novel. According to Sarraute, Proust's explanations are directed toward a world that appears immobile since it is seen in memory and across a great temporal distance. The fault of these explanations is that they incite the reader "to use his own intelligence, instead of giving him the sensation of reliving an experience."[5] Sarraute is defending here the reasons why she and other New Novelists have abandoned psychological analysis. The works of these writers, like the plays of the so-called absurdists, are examples of what has become a fundamental principle of contemporary aesthetics—*faire voir au lieu d'expliquer,* show instead of explaining.

Seen in this light, *A la Recherche* does not give the reader the sensation of reliving an experience in all its immediacy. As dramatic as Marcel's or the narrator's encounters are, they are still set firmly in time; that is, they are dramatizations of evocations. In his efforts to recapture and express the intricate and fleeting movements of consciousness, today's

5. *Age of Suspicion*, p. 93; *L'Ere du soupçon*, p. 117.

novelist is a descendant of Joyce and not Proust. The fact is that Proust was not interested in the "stream of consciousness" or any of its related forms. The very temporal complexity of the Proustian "I" makes it poorly suited to such a purpose. On the other hand, this same complexity shows that the "I" is admirably adapted to the task it was designed to perform, for in *A la Recherche* the point of view is first of all an *instrument* for discovering and examining those truths that Proust was determined to reveal—the laws governing man's existence in time and the nature of the creative process. It is for this reason that Proust needed both a hero and a narrator, an "I" who could "live" in time and an "I" who could judge his life. It is for this reason also that Proust had to incorporate within his novel both the idea and the attributes of a real and independent world to be confronted and explored.

Throughout this study I have shown that the creative encounters always take place within a real context. All of Marcel's impressions never suppress the objective world. The shock of an encounter that suddenly exposes the hidden reality of some person, place, or thing also reveals its autonomous existence. The encounter itself momentarily objectifies the world by placing it at a new psychological or perceptual distance. This does not mean that the New Novelists deny the existence of the real world. Their works, which are sometimes filled with objects and more or less real settings, reflect the lesson Proust learned from Darlu and that the phenomenologists have since developed—that the only way we can know ourselves or be revealed to ourselves is in the way we see the world. But even in the novels of Robbe-Grillet, which contain such detailed descriptions of exterior reality, and where this reality so often functions as a threat to the complex fictions of the imagination, the objective world is still essentially reduced to the role of being the support of a subjective world. Although the exterior world also acts as a support in *A la Recherche,* it remains the *object* of confrontations precisely because *the subjective is itself used as an instrument; a means for investigating the objective.* Just as Proust keeps the two terms of his metaphors separate and distinct in order to show how they are united, so he constantly maintains a distance between self and world in order to reveal and to *renew* their interactions. Without the presence of a real world existing outside the self, encounters would have no meaning, and it is because of these encounters that *A la Recherche* cannot be called a novel of mental space. Like the New Novelists Proust proclaims the artist's creative independence from the contingencies of time and space, but

233

unlike them he presents these contingencies within the novel itself where they form a variety of spaces, objective and subjective, through which the hero-narrator progresses until he discovers his identity. While *A la Recherche* transcends the conflicts that led to its creation, it still describes, as I have noted, a threshold world, and in the New Novel the room of consciousness has no functioning door. When Butor's hero exits from his compartment in *La Modification,* he is lost in a void.

Shortly after the publication of *Du Côté de chez Swann,* Proust insisted in a letter to Jacques Rivière that the subsequent volumes of his novel would show that he had traced the evolution of a man's thoughts. "But," he added, "I did not want to analyze this evolution of a mind in an abstract fashion, but to recreate it, to make it live. I was forced therefore to describe errors, without feeling that I was obliged to say that I held them to be errors."[6] Only later would the reader learn why Swann confides his wife so readily to the care of Charlus, or how the narrator's pessimistic judgment of his life is reversed.

A la Recherche is in fact full of errors of interpretation, faulty judgments, incomplete discoveries, misconceptions, and partial explanations. Although many of these errors are rectified at the end of the novel, their effect on the reader is not destroyed, for he has indeed witnessed the complex and discontinuous evolution of a man's thoughts in time. Sarraute's remark on the immobility of Proust's world is not, therefore, entirely justified. In *A la Recherche* the experiences that do give the reader the sensation of reliving them are more often than not Marcel's or the narrator's *efforts* to explain the world or to understand the meaning of certain impressions. Commenting on Proust's technique of presenting first the impression and not its cause, Samuel Beckett remarks that Proust, like Dostoevsky, "states his characters without explaining them." "It may be objected," he continues, "that Proust does little else but explain his characters. But his explanations are experimental and not demonstrative. He explains them in order that they may appear as they are—inexplicable. He explains them away."[7] It is this experimental nature of Proustian analysis that preserves the mobility of the novel's world. It intensifies both the drama of Marcel's encounters and the mystery of the characters who remain, consequently, and despite all the "laws" that explain their lives, *êtres de fuite.* Writers before Proust and particularly after him have

6. *Marcel Proust et Jacques Rivière: Correspondance,* ed. Philip Kolb (Paris: Plon, 1955), p. 3.
7. *Proust,* pp. 66–67.

attempted to show in their novels some aspects of the process that led to their creation, but none have dramatized as effectively as Proust all the difficulties and joys of autocontemplation and all the different moments of the creative becoming of an artist.

There can be little doubt that Proust lived through some kind of "bedroom drama" as a child, or that he was powerfully impressed at times by the beauties of nature and art, that he had experiences of involuntary memory, suffered moments of intense disappointment, or was struck by sudden revelations of the truth hidden in the lives of others. Yet one can doubt whether these different encounters were always as *dramatically* shocking, revealing, or disruptive as the ones he describes in *A la Recherche*.

In a detailed study of the evolution of involuntary memory in Proust's works, Elizabeth Jackson demonstrates repeatedly that the presentation of involuntary memory in *A la Recherche* cannot be taken as a totally accurate account of what Proust really experienced.[8] She shows that Proust's insistence on the element of chance and on the whole miraculous aspect of involuntary memory was the result of a highly conscious and progressive effort at dramatization. In *Les Plaisirs et les jours,* for example, some of Proust's heroes can will to have experiences by seeking out sensations that provoke memory. Even the subordination of intelligence to sensitivity is not always clearly stated in his earliest writings. As for the increasing attention Proust devotes to failure, this also can be seen as a device he chose to heighten the drama of success and the importance of chance. Finally, Mlle Jackson is correct when she states that there was nothing in Proust's life like the "matinée des Guermantes" if that event is understood as being a moment when all his doubts were suddenly dissipated, when the value of literature was suddenly reaffirmed, and when the whole past was suddenly resurrected.

Given this divergence between Marcel's encounters and Proust's real experience, is one still justified in saying that *A la Recherche* is the description of its own genesis? In other words, through his "invention" of a fictional world did Proust corrupt the "translation" of his experience, so that his novel is no longer a truthful account of how a life was, or could be, transformed into a work of art?

To begin answering this question one must turn not to Proust's life as a man but to his development as a writer. *Jean Santeuil* opens with

8. Elizabeth R. Jackson, *L'Evolution de la mémoire involontaire dans l'oeuvre de Marcel Proust* (Paris: Nizet, 1966).

the following statement which the editor drew from Proust's manuscript: "Should I call this book a novel? It is something less, perhaps, and yet much more, the very essence of my life, with nothing extraneous added [sans y rien mêler], as it developed through a long period of wretchedness. This book of mine has not been manufactured: it has been garnered."[9] Proust could have used these same remarks to describe *A la Recherche,* for there again he makes a distinction between novels that are inventions of the imagination and works like his own, whose material grew within him. Such a distinction explains in fact why the narrator can say in *Le Temps retrouvé* that his life could also *not* be called a vocation since "literature" played no part in it. In *Jean Santeuil,* however, Proust seems to have envisaged a work whose "purity" would be maintained by a refusal to describe anything that was not the result of some powerful, and particularly joyful, impression. After his experience of involuntary memory at Begmeil, for example, Jean even resolves to write "only of what the past brings suddenly to life in a smell, in a sight, in what has, as it were, exploded within me and set the imagination quivering, so that the accompanying joy stirs me to inspiration."[10] Unlike Marcel, Jean conceives of a work in which "intellectual truths" will have no place.

Certainly, *Jean Santeuil* is not based solely on moments of inspiration. It contains not only the description of an "imaginary life" and the account of historical events like the Dreyfus affair, but also a variety of moral and intellectual observations. Proust does seem to have followed, however, his intention of writing a work that would not simply be a novel in the traditional sense of an invented "story" having a predetermined unifying structure. These considerations have led Maurice Blanchot to remark that the fragmentary nature of *Jean Santeuil* is not a result of the fact that Proust never finished it. By constructing a work composed of fragments in which characters appear and disappear and in which scenes are not related to other scenes, writes Blanchot, Proust was attempting to satisfy his desire to write a novel which would avoid the "impurity" of a traditional narration. But the paradoxical result of Proust's efforts was that instead of giving us "moments" he described them as scenes and instead of showing characters in the form of apparitions he presented portraits of them.[11]

Nothing is more different in this respect than *A la Recherche du*

9. *Jean Santeuil,* p. 1; I, 31.   10. *Jean Santeuil,* p. 410; II, 233.
11. Maurice Blanchot, *Le Livre à venir* (Paris: Gallimard, 1959), p. 29.

temps perdu in which Proust relates all the elements of the novel to each other and in which the various impressions, apparitions, and shocks are presented in all their explosive intensity. For example, in *A la Recherche* the "bedroom drama" is precisely that—a beautifully staged and intricately constructed play complete with exposition, development of action, crisis scene, and dénouement. It has what its counterpart in *Jean Santeuil* with its anticlimactic structure lacks, a genuine atmosphere of tension and suspense. But this more dramatic structure cannot alone explain the greater intensity of Marcel's experience, for Proust would not have achieved the same result simply by imposing a similar structure on the event he describes in *Jean Santeuil*. By having Jean's mother *refuse* to go to her son's room until she is forced to do so against her will, Proust may have added more suspense, but this suspense would have had little dramatic value unless Proust had also described in greater detail than he did for Jean the son's anxiety and suffering while waiting for his mother. Much more than in *Jean Santeuil* the real drama in *A la Recherche* takes place *within* Marcel, and the function of the dramatic structure is essentially to reveal the *inner structure* of Marcel's suffering. Did Proust's own mother resist his desires as much as the mother in *A la Recherche*? Was she as sweet and loving as she appears in *Jean Santeuil*? These questions are best left to biographers. What interested Proust was the reality of his own suffering, and when he wrote *Jean Santeuil* this reality had not yet had time enough to be formed in his memory. Also, he himself still needed more time to form the reality of his life through writing, to discover and create the spiritual equivalents, the necessary dramatic and fictional structures without which he could not translate reality into art. All this suggests that it is Marcel's experience and not Jean's or Proust's that is Proust's "real experience."

As I noted earlier, an important element in Proust's fictionalization was his invention of a narrator. In *A la Recherche* the narrator's remarks and explanations serve to "interiorize" the bedroom drama by drawing attention to the nature of Marcel's suffering. It is also the narrator who sets this event in time by making it the focus of a variety of temporal and spatial points of view. He relates the whole episode to the inner becoming of Marcel's life and links it to other events in the novel such as the story of Swann's love. Here again it matters little whether or not Proust's bedroom drama as a child was witnessed by a Swann or by someone like the Doctor Surlande who appears in *Jean Santeuil*. Proust saw in time that the presence of Swann was necessary not only because of the general

themes and structure of his novel, but also because he realized that someone like Swann had been present, if only in spirit. Through his invention of a narrator, Proust also discovered a way out of the dilemma he
had encountered in *Jean Santeuil.* The narrator's remarks are not part
of a traditional narration which "tells a story." Marcel's search for a vocation is presented as a series of experiences that are explored by a narrator
whose own explanations are an inseparable part of the experiences he
attempts to understand. By interiorizing the story of his own quest, the
narrator transforms it from a linear description into a complex temporal
and spatial structure.

Maurice Bardèche remarks that if there was for Proust any "miracle"
or sudden "revelation," it must have occurred when, looking over the
blocks of written material he had accumulated, he discovered the genial
idea of structuring them on the principle of the "psychology of space."
In *Jean Santeuil,* writes Bardèche, Proust was fully conscious of time as
an "element" in which events take place and characters live, but it was
only later that he realized that time could also be an "instrument of control."[12] The "fiction" of *A la Recherche* is not based as in *Jean Santeuil*
on the description of an "imaginary life," but on its far more rigorous
construction.[13] Proust's own development as a writer does indeed resemble the experience of the narrator who after living in time discovers
that time can be an instrument for the creation of his novel. In judging
the material he had written, Proust also made a discovery comparable to
that of the nineteenth-century writers who found "in between" the works
they had already completed the principle of their vital unity. In this way
Proust satisfied his ambition in *Jean Santeuil,* which was to write a work
whose unity would not be imposed from without.

Although Proust constantly rewrote certain parts of his novel, he took
particular care in developing and polishing many of Marcel's important
encounters. Bardèche notes that the encounter with Gilberte at Tansonville is repeated in eight different versions in the manuscripts; the description of the hawthorns was perfected only after several rewritings;
the significance of the Vinteuil sonata developed as it was moved from
one episode of the novel to another; other events like the bedroom drama
haunted Proust throughout his writings.[14] It seems certain that the more
Proust explored the meaning of these events and sought for them a place
in his novel the more he also fictionalized them. There are no "keys" to

12. Bardèche, *Marcel Proust Romancier,* I, 125–26.
13. Ibid., I, 70.   14. Ibid., I, 233.

Marcel's encounters anymore than there are for the characters in *A la Recherche*. Proust insists in *Le Temps retrouvé* that his novel contains "[not a single fact that is not fictitious . . . , everything has been invented for the needs of my demonstration]."[15] He describes and justifies his method again later: "And just as the painter needs to study many churches in order to paint one, even more so must the writer who wishes to acquire volume, substance, generalness, literary reality, study many human beings for a single sentiment." Since we are more faithful to ourselves than to others, says the narrator, and since the nature of our love or jealousy does not change in our different affairs, in order to describe these emotions the writer can "substitute" one woman for another. "These substitutions give the book an impersonal, more general character and this is at the same time a stern admonition that we should not devote our attention to persons but to ideas, which have a real existence and are therefore susceptible of expression."[16]

These remarks, which reveal some of the reasons for Proust's failure in *Jean Santeuil*, where he does not attain the same degree of "generalness" and "impersonality," also explain why he constantly reworked and progressively fictionalized and dramatized Marcel's major encounters. They are the vital pieces of his "demonstration," the forms best suited to the expression of his most important "ideas." In order to make these encounters fulfill their function, Proust had to create composites by drawing on a variety of experiences and memories. He had to make "substitutions" and invent his own writer, composer, and painter since no single one in life could satisfy the needs of his demonstration. He had to dramatize them because that was the only way he could reveal their inner meaning and transform them into revelations for his hero and his readers. Finally, he had to give them "volume, substance, generalness, and literary reality" so that they could become truly *exemplary events* showing the essential form of those reactions that are produced in the mind by the shocks of joy, suffering, and disappointment. Seen in this light, Marcel's experiences of involuntary memory are also exemplary events. The function of the madeleine is not limited to the resurrection of Combray, nor is it placed in the novel simply to show that artistic

15. II, 976; *Temps retrouvé*, III, 846. Blossom translates "pas un seul fait qui ne soit fictif" as "not one fact that is not imaginary," and "tout a été inventé par moi selon les besoins de ma démonstration" as "everything has been invented by me to meet the needs of my story."
16. II, 1021–22; *Temps retrouvé*, III, 907–8.

creation depends on involuntary memory. Critics are correct in doubting whether Proust needed an experience of this kind in order to recall his childhood.[17] Yet what it does show and what Proust meant it to show is that creation depends on certain sensations and impressions, that it involves a plunge into the depths of the self during which all efforts must be made to preserve the activity of the mind from corruption. And it was surely this same activity that Proust himself engaged in as he wrote and developed the material of his novel.

I have tried to demonstrate in this study that all of Marcel's major encounters incorporate with variations the same basic structure Proust first presented in "L'Etranger." Although some aspects of this structure can also be found in *Jean Santeuil*, particularly in Proust's descriptions of involuntary memory, their presence remains rather vague. Jean's privileged moments do most often appear in the form of descriptive scenes. In *A la Recherche* Marcel's experiences are more truly encounters because they are used to sustain the overall structure of the novel based on the principle of the "psychology of space," which can operate only within a context of habits, memories, and expectations that are repeatedly disrupted by unexpected events acting as revelations. It is in fact in his careful placing of Marcel's encounters that Proust's control over the time of the novel is most evident. And since the "psychology of space" also operates *within* the encounters, they themselves are "controlled" by a more rigorous temporal and spatial structure.

But an equally important reason why Marcel's experiences are encounters is once again because Proust wants them to reveal the world of the mind and of the emotions. The structure of Jean's moments is less clearly defined because Proust had not yet fully understood the necessity of using *all* the elements in the novel to present the inner becoming of an artist. In reworking Marcel's encounters, Proust must have discovered the similarities in their structures. He realized, in other words, that while suffering and joy are markedly different reactions, they still represent variations on certain basic mental processes. He also discovered how all these encounters could be presented as variations on certain themes and ideas (the corruption of consciousness, the multiplicity of the self, the role of the will) and certain images (the room and the door). Obviously, in "discovering" these essential elements of his vision, Proust also created them and sought to reproduce them. The end result of all this writing

17. See, for example, Bardèche, I, 253.

and autocontemplation was Proust's realization that the great moments of his existence were by no means limited to his joyful impressions. Unable to write a novel based solely on the inspiration provided by these poetic moments, he succeeded in writing one in which all the different aspects of his life could be expressed in the form of an unexpected and extraordinary event. In this way the bedroom drama, Vinteuil's music, and Albertine's homosexuality could, by becoming the material for encounters, take their place alongside the *moments bienheureux*.

Proust did not live his life and then retire to write it. From before the publication of *Les Plaisirs et les jours* until his death he never ceased to write so that his work constantly enriched his life and became as much a part of it as his experiences in the exterior world. At the same time writing never cut him off from life. Even when he retired almost completely from society and withdrew into his room, Proust continued, like Aunt Léonie in her bedroom at Combray, to stage dramas for himself. He invited friends to dinner in order to observe them. He had concerts performed in his room. He also became, like Charlus, a man who sought out others to act in dramas which could satisfy his darker sexual desires. Whatever their immediate purpose, all these events served as material from which he drew the world of his novel.

While writing about his experiences Proust must have made discoveries that were surprising even to himself. In fact, he suggests in *Le Temps retrouvé* that a writer can adopt an attitude toward his work which can make possible such sudden insights:

> It is quite possible that, to produce a literary work, imagination and sensibility are interchangeable qualities and that the latter can, without much disadvantage, be substituted for the former, just as people whose stomach is unable to digest food charge their intestines with this function. A man born sensitive to impressions but without imagination, might nevertheless write admirable novels. The suffering caused him by others, his attempts to forestall it, the conflicts provoked by his suffering and the other cruel person—all that, interpreted by his intelligence, might furnish the material for a book not only as fine as if it had been imagined and invented, but also as completely foreign to the author's reveries as if he had been absorbed in himself and happy, as surprising to him and as much the product of chance as an accidental caprice of the imagination.[18]

18. II, 1017; *Temps retrouvé*, III, 900–901.

While Proust is defining here the sources of his own creativity, he adds a new twist to his argument by stating that a writer like himself might consider his work "as if" it were an invention unrelated to his experience. He is suggesting that the act of writing must incorporate within itself the very conditions that made it possible for him to begin writing. Just as the narrator must first forget his own past so that it can strike him as something new and revealing, so must the author set his own experience at a distance so that it can strike him "as if" it were something surprising, a product of chance. The creative process must itself reflect the paradox of involuntary memory by confronting the author with a world at once absent, and therefore capable of being imagined, and present to the senses as an authentic impression. It now seems that the presence of an invented narrator enabled Proust to transform his own self into the object of repeated encounters. In this way the activity of autocontemplation became a truly dynamic process involving a constant and startling recognition and rediscovery of the self and its world. Therefore, when Proust speaks of translating his life into a work of art, he means that it must be relived *as a novel* in which the fiction of the "as if" becomes another instrument for the discovery of truth. These considerations reaffirm the validity of Clive Bell's perception that the gift that conditioned Proust's method was his capacity for giving himself shocks.

One could object that the very idea of an artist giving himself shocks either in life or during the process of writing contradicts the principle of an encounter that cannot be willed. Although Proust speaks often of the fact that an artist's first discoveries may be totally unexpected, he also writes that an artist gradually begins to seek out those sites, experiences, and situations in life which contain his "ideal," and which give him the opportunity of rediscovering the *phrases-types* of his vision.[19] The world first revealed by chance encounters is what he now consciously seeks or establishes in his mind so that it can be the object of new encounters. Since it becomes more and more a world to which he is committed, it becomes as well the only world capable of revealing the truth he seeks. All of Marcel's encounters are, after all, with *his* world and fall within the context of an inner commitment to certain special truths. The artist who gives himself shocks is really creating the conditions under which the real shock, that of a sudden insight or discovery, can occur. It is this shock that cannot be willed, but it requires the preceding and subsequent commitment of the artist.

19. See: I, 647; *Jeunes filles,* I, 861.

Although Proust made discoveries while writing, his novel is still the work of a man who knew from the beginning what the narrator understands only at the end. The most troubling paradox of *A la Recherche,* writes Gérard Genette, "is that it presents itself at once as a work of art and as an approach to a work, as termination and as genesis, as the search for lost time and as the presentation of time recaptured." Like the novels of the nineteenth century Proust admired, his also is "marvelously incomplete." For this reason, continues Genette, one can say that each moment in the novel can be read in two different ways—as part of a development that describes the birth of a vocation and also as the exercise of that vocation. The reader, "informed *in extremis* that the book he has just read still has to be written, and that the book to be written is more or less (but more or less only) the one he has just read," is forced to turn back to the beginning to read it again in a different way. Given this perpetual incompleteness of *A la Recherche,* Genette finds that it admirably reflects Sartre's idea: "The literary object is a strange top that exists only in movement."[20] Other critics have also searched for images to describe the paradox of *A la Recherche.* Blanchot calls the novel a "sphere" turning on itself.[21] For Jean Rousset it has the form of a "great buckle" or loop which links the end to the beginning.[22] And Louis Bolle, using a very Proustian image, says that the novel presents the reader with a "mirror" in which at the end he must reread everything backwards.[23]

The reader becomes aware of the novel's paradoxical structure well before he reaches the end. By commenting on the different moments of Marcel's quest and by demonstrating the way each is related to the other, the narrator reveals the form of that quest. But these same explanations, however partial they may be, also force the reader to perceive how the different elements of Proust's *novel* are related to each other. Each encounter, for example, by the meaning it has for Marcel and by the form Proust gives it, recalls the meaning and form of a previous encounter. It also contains within itself the figure of the future, the meaning and form of an encounter yet to be experienced and read, so that *A la Recherche* constantly turns back and forward on itself. The movement of each moment repeats the movement of the whole work, and each moment can

20. Gérard Genette, *Figures* (Paris: Editions du Seuil, 1966), pp. 62–63.
21. Blanchot, pp. 30–33.
22. Jean Rousset, *Forme et Signification* (Paris: José Corti, 1962), pp. 138–45.
23. Louis Bolle, *Marcel Proust ou le complexe d'Argus* (Paris: Grasset, 1967), p. 16.

be read *at the same time* as a stage in Marcel's search and as a stage in the developing form of Proust's novel. Also, in reading the novel we witness the activity of a writer and of a "character" who are completing, discovering, and creating their past through language. *A la Recherche* represents for this reason an extraordinary marriage of form and content, for since the work we read is the story of a man whose life will be at once the source and subject of a similar work, both the language of the novel and what it describes express the same fundamental experience of creative activity. On both levels there is something new coming into being—a novel and a novelist.

The fact remains, of course, that no absolute correlation can be established between the novel Proust wrote and the novel the narrator will write. This is the distance or interval that can never be closed, the real space of tension that keeps the "top" of *A la Recherche* spinning. Yet this distance is as necessary to the meaning of the novel as the distance that must be maintained between the two terms of a metaphor. Proust's experience and the narrator's, the present novel and the future one do indeed exist in a metaphoric relation each with the other. Turning on itself, *A la Recherche* encloses and seals its world and creates its own ultimate autonomy. Its very incompleteness becomes in this way the source of its completeness as a work of art. Its unity is truly organic, because it is a living and dynamic organism in which each part sustains the life of the others.[24]

"No one needs to *search* for paradox in this world of ours," writes Thomas De Quincey. "Let him simply confine himself to the truth, and

24. The new edition of Deleuze's book, *Proust et les signes* (1970), which I received when my own work was all but finished, contains a chapter entitled "Antilogos ou la machine littéraire," in which the author seriously challenges the idea that *A la Recherche* has "organic unity." The problem posed by Proust's novel, writes Deleuze, "is that of a unity and of a totality that would be neither logical nor organic, that is, that would be neither presupposed by the parts as a lost unity or a fragmented totality, nor formed and prefigured by them in the course of a logical development or of an organic evolution" (p. 179). For Deleuze, Proust, like Balzac, was not "preoccupied with harmony," and wrote a work whose unity was the *effect* of the multiplicity of its parts, which retain all their particularity and are not "fused with the rest." Although I believe that part of my disagreement with Deleuze rests on the different meaning I give to the word "organic," I shall not attempt here to refute his argument. To do so would be to repeat all I have said in the course of my discussion concerning the activity of the *esprit,* the structure of Proust's novel, and his conception of *fondu.* I do admire, however, the brilliance with which Deleuze presents his thesis, and I find myself in agreement with many of the points he raises.

he will find paradox growing every where."[25] The paradoxes that characterize Proust's vision are at once the result of his commitment to truth, sustained by his almost obsessive need for purity and intellectual sincerity, and his ambition as a novelist who saw the necessity of giving his readers shocks. Marcel's encounters are for the reader as well moments of heightened consciousness which, by exposing the limits of his habitual responses to life and his ordinary perception of reality, force him to adopt a new and critical view of the world. Like Elstir, Proust gives "unusual images of familiar objects." His method also resembles that of a writer with whom he has little else in common—Bertolt Brecht. As Brecht himself defines it, the much discussed "Alienation-effect" in his plays "consists in turning the object of which one is to be made aware, to which one's attention is to be drawn, from something ordinary, familiar, immediately accessible, into something peculiar, striking and unexpected."[26]

For Proust the transformation of the familiar into the unexpected was essentially a way of converting falsehood into truth, illusion into reality. Referring to the various incarnations his characters would assume in the course of the novel, Proust defined his method again in an interview shortly after the publication of *Du Côté de chez Swann*: "I have tried to imitate life, where the unsuspected aspects of a person suddenly reveal themselves to our eyes. . . . We live next to beings whom we think we know. What is lacking is the event that will make them suddenly appear different from the way we know them."[27] *A la Recherche* gives its readers the sudden events and revelations that are lacking in their lives not because they never occur there, but because they are often lost in time so that their effect and meaning are also lost. Proust's novel is truly "a life redesigned" in accordance with the hidden truth of our existence. The reader is placed in a world where, like Marcel, he can "know" only what strikes his senses and disrupts his habits.

It would be difficult to exaggerate the importance of these shocks and paradoxical revelations. They are essential to Proust's presentation of every idea, person, place, and social group in his novel. Who can count

25. Thomas De Quincey, *Autobiographic Sketches* (Boston: Houghton Mifflin, 1876), p. 229. De Quincey's italics.

26. *Brecht on Theatre: The Development of an Aesthetic,* ed. John Willett (New York: Hill and Wang, 1964), p. 143.

27. Marcel Proust, *Textes retrouvés,* ed. Philip Kolb and Larkin B. Price (Urbana: University of Illinois Press, 1968), p. 222.

the faces of Swann and Albertine, the incarnations of Charlus and Odette, or the metamorphoses of the Verdurin salon? Multiple in time and space, they are the centers of endless and contradictory points of view. In *A la Recherche* one character can also become another, as when Gilberte is confused with Albertine, the Duchess is transformed into a Mme de Villeparisis, or when Marcel finds within himself another Swann and Aunt Léonie. Proust's "paradoxical" vision is supported in this way by a "kaleidoscopic" vision revealing the infinite permutations of the same set of basic human and intellectual elements, and pointing out similarities between things one had thought to be different and differences between others that were accepted as similar. So completely do these shocks pervade the novel that one must consider them not simply as means to an end but as ends in themselves. They *are* the subject of the novel because reality *is* the unexpected. They not only reveal the laws of time and space, they constitute these laws, create their structure within the novel, and force Marcel and the reader to live them. They also "force the mind to think." As Gilles Deleuze admirably demonstrates, it is this *necessity* of thought that is produced by Marcel's *chance* encounters. In *A la Recherche* the fortuitous and the inevitable thus exist as the two inseparable aspects of the same noetic process.[28]

Given the extraordinary number of these surprises, it is nevertheless a mark of Proust's genius that so few of them seem contrived. Although the reader's belief may be strained at times by certain revelations of homosexuality, he seldom if ever doubts the accuracy of Proust's vision. He accepts the surprises because he learns to expect them, and he expects them because these discontinuous shocks and explosions create, like the other elements in the novel, a deep continuity of meaning, and establish what Michel Raimond has recently called a "logic of the unexpected."[29] Indeed, the reader discovers that *A la Recherche* contains within its very structure the lesson of how it should be read.

In the preface to his translation of *The Bible of Amiens* Proust writes that whenever the text aroused in his memory passages from Ruskin's other books, he inserted these passages in notes so that the reader, making Ruskin's acquaintance for the first time, might still recognize the permanent and fundamental aspects of his vision. "In this way," he con-

28. Deleuze, *Proust et les signes,* p. 195.
29. Michel Raimond, "Le Récit proustien dans le *Côté de Guermantes*" (paper presented at the Proust Centennial Commemoration at the University of Illinois, Urbana, May 6, 1971).

tinues, "I have tried to equip the reader with, as it were, an improvised memory, furnishing it from Ruskin's other works—a kind of whispering-gallery [caisse de résonance] in which the words taken from *The Bible of Amiens* may establish themselves in his mind by dint of calling forth related echoes." Proust adds immediately, however, that this procedure can only partially create the desired result:

> But these echoes of what is written in *The Bible of Amiens,* will not, as when memories spring unprompted to the mind, tell of those horizons, some near, some far, of which, since they are habitually hidden from us, our life, as it is lived day by day, is the measure of the intervening distance. Between them and what we find written here, what, precisely, has called them forth, will be none of that element of gentle resistance, as of a layer of atmosphere interposed, which is co-terminous with our existence and comprises the whole of the poetry of memory.[30]

This passage provides one of the keys to the form of Proust's novel, which perhaps more than any other is consciously constructed so as to transform the reader's mind into a *caisse de résonance. A la Recherche* is a long novel composed of many "books" not simply because Proust wanted to capture the totality of his experience in life or to show man in time, but also because he wanted to be sure that the reader would discover the fundamental characteristics of his art and the essence of his vision. Moving from page to page, from one encounter to another, from one volume to the next, the reader does acquire a memory which is aroused across an inner distance each time he himself encounters some "new" object, character, or situation. Just as the narrator discovers at the end the inner necessity that binds together all the chance encounters of his existence, so the reader gradually recognizes "in-between" the recurrent elements of the novel the *phrases-types* of Proust's vision. Through the activity of his own creative *esprit* the reader discovers that Proust has made each encounter and experience the metaphor for another. As I noted earlier, it is this metaphoric extension of all the elements of the novel that creates its unity and assures its autonomy as a work of art.

But the *esprit* is not the most fundamental mode of consciousness. Behind the "philosopher" who is not happy until he has discovered something common between two things, Marcel finds within himself a "little fellow of the barometer" who is sensitive to the slightest changes

30. *Proust: A Selection,* p. 24; *Pastiches,* p. 108.

in the weather. There are other names Proust gives to this basic sensitivity. In the *Contre Sainte-Beuve* he identifies it with his own "ear" for the music of a writer's style: "When I began to read an author I very soon caught the tune of the song beneath the words, which in each author is distinct from that of every other; and while I was reading, and without knowing what I was doing, I hummed it over."[31] Proust adds that it was this ability that enabled him to write his pastiches of Balzac, Flaubert, and others. Anyone attempting to write a pastiche of *A la Recherche du temps perdu* would have to reproduce the "song" of Proust's sentences, their discontinuous movements, and their strong resolutions. He would also have to recapture those "explosions" which establish the basic tempo of the novel and measure its intervals. Beneath all the images and ideas, laws and explanations, scenes and descriptions there is the flow of the sentences themselves leading from one explosive revelation to another. Attuned to the novel's inner "song" the reader's ear soon learns to anticipate these explosions and to hear their immanent arrival; but as with any great work, familiarity does not destroy the element of surprise. The reader expects, and takes delight in, the unexpected. And it is in moving from one *tout d'un coup* to the next that he acquires, at a level of consciousness that escapes analysis, a sense of the novel's time.

31. *Proust on Art*, p. 265; *Sainte-Beuve*, p. 301.

Index

Listed here are names mentioned in the text or in the notes; works by Proust other than *A la Recherche du temps perdu;* and the major discussions of encounters and related experiences, entered under the principal character or place with which they are identified.

Racine, Jean, 97–98, 102, 104, 216

Raimond, Michel, 231 n, 246

Rembrandt, 128, 229

Renoir, Auguste, 212

Ribot, Théodule Armand, 27

Rivière, Jacques: Proust's letter to, 234

Robbe-Grillet, Alain, 230, 233

Rousset, Jean, 243

Ruskin, John, 36, 62, 112; and idolatry, 115–21, 116 n; and Proust's narrative techniques, 138–40, 142 n, 208, 223; and the structure of *A la Recherche*, 246–47

Sainte-Beuve, Charles-Augustin: attack on method of, by Proust, 223–25

Saint-Loup, Robert de: abdication of Marcel to friendship of, 69–70

Saint-Saëns, Camille, 136

Saint-Simon, Duc de, 121

Sand, George: *François le Champi*, 185, 186, 187

Sarraute, Nathalie, 231–32, 234

Sartre, Jean-Paul, 48, 168, 243

Schiff, Mme Sydney: Proust's letter to, 140

Schopenhauer, Artur, 21, 27–28

"Sentiments filiaux d'un parricide," 29 n

Sesame and Lilies (Proust's translation of), 62; reading defined in, 112–15; use of the "I" in, 138–39, 225

Sévigné, Mme de, 7, 106, 208

Shattuck, Roger, 188 n

Simon, Claude, 230

"Spiritualité de l'âme, La": Proust's philosophy of the *esprit* defined in, 18–20

Stendhal, 2, 224

Strauss, Walter A., 2 n

Sturrock, John, 230

Swann, Charles: role of, in the "bedroom drama," 41–42, 237–38; relation of, to Proust's criticism of Ruskin's idolatry, 120–21, 136–40; and Vinteuil's sonata, 121–24; consciousness of music of, corrupted by Odette, 124–27; Odette and Botticelli idolized by, 127–33; past of, and last encounter with the sonata, 133–36; attitude of Proust toward, 140–41; story of his love haunts Marcel, 152, 156–57; his experience with music compared with Marcel's, 172–75, 177

Tadié, Jean-Yves, 75, 78, 81 n

Taine, Hippolyte, 16

Turner, J. M. W., 45, 208

Velasquez, 128

Venice: transformed by mother's departure, 44–46; reborn through involuntary memory, 184

Verdurin, M. and Mme: salon of, described in the *Goncourt Journal*, 180–81, 214–15; salon of, as seen by Brichot, 218–19

Vermeer, Jan, 132, 205, 206, 228, 229

Vinteuil: sonata of, Swann's first encounters with, 121–27; last encounter with, 133–36; music of, compared with music in *Jean Santeuil*, 136–38; septet of, Marcel's encounter with, 170–71; music of, and the forms of love, 171–73; music and true self of, 174–75; septet of, and themes of *A la Recherche*, 175–78; value of music of, 178–80; music of, and involuntary memory, 184. *See also* Swann, Charles

"Violante ou la mondanité," 25–26, 27, 31, 34, 35

Virgil, 27

Wagner, Richard, 192

Wilde, Oscar, 121

Wilson, Edmund, 29

Wimsatt, W. K., Jr., 209